The Campus History Series

JOHN CARROLL UNIVERSITY

On the Front Cover: On October 7, 1935, students cheered as classes finally began at John Carroll's new University Heights campus.

On the Back Cover: The handsome building that was completed in 1891 and once housed Saint Ignatius College is now the heart of the Saint Ignatius High School campus.

The Campus History Series

JOHN CARROLL UNIVERSITY

MARIAN J. MORTON

ARCADIA PUBLISHING

ISBN 978-0-7385-9074-5

Published by Arcadia Publishing
Charleston, South Carolina

Printed in the United States of America

Library of Congress Catalog Card Number: 2012948118

For all general information, please contact Arcadia Publishing:
Telephone 843-853-2070
Fax 843-853-0044
E-mail sales@arcadiapublishing.com
For customer service and orders:
Toll-Free 1-888-313-2665

Visit us on the Internet at www.arcadiapublishing.com

This book is dedicated to the John Carroll community with great respect and deep affection.

Contents

ACKNOWLEDGMENTS

Special thanks to these people: Rev. Robert L. Niehoff, SJ, for his generous support of this book; Dr. Jeanne Colleran for getting it going; the late Dr. Donald P. Gavin, whose *John Carroll University: A Century of Service* has been invaluable; university archivist Laurene DiCillo for her expertise, energy, and hospitality; Dr. James Krukones and Dr. Paul V. Murphy for catching some of my mistakes; and Marcia Aghajanian and Laurie A. Frantz for catching others and adding valuable insight. Like most things at John Carroll, this book was made possible by our wonderful and talented staff: Patricia Harris, Cheri Slattery, John Carfagno, Marilyn Valencia, Peter Bernardo, Paula Fitzgerald, John Walsh, Brian Fitts, Samantha Schneider, Kathryn Y. Schiffer, Pat Hoffman, Kathleen DiFranco, and Tracee Patterson. Thanks also to Sr. Colette Livingston, OSU, archivist for the Ursuline Sisters of Cleveland; Sherri Wisnieski, City of University Heights; Aurora Martinez, Cleveland Heights–University Heights Public Library; and Judith Gedeon, Saint Ignatius High School.

Unless otherwise noted, all photographs appear courtesy of John Carroll University.

FOREWORD

Certain life events prompt us to pause and reflect. John Carroll University recently celebrated one of those milestones—its 125th anniversary in 2011—so it is the perfect time to write this abbreviated history.

In reviewing John Carroll's founding, one finds distinct parallels with the origin of the Society of Jesus (the Jesuits). The university was established at the request of Cleveland's bishop Richard Gilmour, who encouraged Rev. Henry Behrens, SJ, superior of the Buffalo Mission of the Jesuits, to establish a Catholic college in Cleveland. Rev. Behrens sent Rev. John Neustich, SJ, to purchase land where they could build the school.

Rev. Behrens arrived in Cleveland in 1886 and brought three other Buffalo Jesuits with him for Bishop Gilmour's approval. This small group, including Rev. Neustich, became the first faculty at Saint Ignatius College, named for Ignatius of Loyola, who founded the Society of Jesus.

Similarly, more than 475 years ago, when Ignatius of Loyola was a graduate student at the University of Paris, he frequently led a small group of friends in prayer. They called themselves "amigos en el Senor," meaning "friends in the Lord," and ultimately were ordained to the Catholic priesthood. In 1540, Pope Paul III approved the Institute of the Society of Jesus; Ignatius was elected Superior General and served in that post until his death in 1556.

As you will read in the subsequent pages, Saint Ignatius College opened its doors on September 6, 1886. In 1923, it was renamed John Carroll University after the first archbishop of the Catholic church in the United States.

The Jesuit visionaries who created and shaped our university would be proud to see John Carroll today. Since its founding, John Carroll has grown into an institution widely recognized for excellence in learning, leadership, and service.

Generations of outstanding students, alumni, faculty, and staff blessed our campus in the first 125 years. The quality of their character and their dedication to Carroll are inspiring. With God's grace, may we continue to serve Him and each other as we work to fulfill the mission of John Carroll University and as we commence its next 125 years.

—Rev. Robert L. Niehoff, SJ

INTRODUCTION

John Carroll University began in 1886 as Saint Ignatius College in an unpretentious wooden building in a working-class neighborhood on Cleveland's west side. It had a few dozen male students and a faculty of four Jesuits. Its opening went unnoticed by Cleveland newspapers, except for the Catholic weekly newspaper. Today, John Carroll sits on 64 landscaped acres in suburban University Heights. In 2011, its graduate and undergraduate students—male and female, Catholic and non-Catholic—numbered 3,709, and its full-time faculty was 204. The university, its faculty, and its students have won national and regional recognition. Getting there has not been easy; John Carroll faced challenges from local circumstances and prejudices as well as national events and emergencies.

Reflecting the religious pluralism of this country, most American private colleges were closely tied to Protestant denominations. The founding of the colleges was inspired by enthusiastic sectarian (and regional) rivalries, as Protestants of all kinds sought to establish spiritual and secular hegemony—first over the new colonies and then over the new republic. By 1850, in Ohio alone, Congregationalists had founded Western Reserve (now Case Western Reserve University) and Oberlin Colleges; Episcopalians, Kenyon College; Disciples of Christ, Hiram College; Baptists, Denison University; Methodists, Ohio Wesleyan University, Mount Union College, and Baldwin University (now Baldwin Wallace); and Lutherans, Wittenberg University. College presidents, and often faculty, were Protestant ministers whose goal was to educate clergy and other men headed for public life. Initially, colleges taught a classical curriculum derived from English universities with an emphasis on Greek and Latin. Although the smaller colleges were perennially strapped for money, and many failed, the survivors got a healthy head start on Catholic institutions and were more likely to win financial support from wealthy benefactors—and sometimes from state or local governments, at least through the 19th century.

Catholic colleges, beginning with Georgetown University in 1789, were a logical response to this rapid proliferation of denominational colleges. Rightfully fearful of Protestant proselytizing, Catholics tried to beat Protestants at their own game, founding 92 colleges by the end of the 19th century. Most were established at the request of local bishops, who wanted an educated clergy and the social and economic benefits of higher education for their flocks, which often contained recent immigrants.

The Jesuits were the best-known Catholic educators in the United States. They founded colleges ranging from Georgetown University and Boston College on the East Coast to Santa Clara College on the West Coast. In 1876, Cleveland's bishop, Richard Gilmour, asked the Jesuits' Buffalo Mission of the German Province for priests to serve Saint Mary of the Assumption Church on the city's near west side and to establish a college there.

Like other Catholic colleges of the era, Saint Ignatius had a small student body of first- and second-generation Americans. To avoid the public high schools, which, like the public elementary schools, were Protestant in tone and substance, students attended Saint Ignatius College for seven years; the first four years would be roughly equivalent to grades 9 through 12 in high school today. As at the Protestant colleges, the focus was on the classics, rhetoric, and philosophy, and the intent was to educate men for the church and other public positions. Tuition was low, although most Catholic colleges were tuition-dependent. The most important requirements for admission were a good recommendation from the applicant's parish priest and some minimal academic preparation.

By the end of the 19th century, in a rapidly industrializing economy, science and technology became increasingly attractive to Americans searching for success in the secular world, encroaching into colleges' classical curriculums and challenging the initial pious intentions of small private colleges. State universities also challenged the small private colleges' curriculum and intentions, as did the great research university, Johns Hopkins (founded in 1876), which became a model for higher education. The close denominational ties of Protestant colleges began to fray as they, too, aspired to become nominally nonsectarian universities that were Protestant in orientation.

In 1896, Harvard Law School decided that only under special conditions would they admit students from all but three Catholic colleges (Georgetown University, Boston College, and the College of the Holy Cross), maintaining that the students were academically unprepared. This decision, and pressure from the Catholic Educational Association, forced Catholic colleges to seek accreditation from national organizations and to adopt a standard credit system. In 1902, Saint Ignatius High School and Saint Ignatius College were separated to conform to the national model of secondary and higher education. The college received accreditation from the North Central Association of Colleges and Schools in 1922. Faced with local competition from Western Reserve University and the Case School of Applied Science, Saint Ignatius College applied for a new charter from the state of Ohio that allowed the college to become a university. Hence, after a very brief interlude as "Cleveland University," Saint Ignatius College became John Carroll University in 1923.

During the Depression and World War II, the goal of most colleges, regardless of religious inclination, was simple survival. The loss of already precarious financial backing during the 1930s was compounded by the loss of students to military service during the war years. Construction began on a new John Carroll campus in University Heights in 1931, but the school was forced to halt the process until 1935, when the university was able to borrow enough money to pay the contractors. A Navy V-12 college training program kept the university alive during World War II.

The GI Bill, which allowed thousands of veterans to begin or finish educations, breathed new life into colleges and universities. Catholic institutions benefited from the postwar prosperity of Catholics, who, like other Americans, moved up the social ladder and into the suburbs. In 1946, John Carroll's enrollment was 1,921; in 1960, it was 4,028.

The 1960s and 1970s were tumultuous times. The civil rights and antiwar movements, as well as the second wave of feminism, created student and faculty unrest that challenged long-standing academic traditions. Two Catholics also challenged traditions and helped to propel Catholic colleges and universities into the mainstream: John F. Kennedy, the first Catholic president of the United States (educated at a non-Catholic university), and Pope John XXIII, whose encyclicals advocated a greater role for laypeople in the church and a greater rapport with Protestants. Also, in order to receive federal funds, Catholic universities had to incorporate separately from their founding religious orders to become independent not-for-profit entities, though "under the sponsorship" of the religious order—Jesuits, in the case of John Carroll. In 1969, the university established a board of trustees primarily composed of laypeople. In 1968, following the lead of other Jesuit institutions, John Carroll began to admit women as full-time undergraduate students.

Since the last decades of the 20th century, Catholic colleges and universities have made the transition "from backwater to mainstream," according to sociologist Andrew M. Greeley. As they became more like their Protestant and nonsectarian counterparts, achieving high national rankings and producing distinguished graduates, they also struggled to retain or discover what made them uniquely Catholic. At John Carroll, as at other Catholic universities, the search for a unique Catholic identity took two directions: a look inward at the Jesuit tradition and mission and a movement outward to engage the community and the world.

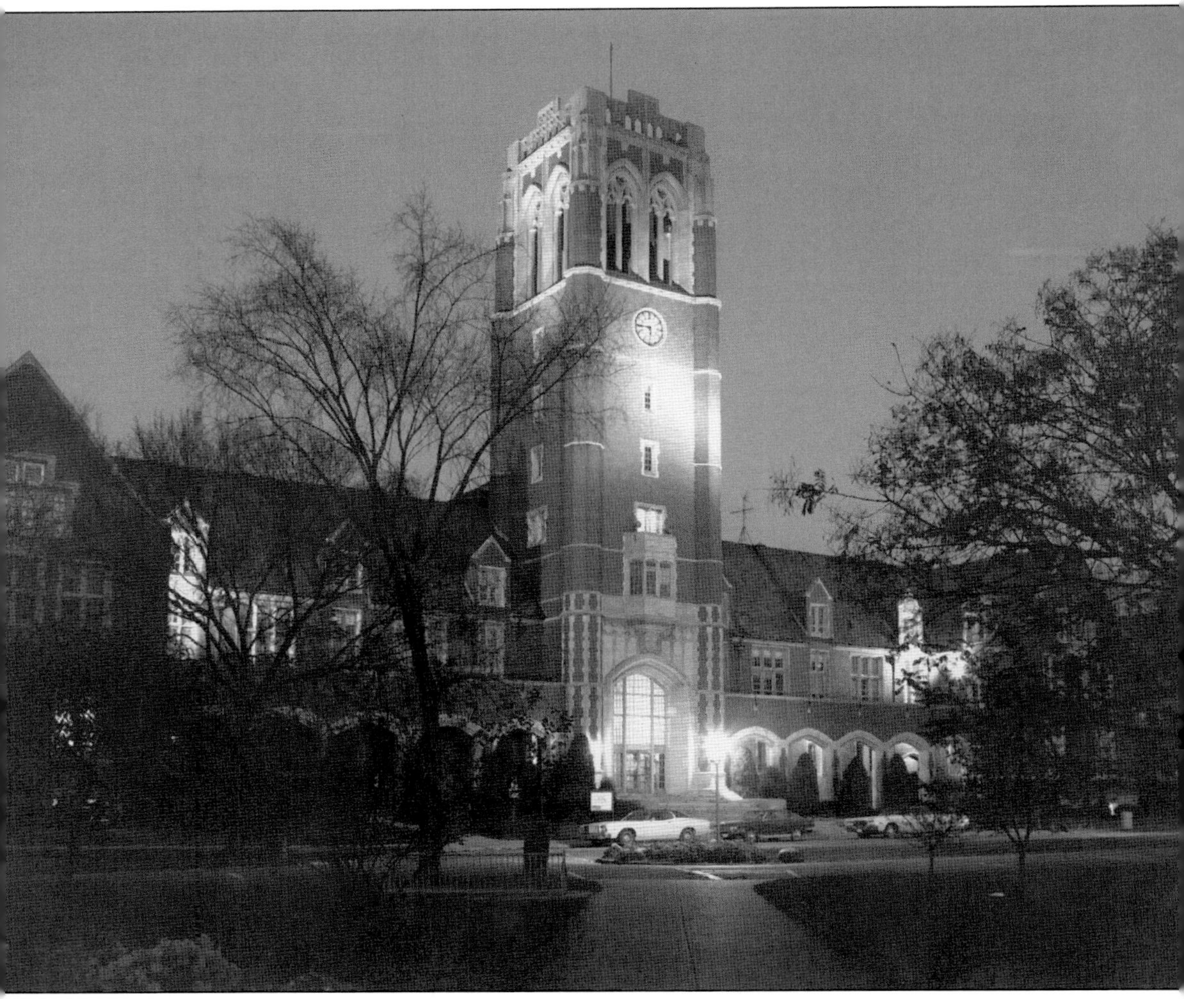

The Grasselli Tower of the Administration Building is John Carroll's signature structure. The tower announces the university's presence, and its bells announce the time to the university and the community.

One

West Side Beginnings 1886–1906

In 1886, when Saint Ignatius College opened on Cleveland's near west side, the city was on the move. Its population reached 261,353 in 1890. Its bustling mills and smoky factories produced iron and steel and offered jobs for immigrants from all over Europe. Catholics became the largest single religious group, although they were still outnumbered by Protestants of many denominations, who distrusted Catholics' religion, class, and ethnic backgrounds. The first and second bishops of the Diocese of Cleveland, Bishop Amadeus Rappe (who served from 1847 to 1870) and Bishop Richard Gilmour (who served from 1872 to 1891), built dozens of churches, schools, social service agencies, and one Jesuit college to serve their growing flocks and preserve their faith in a staunchly Protestant city.

In 1876, Bishop Gilmour invited the Jesuits of the Buffalo Mission of the German Province to Cleveland to serve the congregation of Saint Mary of the Assumption church and to start a nearby school, which became Saint Ignatius College. The Jesuits took charge of the church in 1880, but the college did not get underway for six more years because of disagreements over its location.

The college's Ohio City neighborhood was densely settled and contained apartments and frame homes on narrow lots, small factories, a brewery, the Pearl Street Market, stores, and saloons. The residents were working-class Irish and German immigrants.

As few as 76 students ultimately enrolled during the college's first semester in 1886. Many dropped out before completing the four years of preparatory work and three years of advanced work needed for a bachelor of arts degree. The $40 annual tuition created financial hardships for some families. In 1902, Saint Ignatius College and Saint Ignatius High School were formally separated, although the two remained on the same campus.

Most of the first faculty members were German Jesuits. Many did not speak English well, which did not please the English-speaking students or Bishop Gilmour, who wanted to hasten the Americanization of his flock. The classical course of study was intended to prepare priests for the seminary, although graduates went into other professions as well. The college also offered a commercial curriculum for students interested in business.

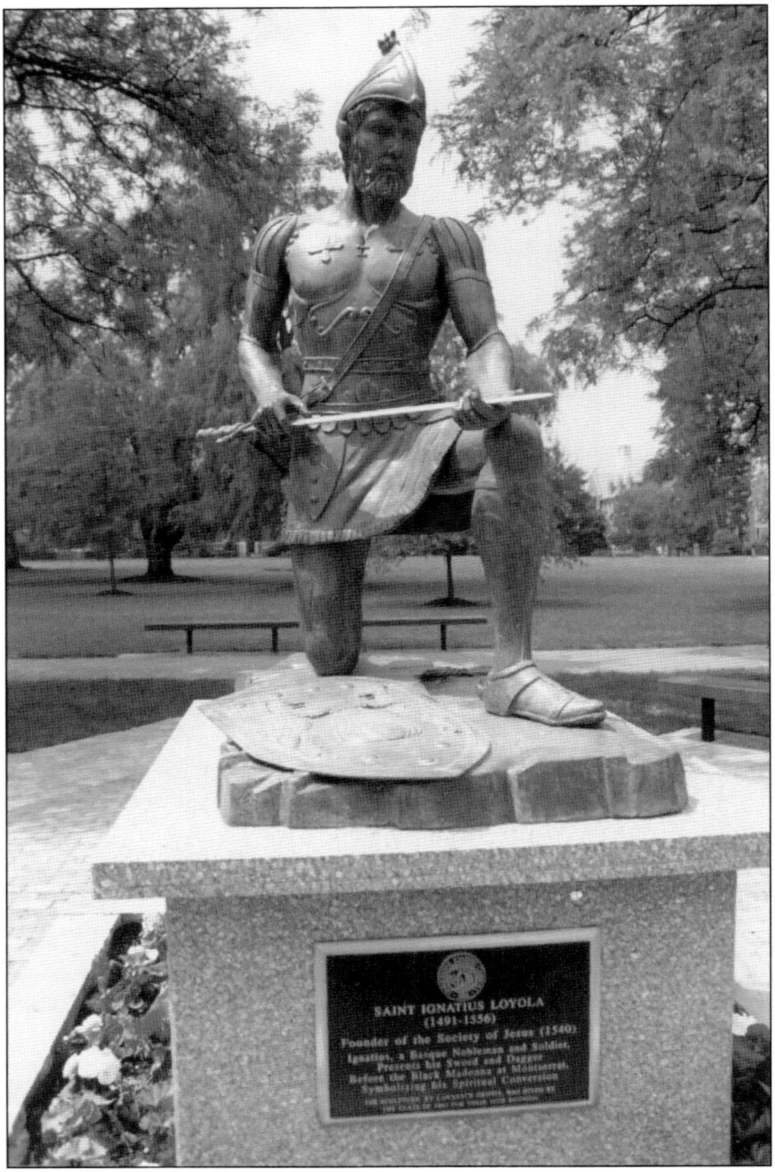

This sculpture of Saint Ignatius of Loyola, just to the west of Saint Francis Chapel on the John Carroll campus, celebrates the founder of the Society of Jesus, the order that established and sustains the university. Ignatius (1491–1556) became a soldier first and an educator second, following his own education in European universities. The schools the Jesuits founded combined a strict plan of study, the *Ratio Studiorum*, with an ability to adapt the teaching to their times, people, and places. The combination enabled the Jesuits to found colleges and universities around the world—and more in the United States than any other order, including the first Catholic college, Georgetown College (now Georgetown University), in 1789. Jesuits became the bellwethers of American Catholic education in a Protestant country that sometimes admired and sometimes disliked them. John Carroll reaffirms its Jesuit Catholic identity not only with this sculpture but also with a robust presence of Catholic thought, rich opportunities for worship, regular offering of the Ignatian Spiritual Exercises, and service opportunities rooted in the Ignatian tradition.

In 1876, Bishop Richard Gilmour, the second bishop of the Cleveland Diocese (1872–1891), issued the invitation to the Buffalo Mission of the German Province of Jesuits to staff Saint Mary of the Assumption and to open a college in Cleveland. The Basilian Fathers' Saint Louis College in Louisville, Ohio, closed in 1873, and the Franciscans' Saint Joseph's College in Cleveland closed in 1879. Misunderstandings and disagreements between the Jesuits and the bishop slowed down negotiations about when Saint Ignatius would open.

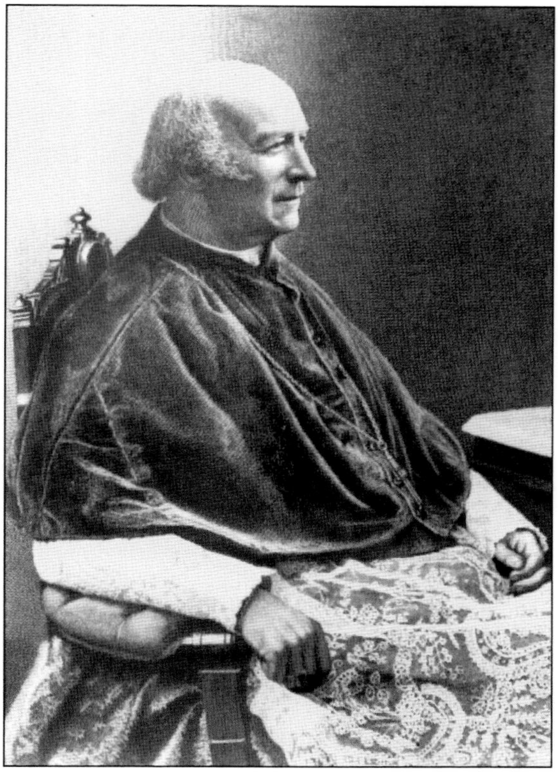

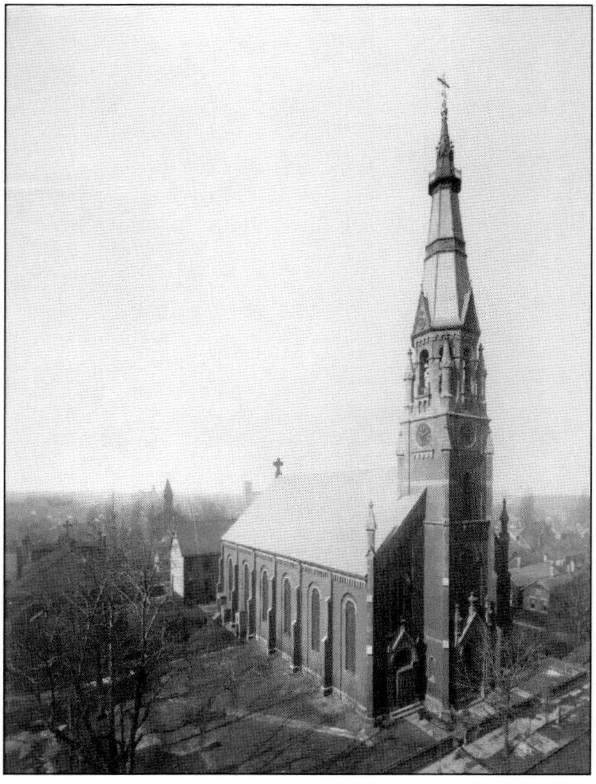

The Jesuits took charge of Saint Mary of the Assumption in Ohio City in 1880. The congregation was organized by Bishop Amadeus Rappe in 1854 for the Germans living in the area. The church's Gothic building was completed in 1865. Its tall spire stood out in the neighborhood of modest homes. After a 1925 fire, this spire was replaced by a Romanesque dome.

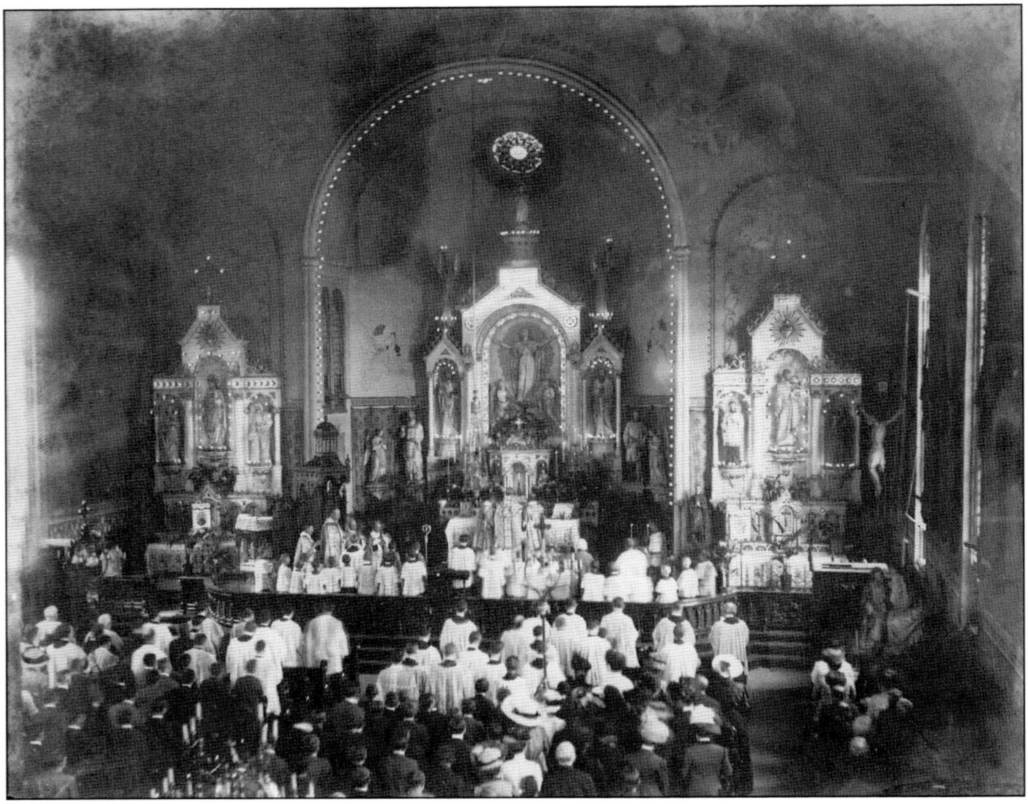

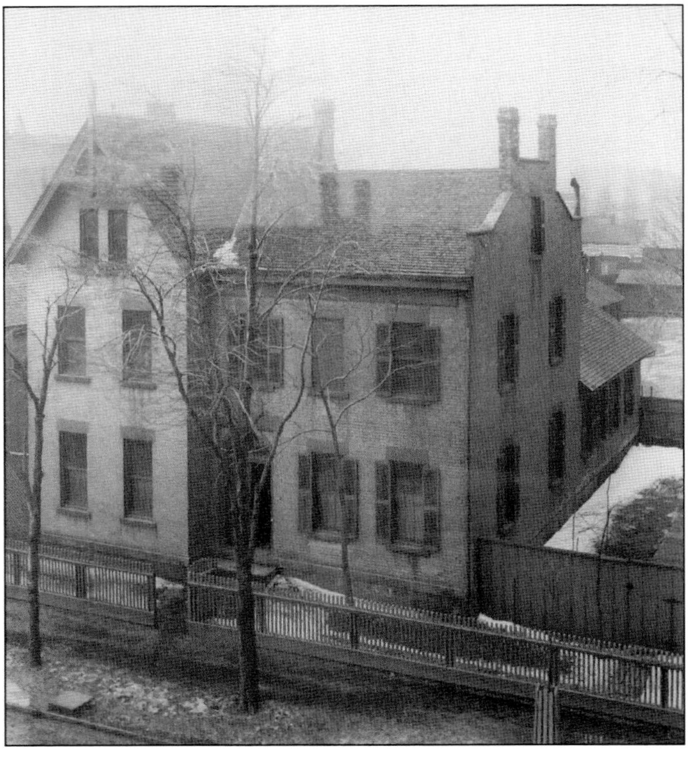

The interior of Saint Mary of the Assumption was as handsome as its exterior, and the priests' robes and the age-old ritual of the Mass provided parishioners with color and drama as well as spiritual solace. The church, which stood for more than a century, was demolished in 1968.

At first, the Jesuits lived in the church's parish house (pictured) in Ohio City, across from the college. Bishop Richard Gilmour insisted that the Jesuits' church and college be close to each other. This photograph provides a glimpse of the crowded urban neighborhood.

Ohio City was a predominantly German neighborhood. Trinity Evangelical Lutheran Church, established in 1873, sat almost directly across Lorain Avenue from Saint Ignatius College. Like Saint Mary of the Assumption, this church served a German congregation and was designed in the Gothic style. It remains on this site at 2057 West Thirtieth Street. (Cleveland State University Special Collections.)

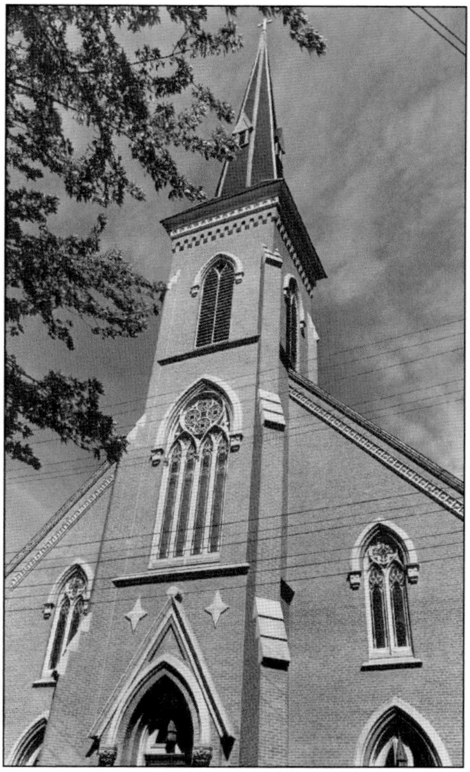

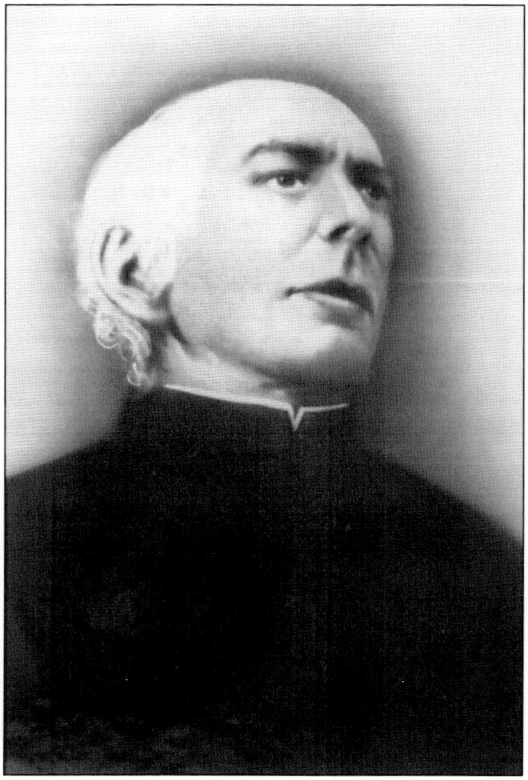

Rev. Henry Behrens, SJ, superior of the Buffalo Mission of the German Province of Jesuits, is credited with finally achieving an agreement with Bishop Richard Gilmour in April 1886 to open the college in September of that year. Behrens asked the bishop to keep the college's opening a secret until some of the property had been purchased.

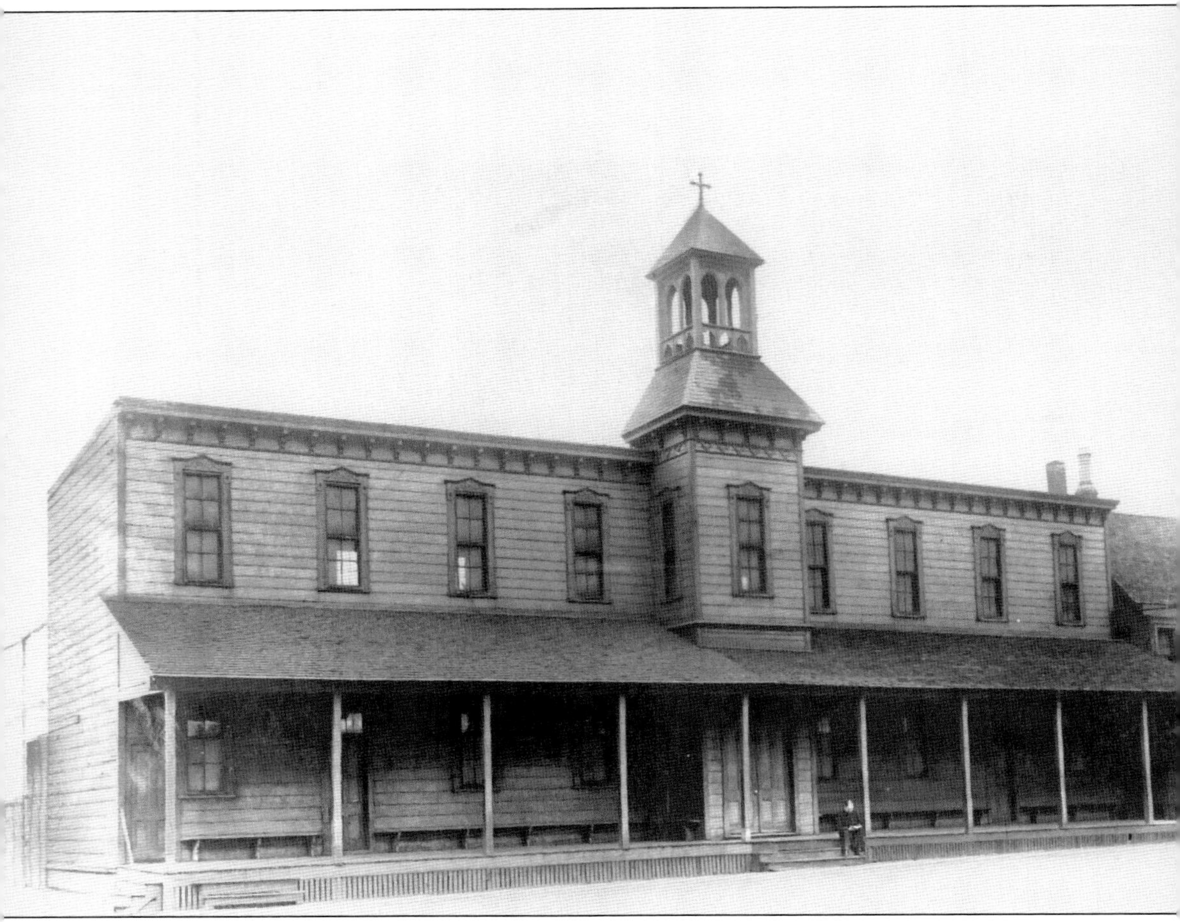

This first classroom building of Saint Ignatius College, constructed across from Saint Mary of the Assumption on lots purchased by the Jesuits from April to July in 1886, was finished two days before classes were set to begin in September 1886. Inside were four classrooms, providing ample space for the first four faculty members and the first students. Although the building is simple, the cupola, the dentils along the roofline, and the ornamented windows distinguish it from neighboring homes. The college opened with 40 students, and enrollment doubled by February 1887. The surrounding neighborhood was crowded with homes, commercial structures, and small factories. A brewery wagon yard was very close to the classroom building.

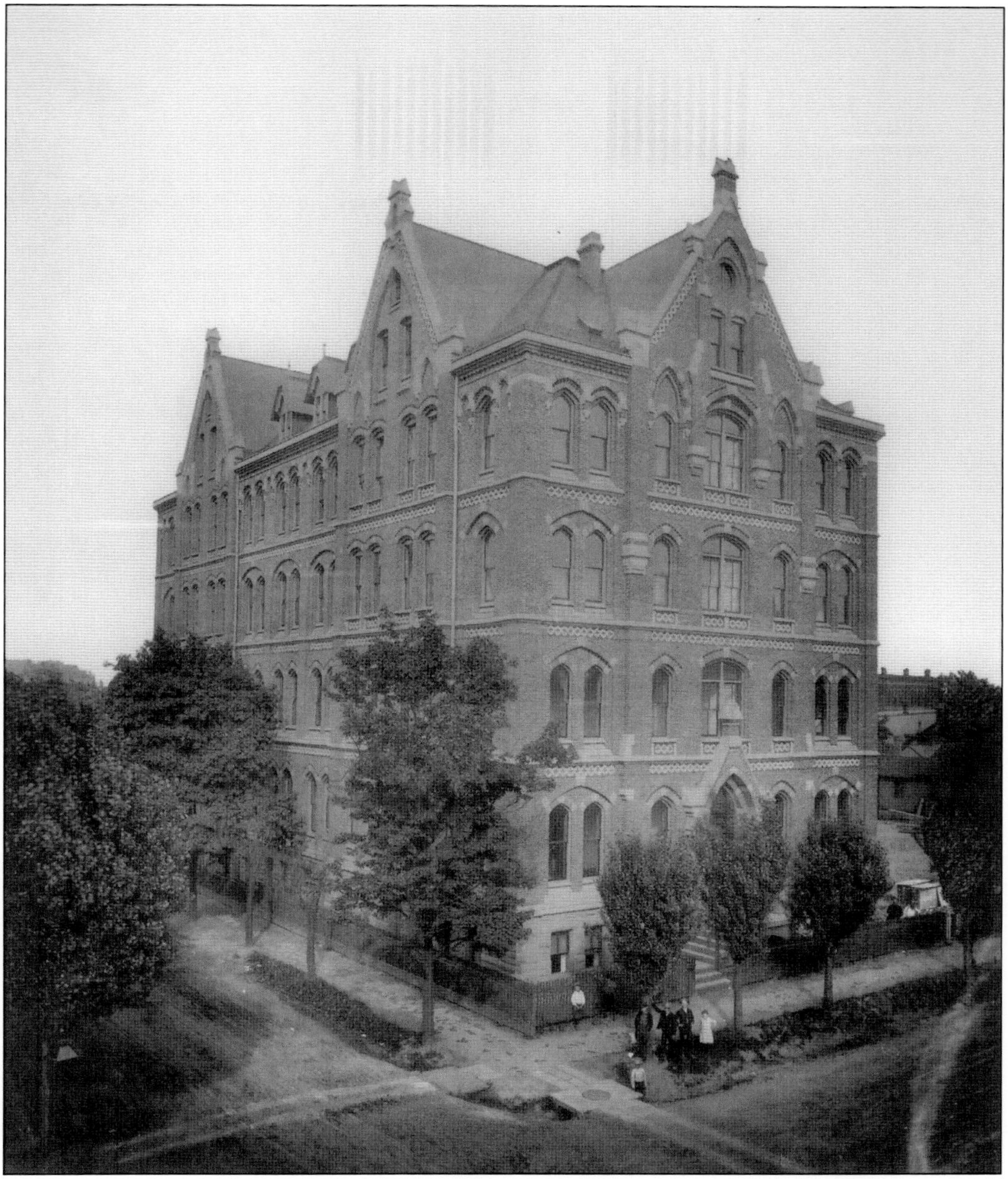

This imposing brick building constructed in 1891 was the second and permanent home of Saint Ignatius College. It was designed by Jesuit brother and architect Frederick Wipfler, who came to Cleveland from Holland in order to construct the building. Other Jesuit brothers who were also skilled craftsmen aided in the building's construction. The turret, the prominent pointed arches that punctuate the roofline, and the symmetrical rows of ornamented windows were typical of the collegiate Gothic style seen at other Jesuit colleges. The building housed the Jesuit residence, classrooms, and the library and rose to an impressive six stories, dominating the surrounding landscape, which it still does. The building's handsome entrances and windows framed with decorative stone added dignity and grace. Since the college only had 178 students in 1891, the ambitious building probably said more about the Jesuits' hopes than the college's realities. The current John Carroll Administration Building is a modified 1930s version of this grand structure.

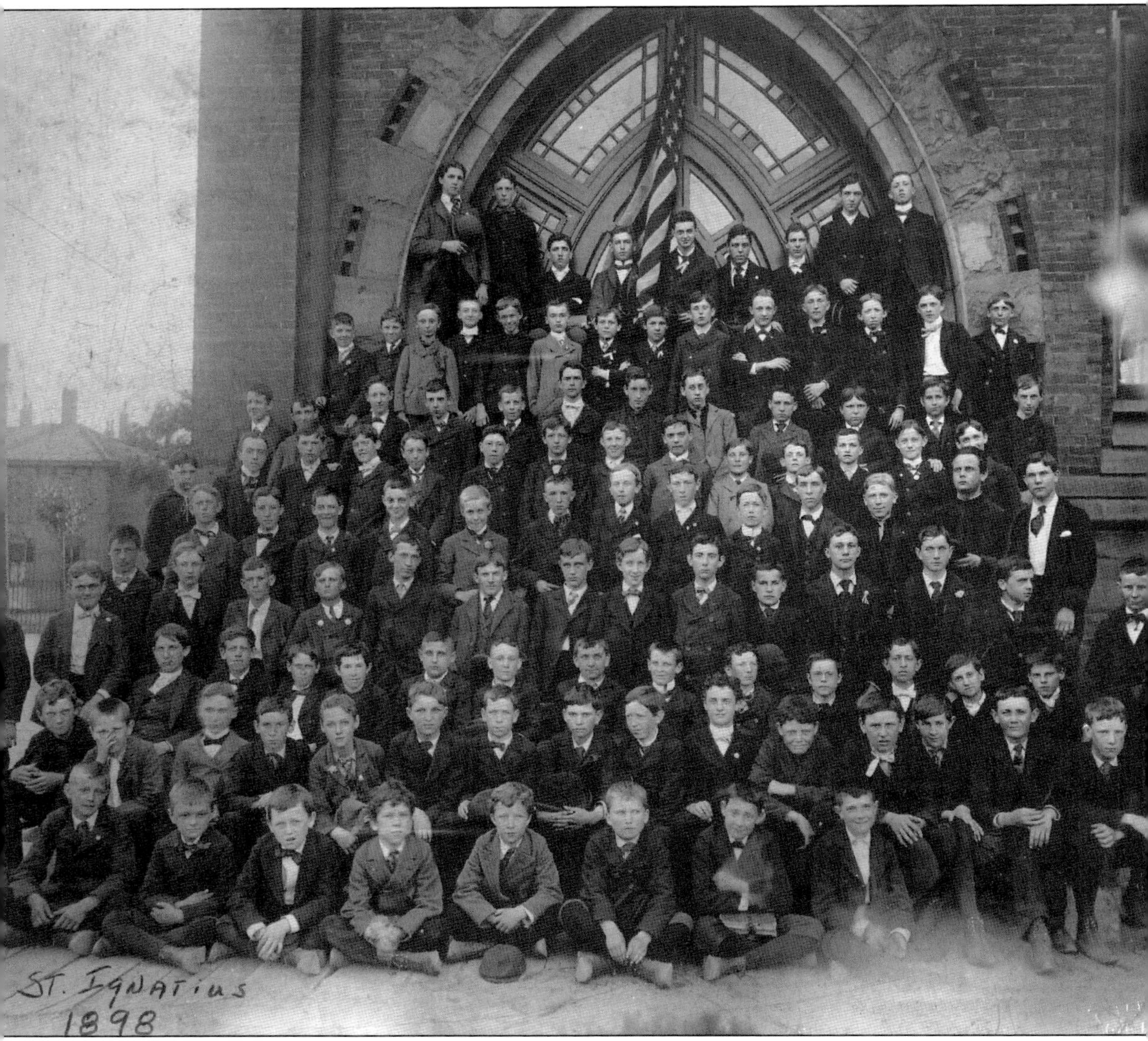

These Saint Ignatius College students, framed by the school's stately entrance, posed for the camera in 1898, when the total student body numbered only 195. Most had German or Irish backgrounds, and they came from all over Cleveland—from the east side to Lakewood, which was on the west side—to study with the Jesuits. There were no other Catholic boys' schools in the area, and public schools were free but permeated with Protestantism. Presumably, the youngest students sat in the first row and the graduating class stood in the last. Since the college and the high school were not separated until 1902, when this picture was taken, the school might include boys as young as 11 or 12 and as old as 20 or 21. All were formally attired in coats and ties, indicative of the level of deportment that the college expected of its students, who were intended to enter the priesthood or other scholarly professions. The college catalogue warned that "any conduct unbecoming to the character of a gentleman is regarded as a violation of the college rules." (Courtesy of Saint Ignatius High School.)

Rev. John B. Neustich, SJ, was named the first president of Saint Ignatius College and pastor of Saint Mary of the Assumption. He had been the treasurer of Canisius College and helped to purchase the properties for Saint Ignatius College. Neustich served as president of Saint Ignatius from 1886 to 1888, left the college, returned in 1906, and became its treasurer in 1922. Like many of the first Jesuits at Saint Ignatius, Neustich was born in Germany.

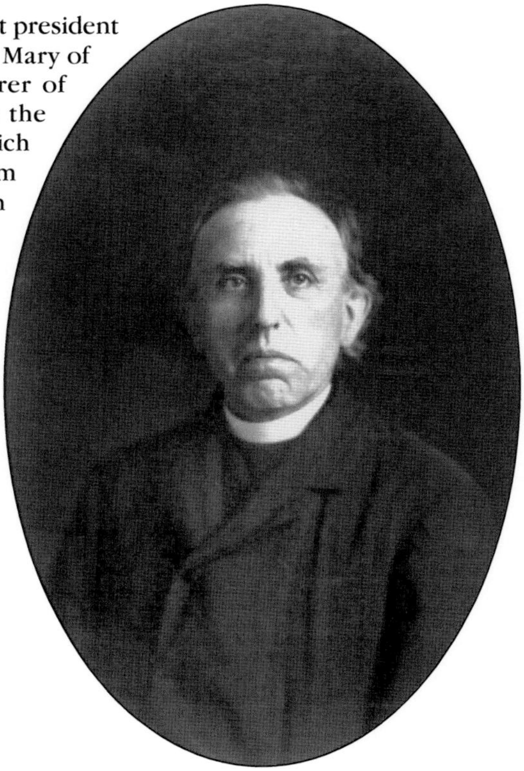

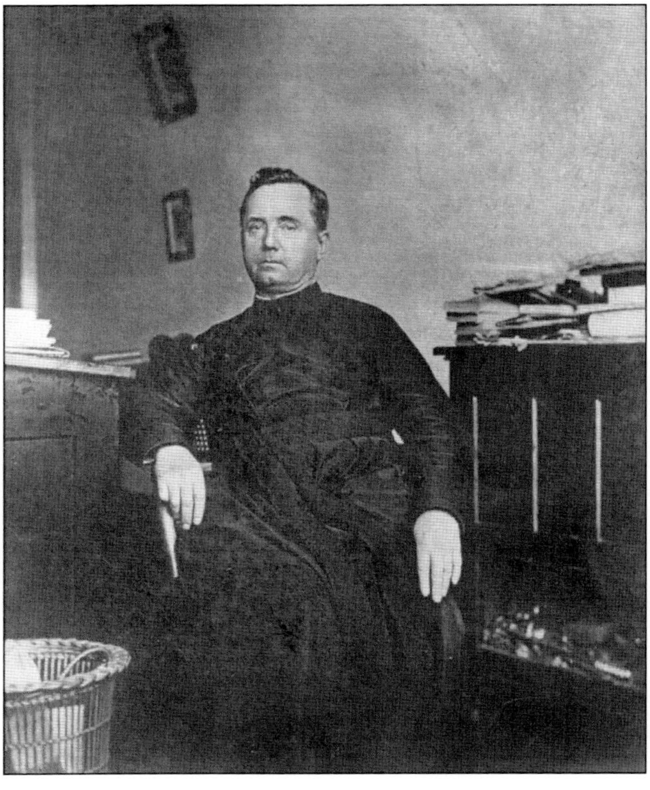

Rev. Henry Knappmeyer, SJ, succeeded Neustich, serving as president from 1888 to 1893. He was also a native of Germany. Some of the college's first faculty members were puzzled by American customs and behavior; some did not speak English well, confusing the English-speaking students and annoying Bishop Richard Gilmour, even though he himself had asked the German Jesuits to pastor a German church and start a college in a German neighborhood.

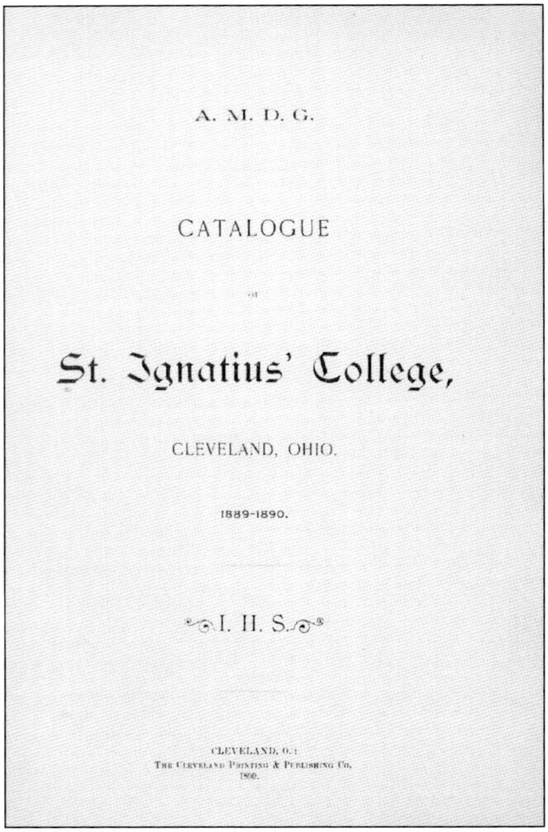

A. M. D. G.

CATALOGUE

OF

St. Ignatius' College,

CLEVELAND, OHIO.

1889-1890.

I. H. S.

CLEVELAND, O.:
The Cleveland Printing & Publishing Co.
1890.

This 1889–1890 college catalogue described the classical curriculum. Students took classes in Latin, Greek, English, German, French, rhetoric, poetry, elocution, English literature, mathematics, natural philosophy, chemistry, history, geography, bookkeeping, and penmanship. The commercial course was shorter and intended for those who planned to go into business.

This library, a quiet, book-lined spot for studying, was located on the third floor of the 1891 building. Classical busts and religious sculptures reinforced what the students learned in their classrooms. Every year, the college set aside $100 for the purchase of new books for the library. (Courtesy of Saint Ignatius High School.)

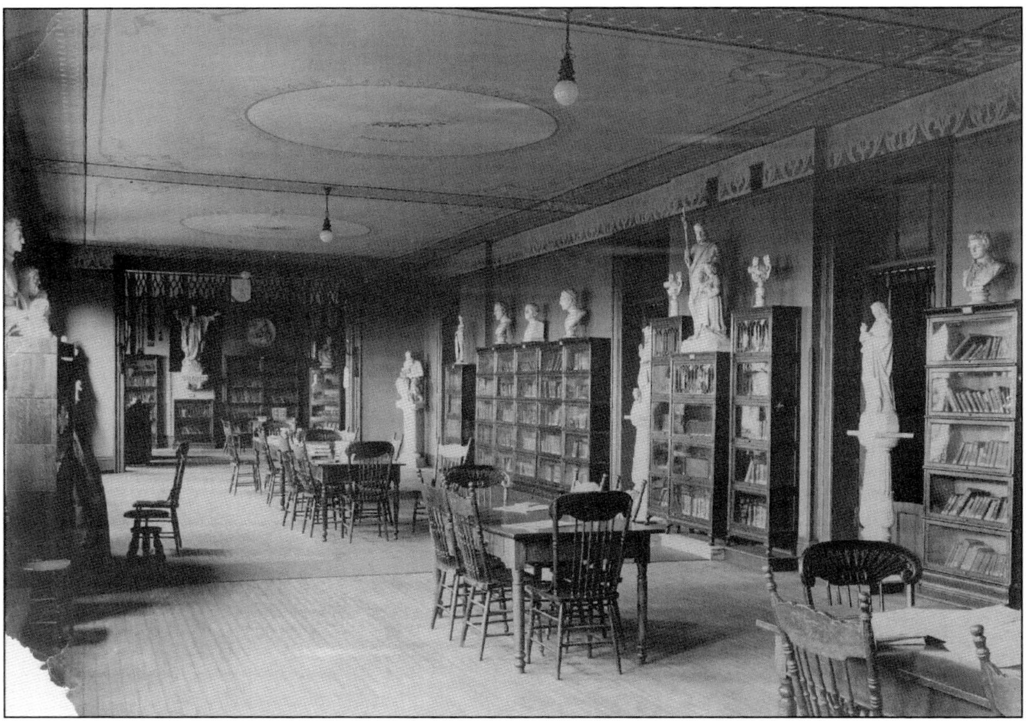

The future looked bright for this Saint Ignatius class of 1902. A 1925 survey of students who had graduated since 1894 indicated that the majority had gone into law, medicine, or business; fewer than 20 percent of graduates went into the priesthood, but this figure did not include those who left the college for the seminary or a religious order. (Courtesy of Saint Ignatius High School.)

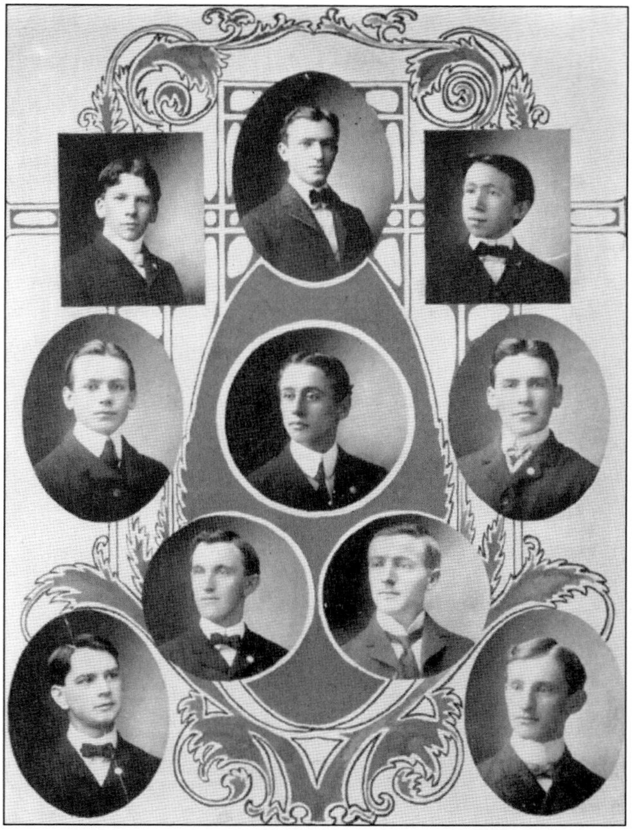

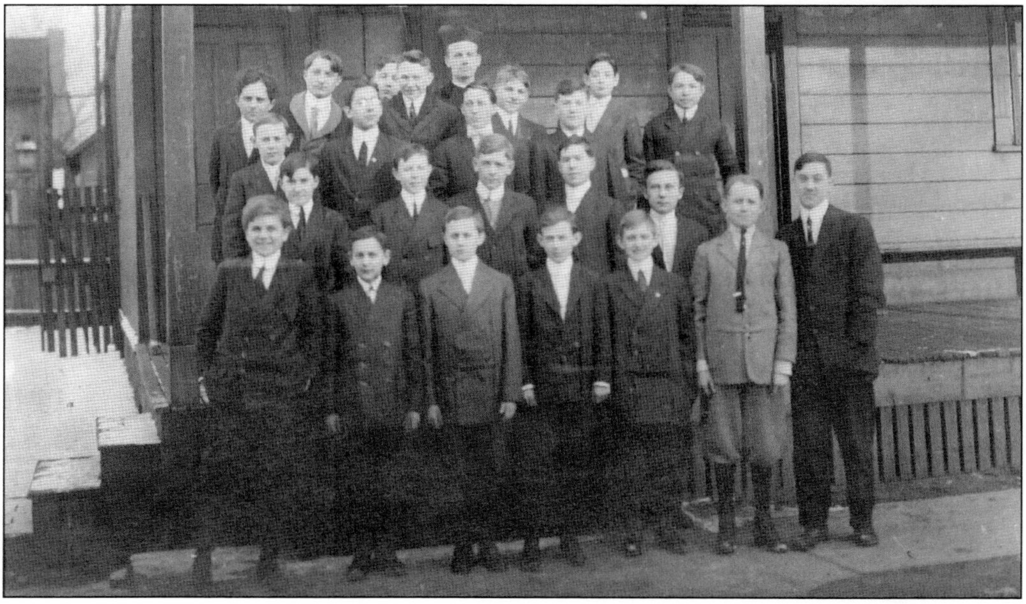

These students gathered in front of the college's first building, which served as a gymnasium after 1891. The man at far right in the first row may have been a lay teacher. Although most of the faculty were Jesuits, a few laymen taught specialized classes in music or science, but never philosophy or religion. (Courtesy of Saint Ignatius High School.)

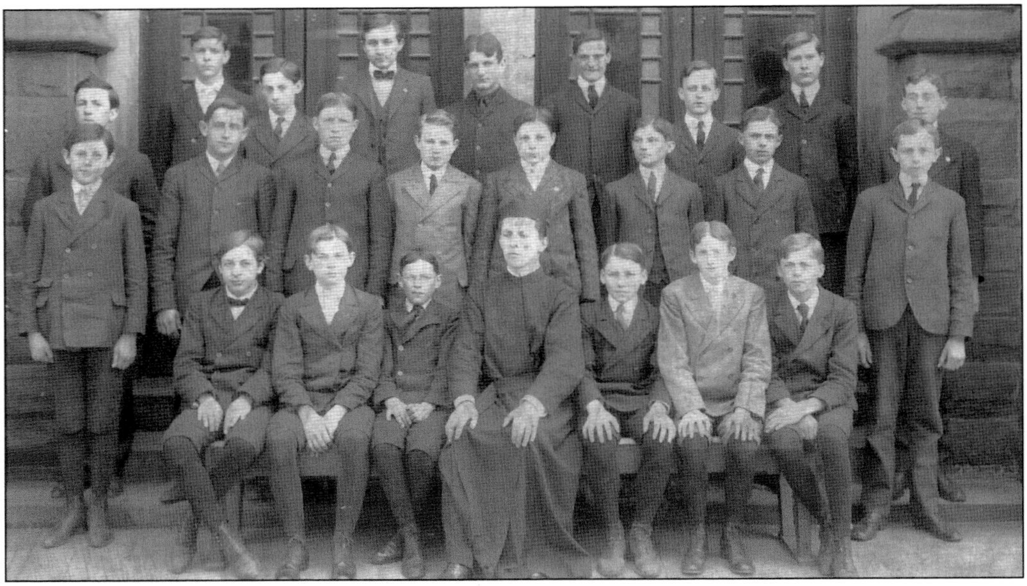

This faded photograph of some very young college students is dated 1905. Until 1893, the priest in the front row taught all the subjects required for students to study in a given year. The separation of the faculty into departments like mathematics, chemistry, or English literature brought the college's curriculum more into line with the American model for high school and college. (Courtesy of Saint Ignatius High School.)

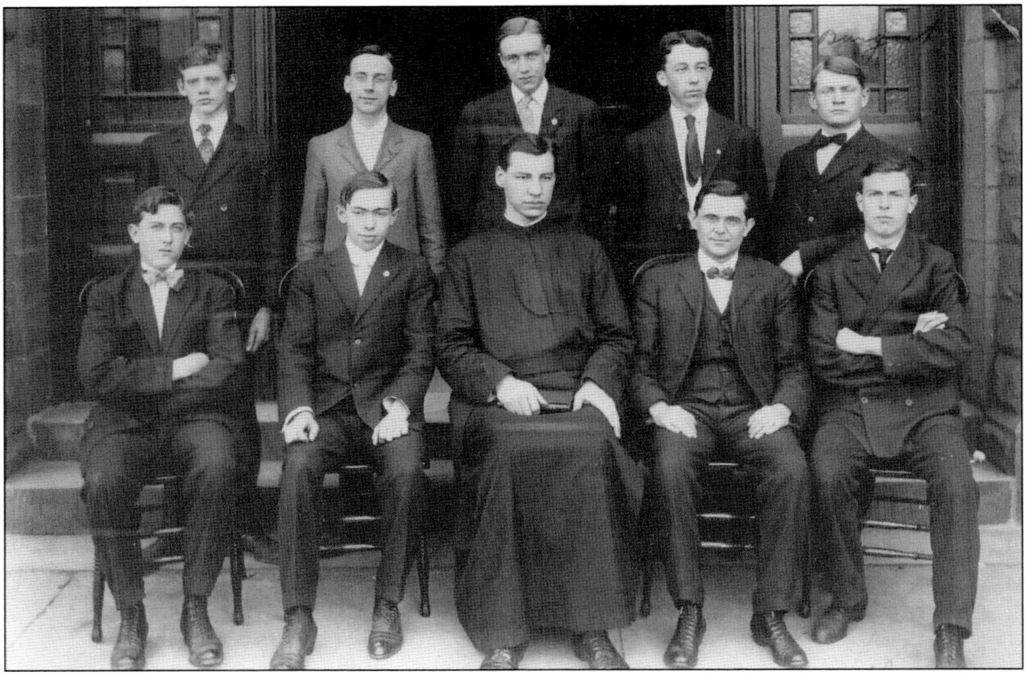

This somber 1907 photograph reminds viewers that at Saint Ignatius College, "the moral and religious training of the scholars [was] the most important part of education; the pupils are required to be present at Mass every day, to make the annual retreat, and to go to the Sacraments at least once a month," according to the college catalogue. (Courtesy of Saint Ignatius High School.)

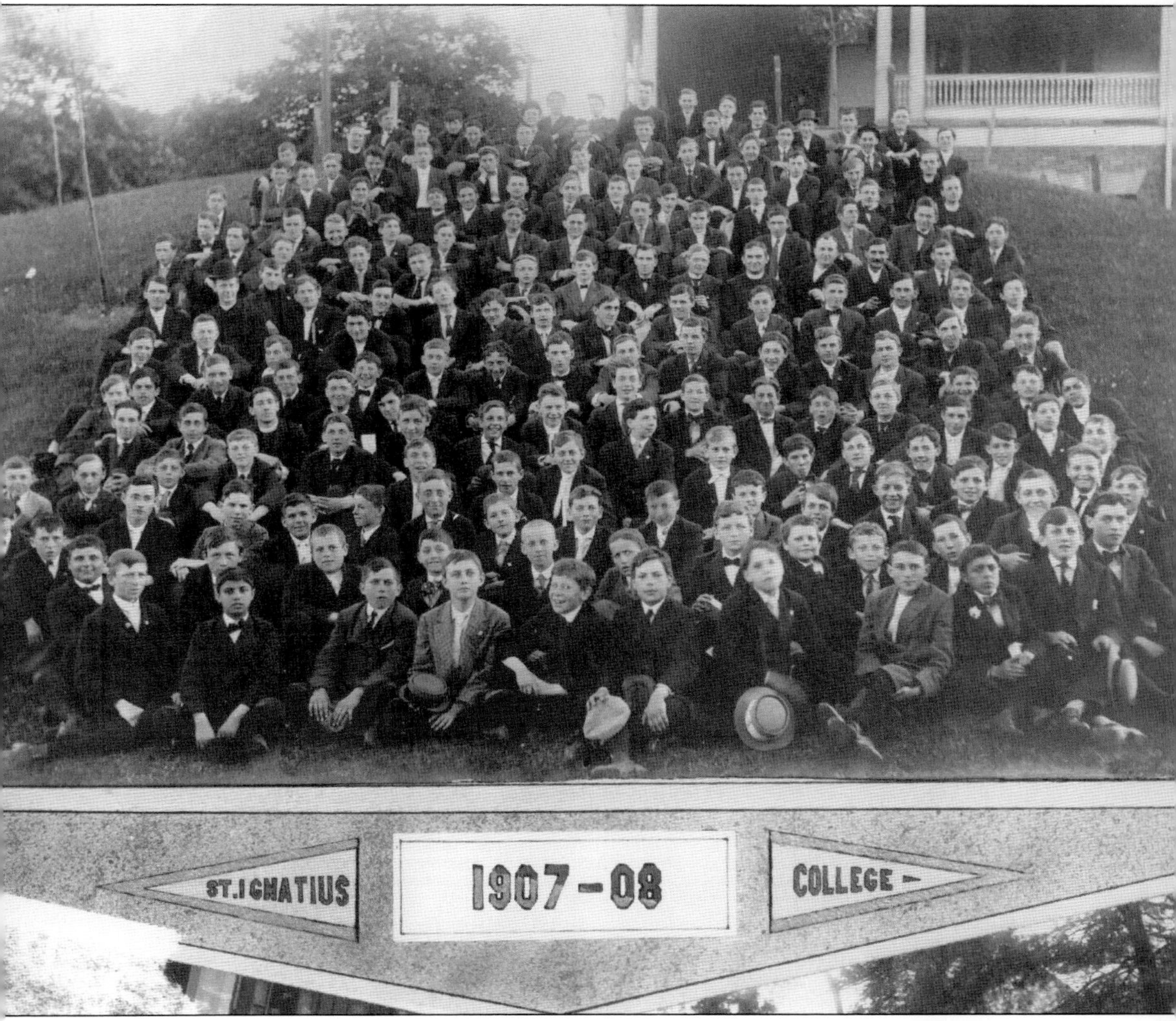

Although the high school and the college were formally separated in 1902, the two student bodies must have posed together for this photograph. Saint Ignatius prided itself on the strictness of its discipline and its adherence to the classical curriculum in both the high school and the college. These characteristics always attracted a few non-Catholic students. At the time this photograph was taken, there was no chance of the college admitting women. In Cleveland, Catholic women could attend schools and colleges run by the Sisters of Notre Dame or the Ursuline Sisters. Regardless of the college's strict rules, these young men appear to be enjoying themselves. (Courtesy of Saint Ignatius High School.)

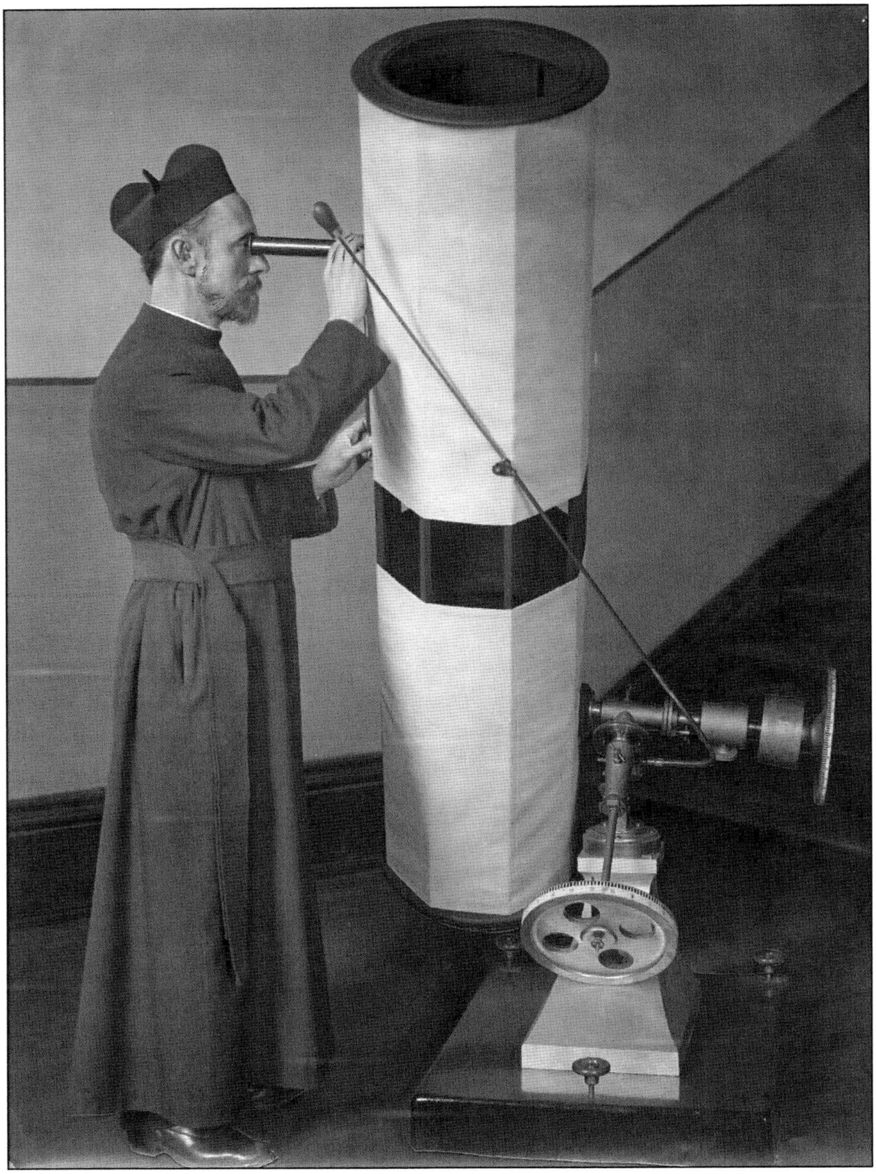

Rev. Frederick Odenbach, SJ, a graduate of Canisius College, arrived at Saint Ignatius in 1893 after completing his Jesuit training and quickly became a public figure. He was noted for his meteorological observatory, from which he and his students flew instrument-bearing kites that recorded temperature and wind velocity. They then flew flags from the top of the building that provided the neighborhood with a weather forecast. Odenbach was a pioneer in seismology and helped found the Jesuit Seismological Service in 1911. He was often quoted in the *Cleveland Plain Dealer*, which came to him for information about everything from insects, planets, and meteors to eclipses and earthquakes. When construction was halted on the University Heights campus in 1932, Odenbach moved into the tower of the unfinished administration building. To commemorate his 75th birthday, the *Cleveland Plain Dealer* interviewed Odenbach on October 21, 1932, in his makeshift living quarters. When asked about humans reaching the moon, he replied, "nonsense." His March 16, 1933, obituary described him as "the best-known educator in Cleveland."

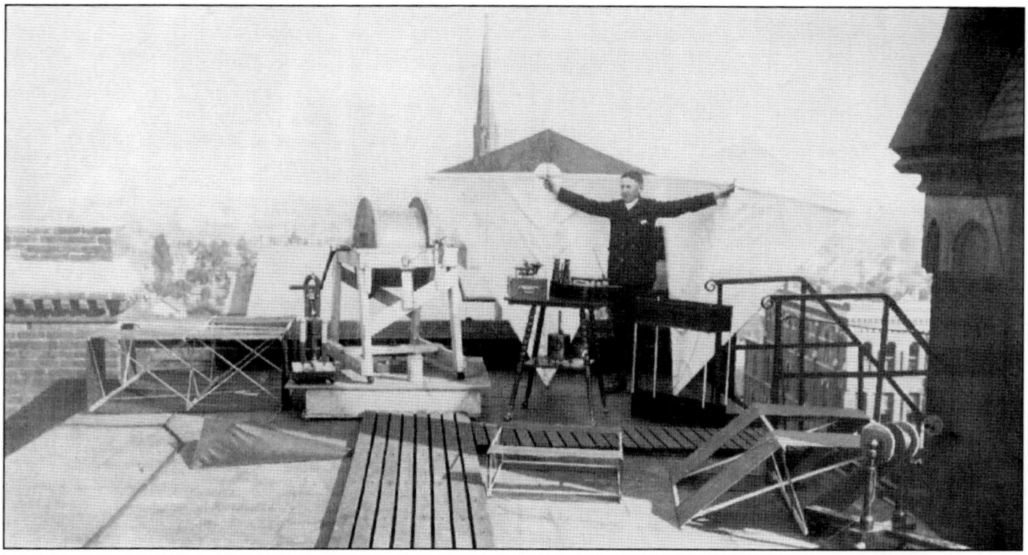

Rev. Frederick Odenbach and his students built kites that gathered weather information. This perch at the top of the 1891 building looks perilous. The steeple of Saint Mary of the Assumption is visible in the background.

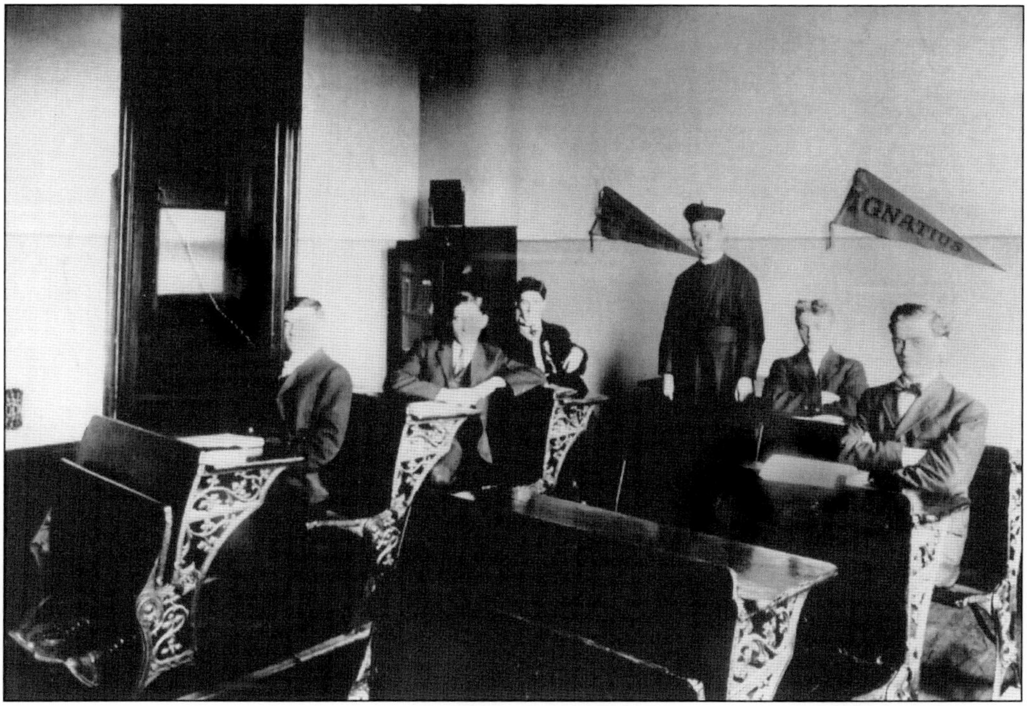

Rev. Francis J. Haggeney, SJ, professor of philosophy and secretary of the board of trustees, taught at Saint Ignatius College from 1892 to 1926. Like some of the other Jesuits, he did not support the curriculum changes necessary for the school to earn accreditation in the early 1920s. In this photograph, he is standing at the back of the classroom.

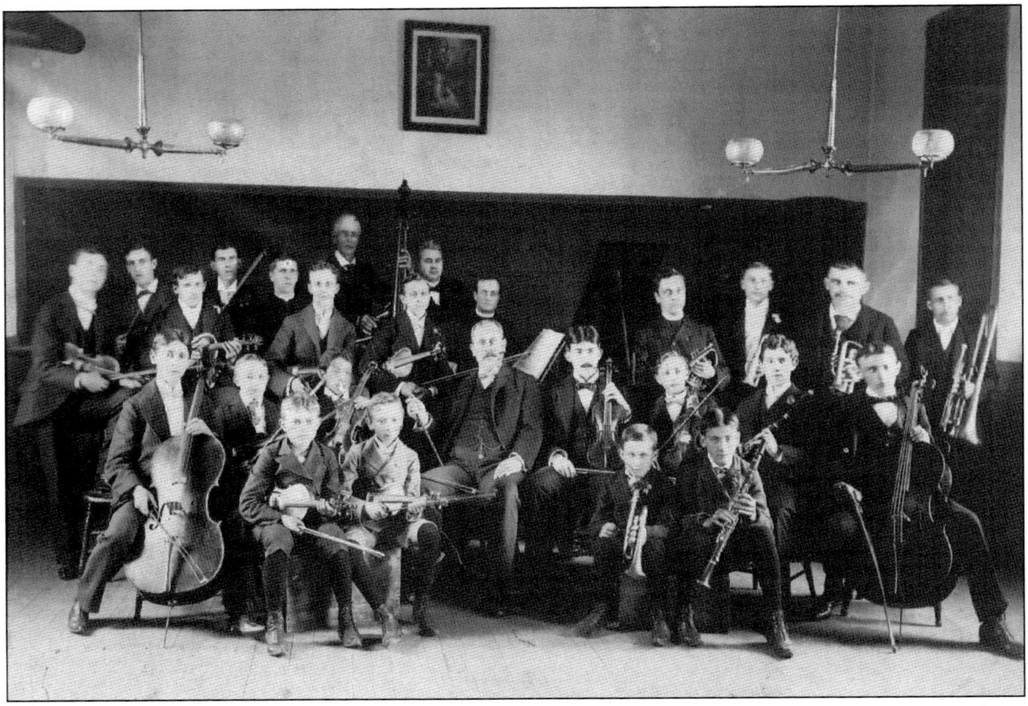

The Saint Ignatius Orchestra was created shortly after the college's founding. Its members played on holidays and at commencements and gave public concerts. In April 1900, the orchestra presented a program of instrumental and vocal music in the auditorium of the Cleveland Chamber of Commerce, and the *Cleveland Plain Dealer* praised the program: "The various selections were admirably rendered."

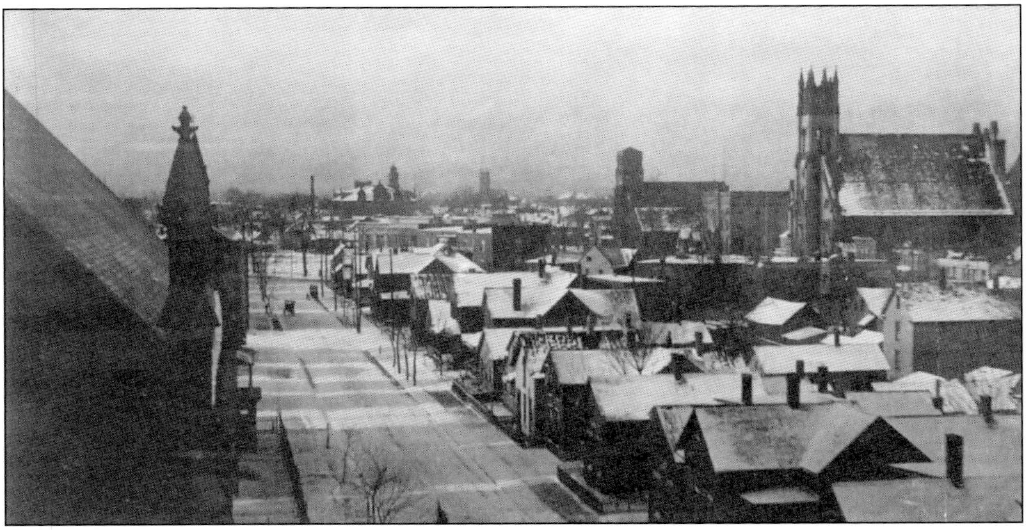

In this grainy, undated photograph, the Ohio City skyline is punctuated with church steeples that represented the religious and ethnic diversity of the neighborhood. To the right is Saint Patrick's, an Irish congregation, and in the distant center is Saint John's Episcopal Church. The Jesuits aspired to move from this neighborhood of small homes, commerce, and light industry to a more affluent setting. (Courtesy of Saint Ignatius High School.)

Two

MOVING EAST
1907–1929

In the first decades of the 20th century, Clevelanders were on the move—to the east. The factories, mills, and refineries that attracted immigrants to the city had begun to repel those who could afford to live elsewhere. By 1900, Western Reserve University and Case School of Applied Science had already relocated to University Circle on the city's east side. The Jesuits followed, but only after a prolonged conflict with Bishop John P. Farrelly.

In 1907, the Jesuits opened Loyola High School, an east side satellite, near University Circle. The high school closed in 1922, ostensibly because the Jesuits could not staff it. Coincidentally, in 1918 Bishop Farrelly had opened a free Catholic high school, Cathedral Latin, in the area.

During World War I, the students at Saint Ignatius College and High School formed a drill team, sold Liberty Loan Bonds, and volunteered for military service, emphasizing the school's patriotic character. Successful baseball and football teams and a talented symphony orchestra also garnered local acclaim for the college.

In 1920, Saint Ignatius College added a fourth year, making it easier for graduates to be admitted to professional schools. In 1922, the college earned accreditation from the North Central Association of Colleges and Schools. In 1923, the Jesuits received a charter that allowed the college to become a university, and Bishop Joseph Schrembs gave them permission to move even farther east. The Jesuits purchased a property just to the north of Shaker Heights in Idlewood Village, which became University Heights two years later.

A 1923 fundraising drive for the new campus fell flat, possibly because the Jesuits considered naming the new institution "Cleveland University" when there was already discussion of a non-Catholic University of Cleveland set to be located in University Circle. The Jesuits quickly renamed the new university John Carroll after the first American archbishop, who was a Jesuit and the founder of Georgetown University.

School officials hoped the proposed move would make the university more attractive to affluent east siders. Despite the setbacks, the college's enrollment increased throughout the prosperous 1920s, climbing from 146 in 1920 to 468 by 1929. In the spring of 1929, a second fundraising drive successfully began with significant support from both Catholics and non-Catholics.

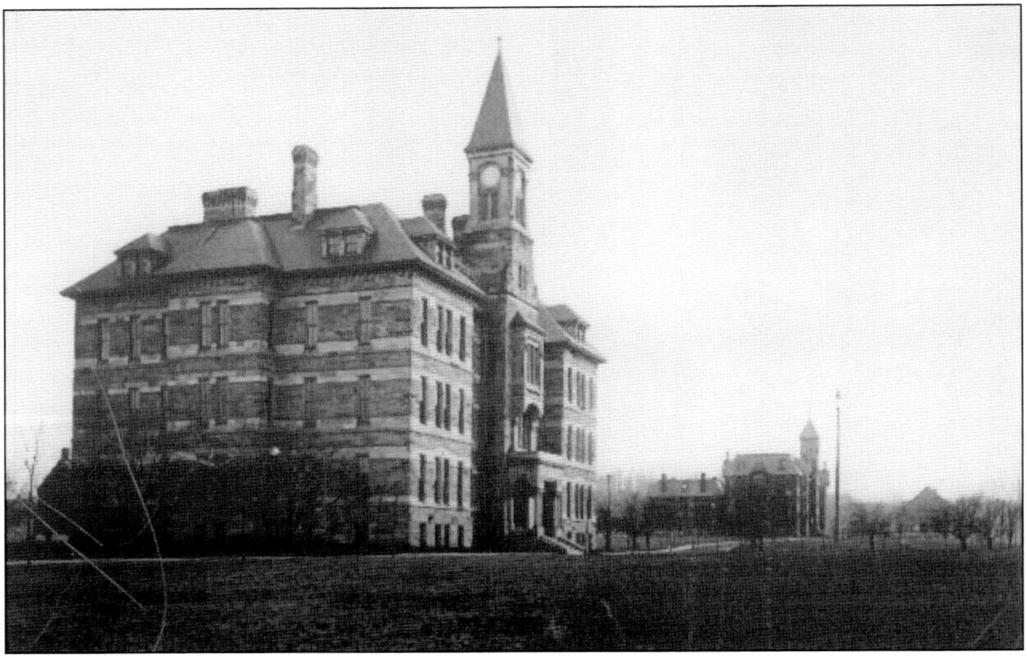

Two Cleveland colleges led the way east. In 1882, Western Reserve College (now Case Western Reserve University) relocated from Hudson, Ohio, to Cleveland's Euclid Avenue, across from the area donated to the city by Jeptha Wade (Wade Park) in the neighborhood that became University Circle. The college, originally sponsored by Congregationalists, became a university when it added its law school in the 1890s. Adelbert Hall, which still stands, is pictured here. (Courtesy of Case Western Reserve University Archives.)

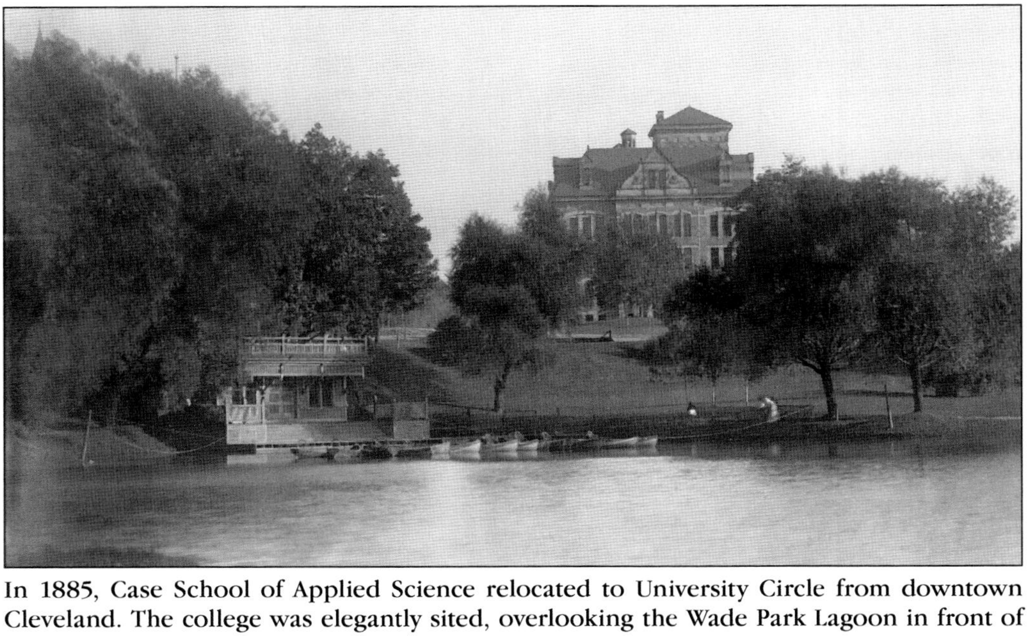

In 1885, Case School of Applied Science relocated to University Circle from downtown Cleveland. The college was elegantly sited, overlooking the Wade Park Lagoon in front of what would become the Cleveland Museum of Art. After existing side by side for decades, the two universities federated in 1967 as Case Western Reserve University. (Courtesy of Case Western Reserve University Archives.)

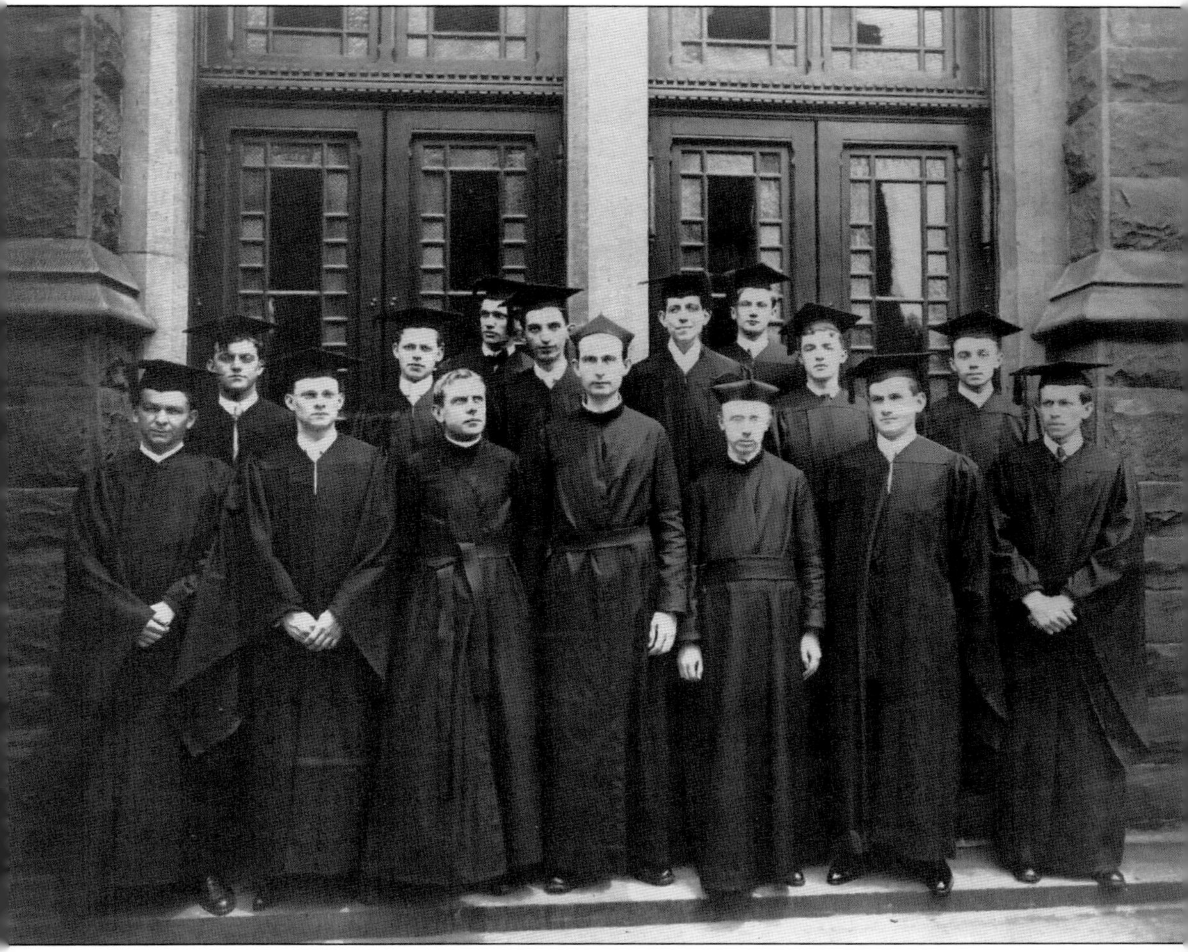

Rev. George J. Pickel, SJ, who stands in the center of the photograph flanked by recent Saint Ignatius College graduates, wanted Saint Ignatius College to move to the east side. Pickel served as president of the college from 1906 to 1910. He got permission from Bishop Ignatius F. Horstmann to open Loyola High School in 1907 near University Circle at E. 106th Street and Cedar Avenue. For the next several years, Pickel battled with Bishop John P. Farrelly over a permanent east side location for the college. Pickel left Saint Ignatius College but returned in 1927 after the college had become John Carroll University. His dream of an east side college was fulfilled when John Carroll moved to University Heights. Pickel again served as president of the university for a brief period in 1937.

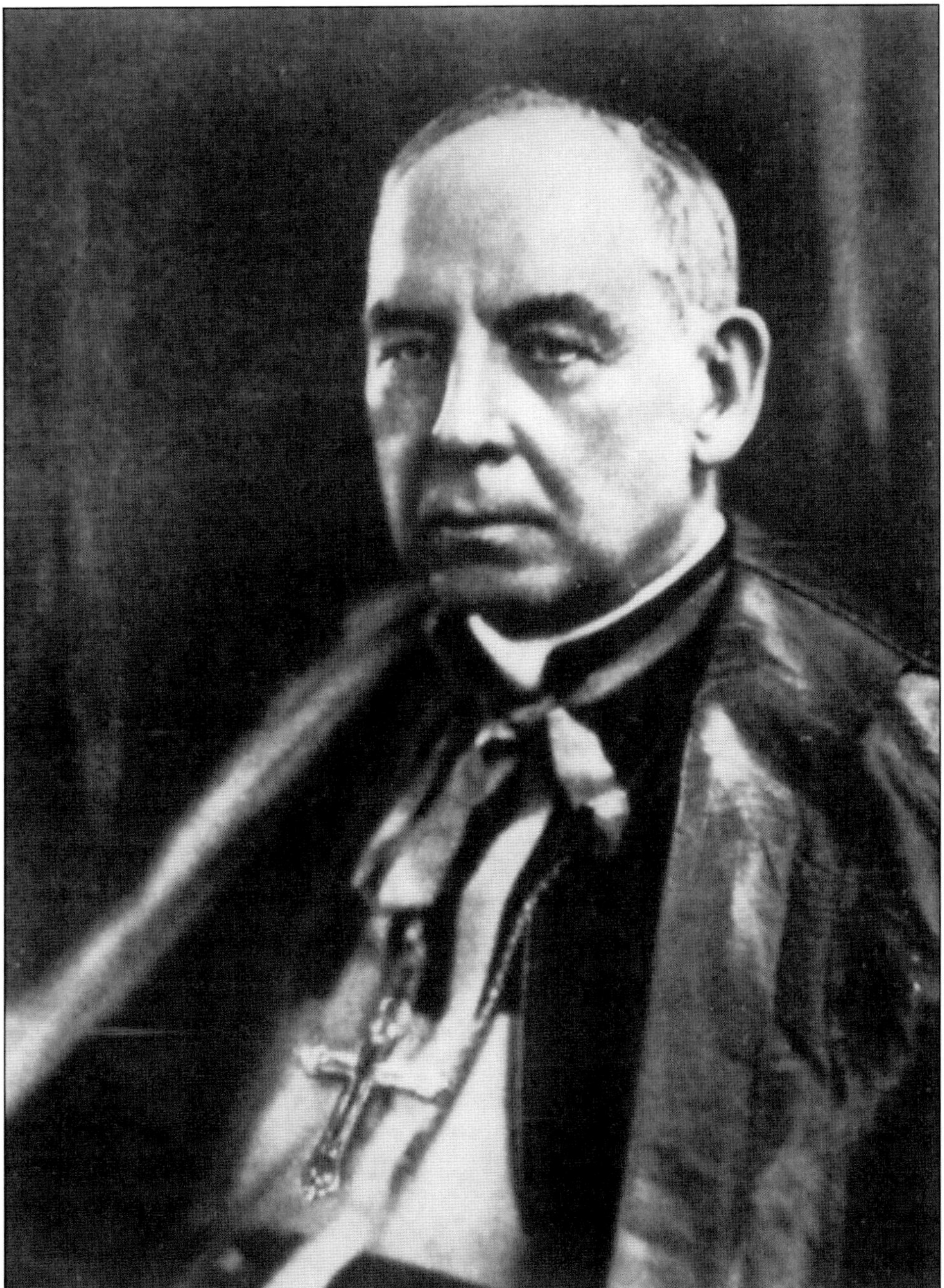

John P. Farrelly became bishop of Cleveland in 1909. Farrelly hoped to relocate Saint John's Cathedral to University Circle and to open a free Catholic boys' school nearby. The plans for the cathedral fell through, but Cathedral Latin High School opened in 1918 just a few blocks from Loyola High School. Two years later, Cathedral Latin had 500 students. Consequently, Farrelly did not support Loyola High School and, until his death in 1921, opposed the Jesuits' efforts to establish a college and a parish on the east side. However, his successor, Bishop Joseph Schrembs, gave the Jesuits permission to establish John Carroll in what would become University Heights.

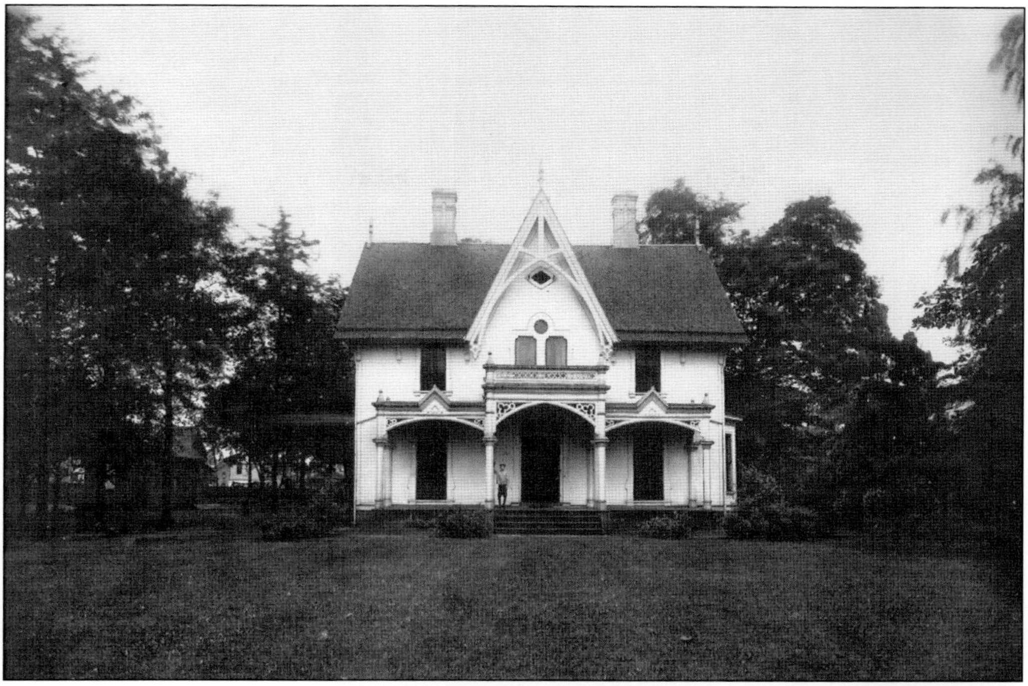

The Barnett home served as the Loyola High School faculty building. Since the school was considered a temporary solution, its site was initially leased. The Jesuits, fearing that other religious orders would come into Cleveland and wishing to solidify their east side position in the face of continued opposition from Bishop John P. Farrelly, purchased the property in 1915. The school closed seven years later.

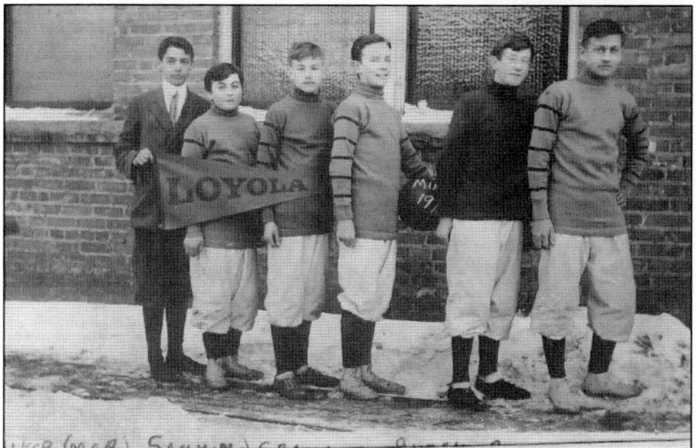

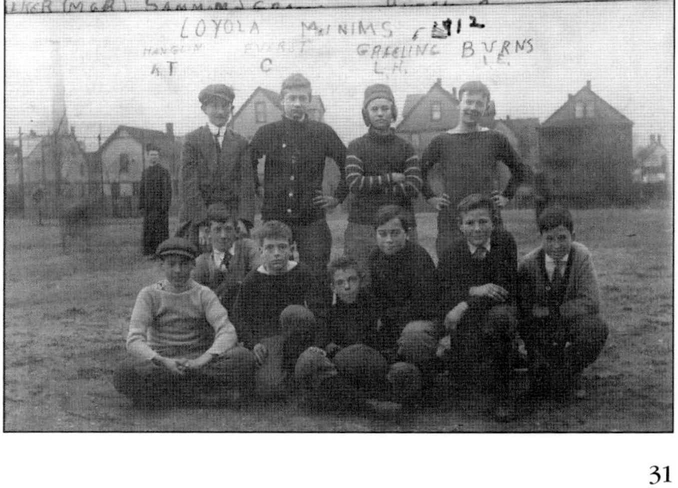

Loyola High School opened in 1907 with only one class and added a class each subsequent year. The school quickly fielded sports teams. The varsity teams called themselves the "Maxims." The "Minims," pictured below at right, may have been the junior varsity team. (Courtesy of Saint Ignatius High School.)

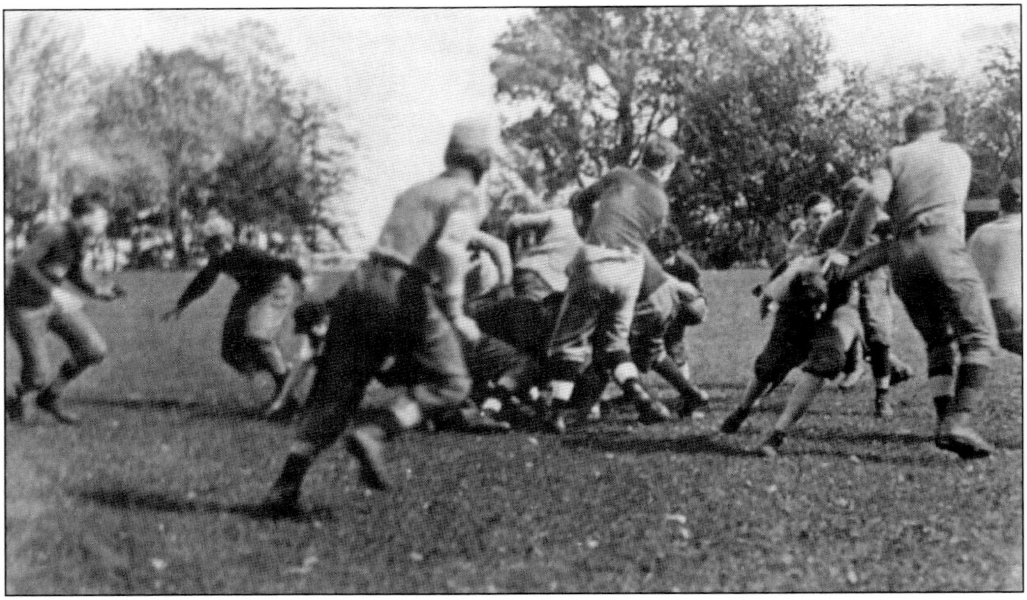

Loyola and Saint Ignatius High Schools played each other every year in football and baseball. In 1910 and 1915, the Loyola football team defeated Ignatius handily, but in 1917, the Saint Ignatius Saints swamped Loyola 68–0 at Gordon Park. This image is from 1911.

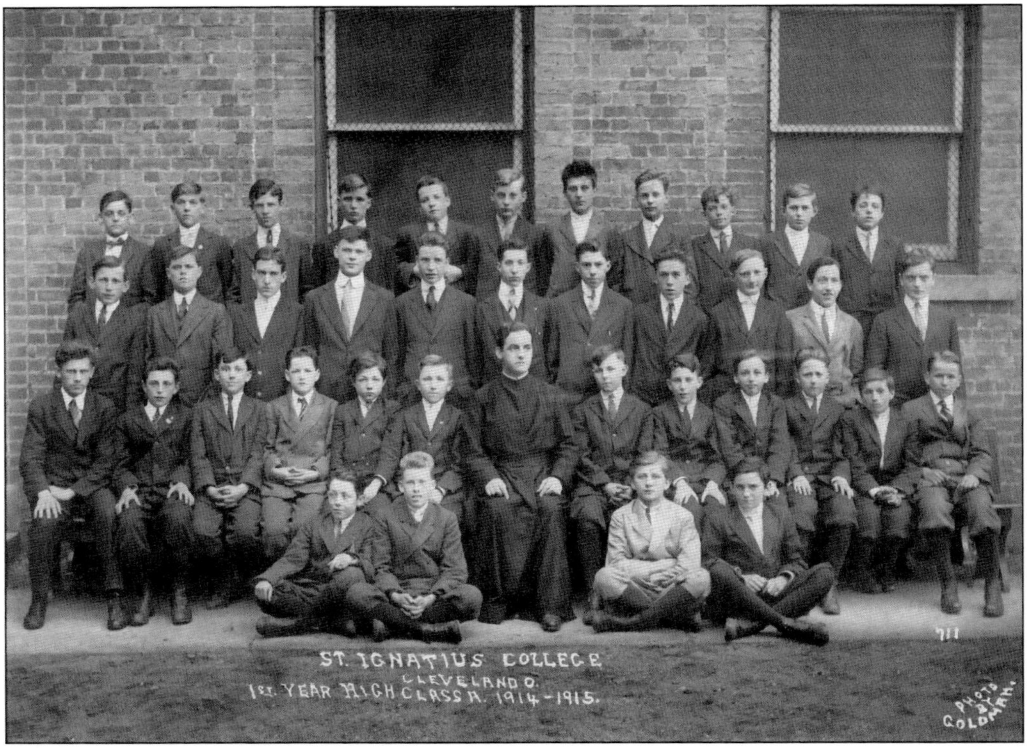

Despite competition from Loyola, Saint Ignatius High School continued to attract students like these young men in its first-year class of 1914–1915. Many of these students later entered the college, since the high school acted as a feeder, much like the preparatory departments at other private colleges. (Courtesy of Saint Ignatius High School.)

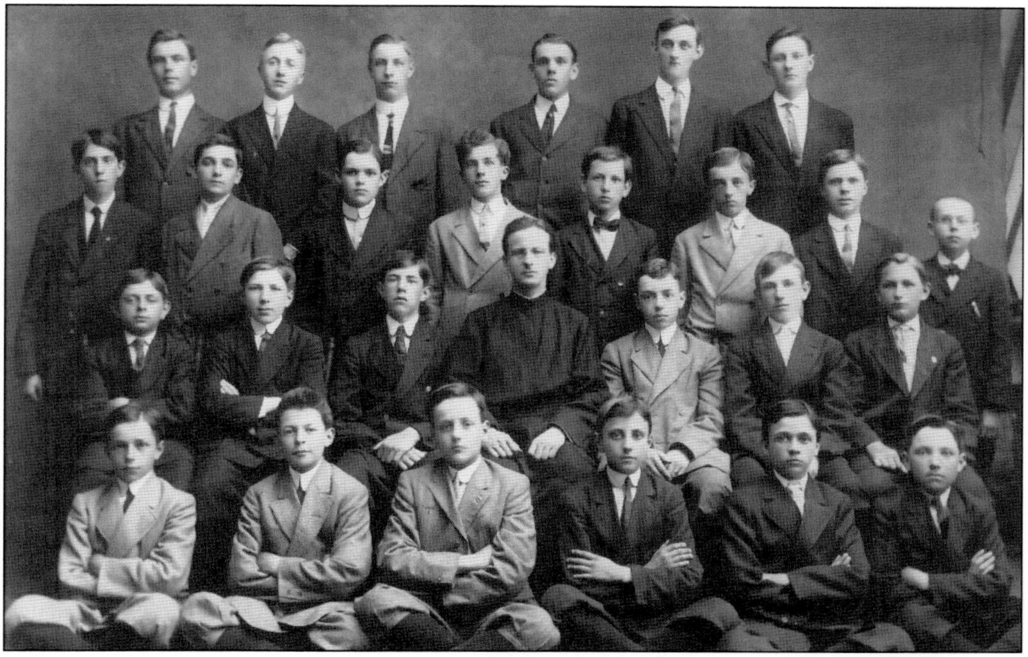

In 1910, Saint Ignatius College had an enrollment of only 58, including these young freshmen. College officials sometimes blamed its low enrollment on Catholics' failure to appreciate higher education. Another explanation might have been the need for young men to support their families. (Courtesy of Saint Ignatius High School.)

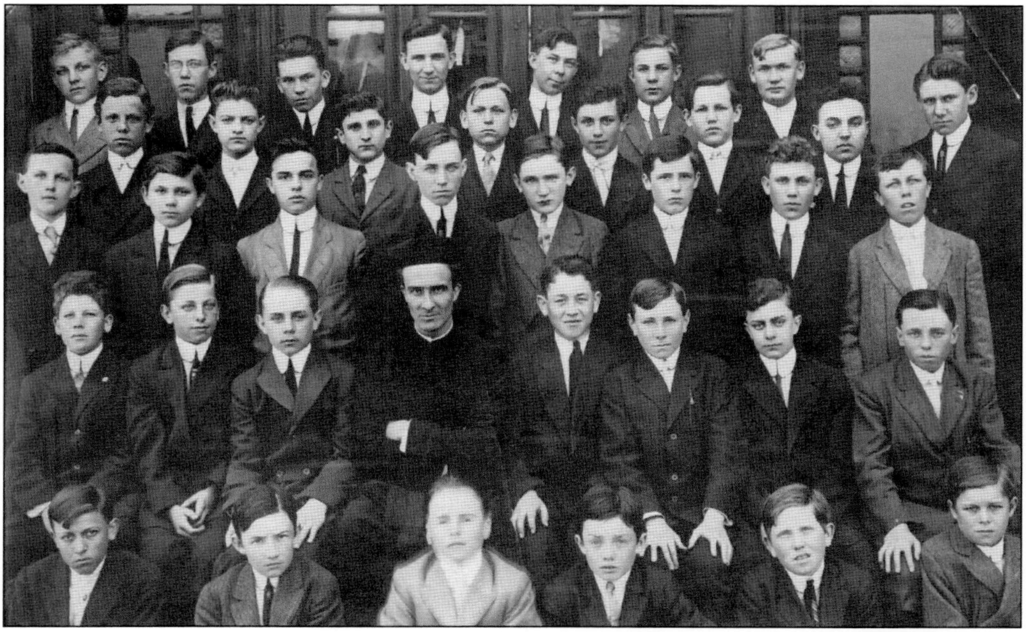

These 1912–1913 college students experienced the college's rising costs, which included tuition plus fees for admission, the library, and the laboratory. Some students received tuition discounts, and others received scholarships donated by diocesan clergy and generous individuals. Even so, many students had to drop out to go to work. (Courtesy of Saint Ignatius High School.)

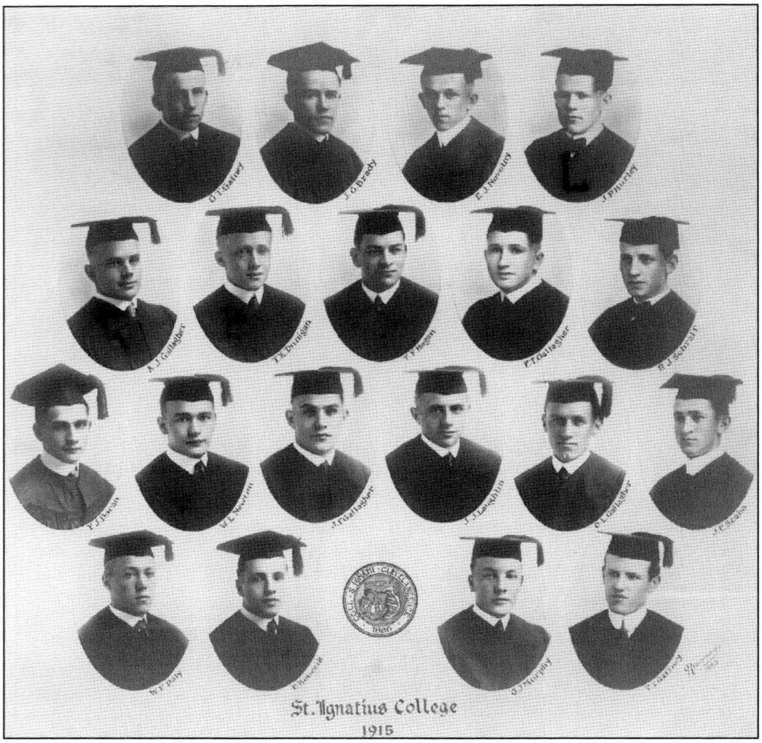

These 19 men graduated from the college in 1915. Two went to Saint Louis University Medical School, and others went to Western Reserve Medical School. One went to Harvard Law School and one entered Saint Mary's Seminary. Every graduating class was known as the "class of Philosophy." (Courtesy of Saint Ignatius High School.)

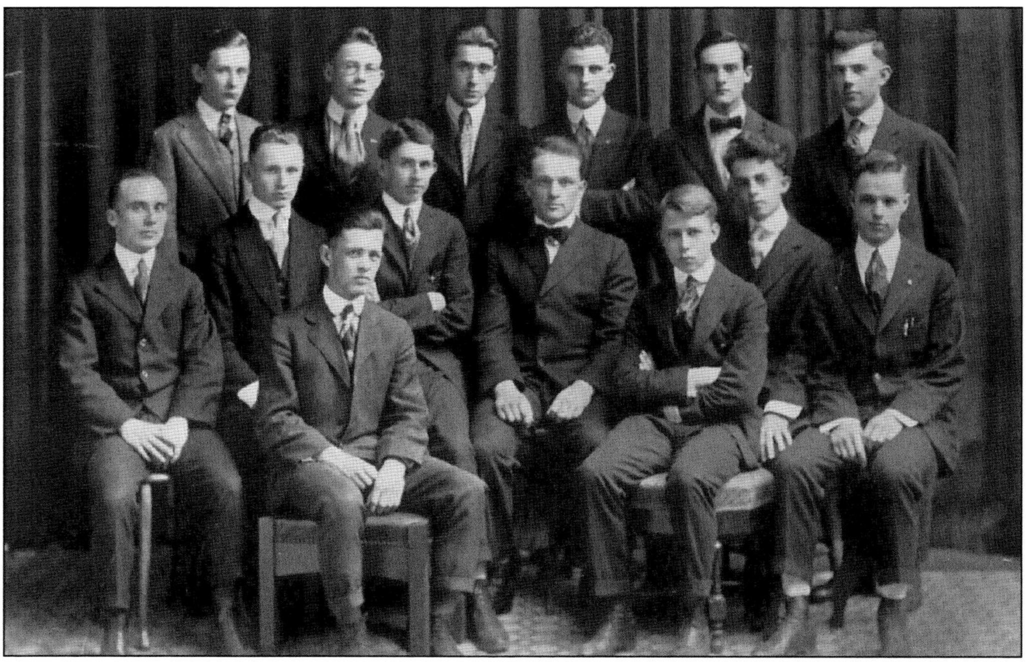

From October 1915 to June 1919, the *Lumina*, the college's literary magazine, was published five times a year. The staff wrote essays on a wide range of topics, including current events and alumni news, as well as poetry. The magazine was replaced by the school newspaper, *The Ignatian*, which became *The Carroll News* when the college changed names in 1923. (Courtesy of Saint Ignatius High School.)

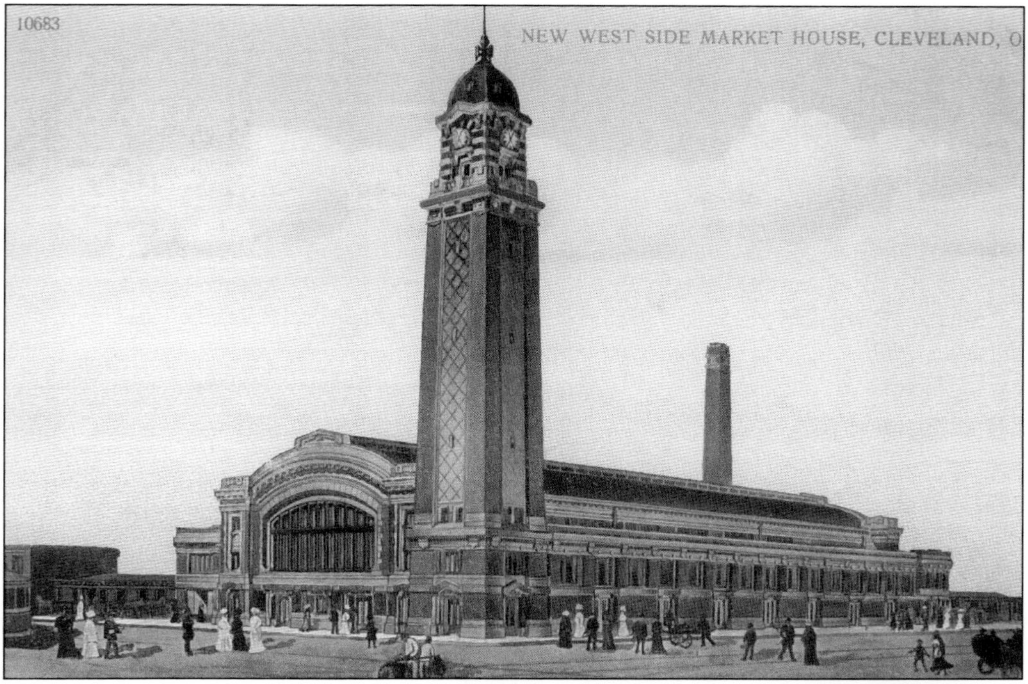

Just to the east of the college, the city of Cleveland gave the neighborhood a boost when it opened the West Side Market in 1912. The market has served as the commercial anchor of Ohio City ever since. The imposing building was designed by the architectural firm of Hubbell & Benes, which also designed the Cleveland Museum of Art. (Courtesy of Cleveland State University Special Collections.)

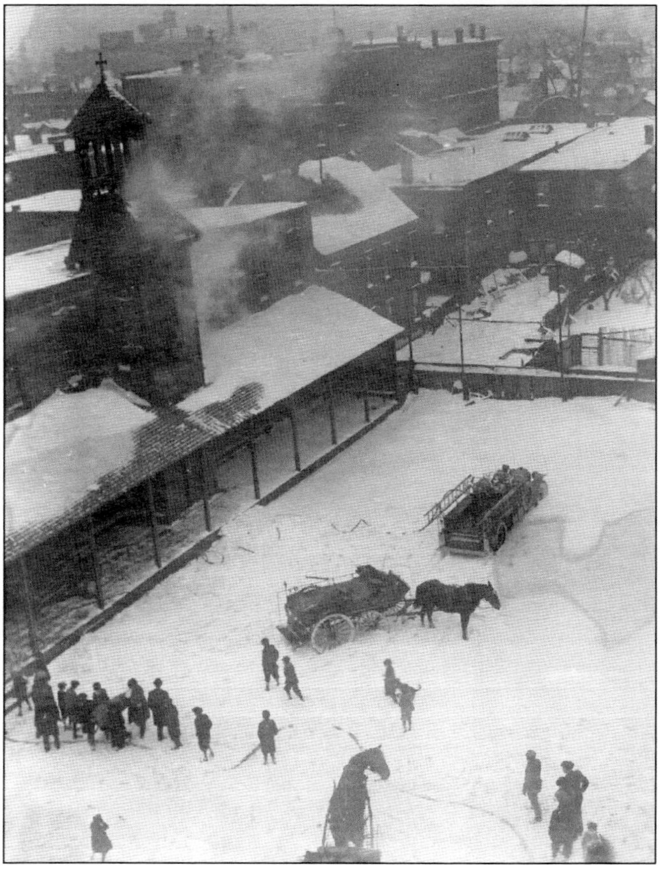

In 1914, fire swept through the college's original building, which was then serving as a makeshift gymnasium. The building was torn down and replaced with a new gymnasium, demonstrating the college's commitment to an energetic athletic program.

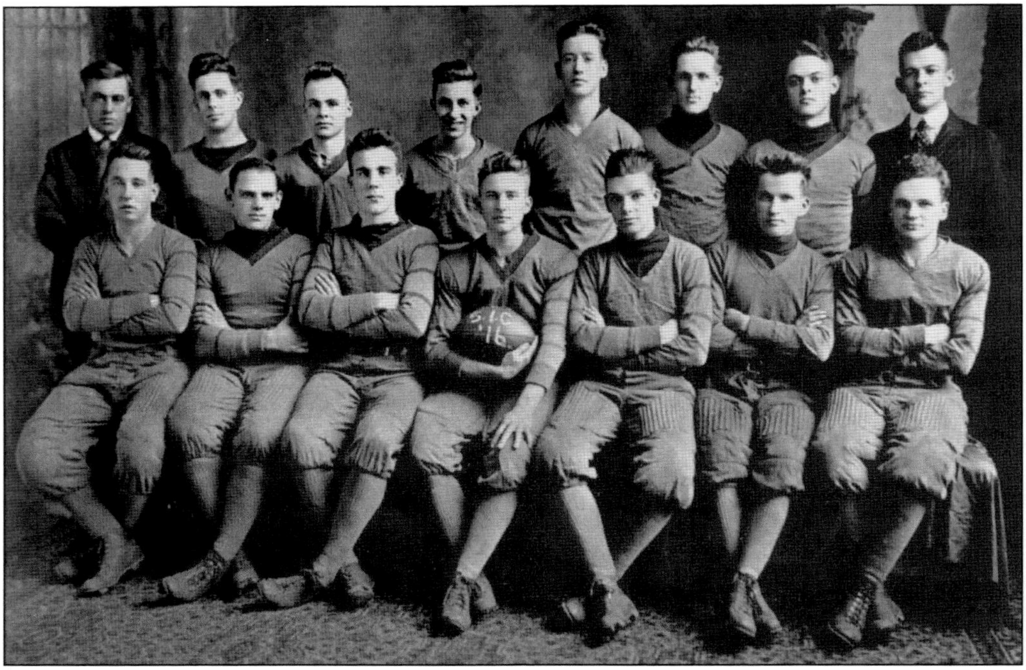

Saint Ignatius College fielded its first varsity football team in 1916, winning three games and losing two against local colleges in its first season. After being discontinued during World War I, the team was revived in 1920. The team's 4–2 season that year was widely celebrated by students, but caused some administrators and faculty members to worry, as they do today, that too much emphasis was being placed upon athletics.

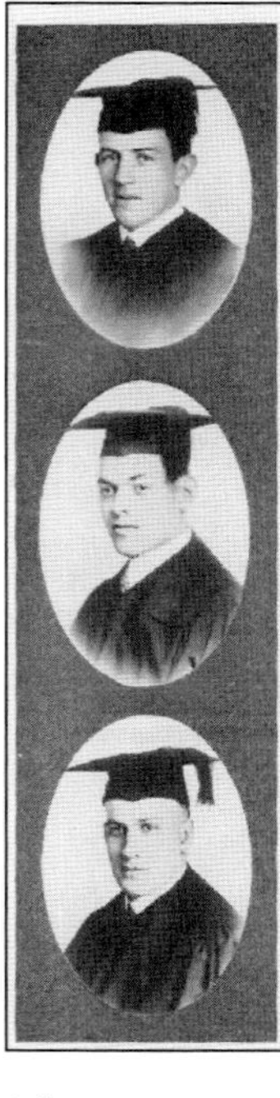

Arthur C. J. Brickel—"Art"

President of class of '17. Lumina Editor. Manager of Varsity Basketball. Pitcher for the Varsity nine. One of the best spitball artists in Cleveland. A versatile and all 'round capable chap. Noted above all for his weird comparisons. Art was juggling hay cocks out Avon way last summer, and during spare moments he studied comparative anatomy in the field. Art was always citing monstrosities who lived on his street. "Well, but Father, a woman on our street used to curse people, and then some one always died"; or, "Father, we had a dog on our street which killed cats and laid their heads across the car tracks,—now, was that instinct, or the result of training?" Art intends to follow the profession of looking at tongues at five dollars a throw.

George L. Warth—"Coxey," "Sox," "Baron," "Carter"

Officer in the Sodality, President of the Debating Society. Hails from Massillon, O. A real Bohemian, noted for bizarre cravats, stale jokes, and a song entitled "Ezzie Wheezzie." Played second fiddle in Jim Deering's snorous orchestra. "Coxey" is a devoted follower of Terpsichore, knows all the latest steps, and has invented a few all his own,—at least so we have been told. A lover of good cigars and Cadillacs. An artist in pulling the unexpected; he'll surely do something to startle us.

Charles Nelan—"Chollie"

One of the prairie chickens from Campion. All 'round athlete, good student, social star. Hails from Akron, but you would never suspect it. Although "Chollie" was with us only a year, he became one of the most popular fellows in school. If "Chollie" unravels the skein of legal lore as well as he studies philosophy we can assure him a successful career. Good luck, "Chollie"!

In 1917, 21 students—including these three men—graduated from the college, the largest graduating class in its history. In 1920, however, only three students graduated, because the college had added a fourth year in order to get accreditation. Students completed the required courses in their first two years and chose electives and their majors and minors in the last two. (Courtesy of Saint Ignatius High School.)

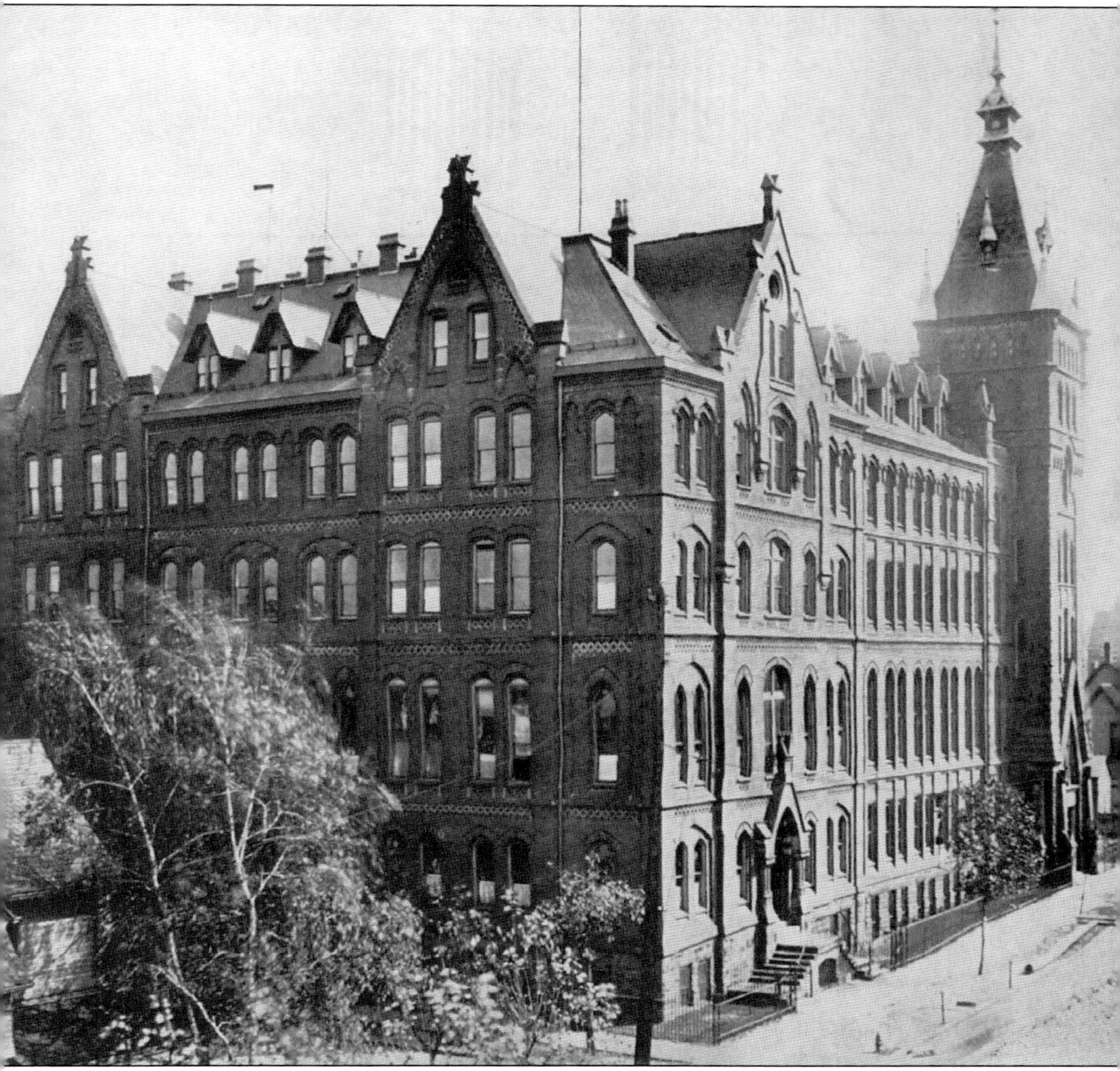

In 1917, Saint Ignatius College celebrated its first 30 years with the *Historical Review of Saint Ignatius College*. The book included this photograph of the 1891 building and dozens of other images that provide a snapshot of life at the college and Saint Ignatius and Loyola High Schools. The lines of poetry that describe the building—"Sun-kissed walls of learning, a grandeur more enduring/Than the bloodstained walls of ancient citadels"—pay tribute to the presence of this grand building and the college in its working-class neighborhood as the country was on the verge of entering World War I.

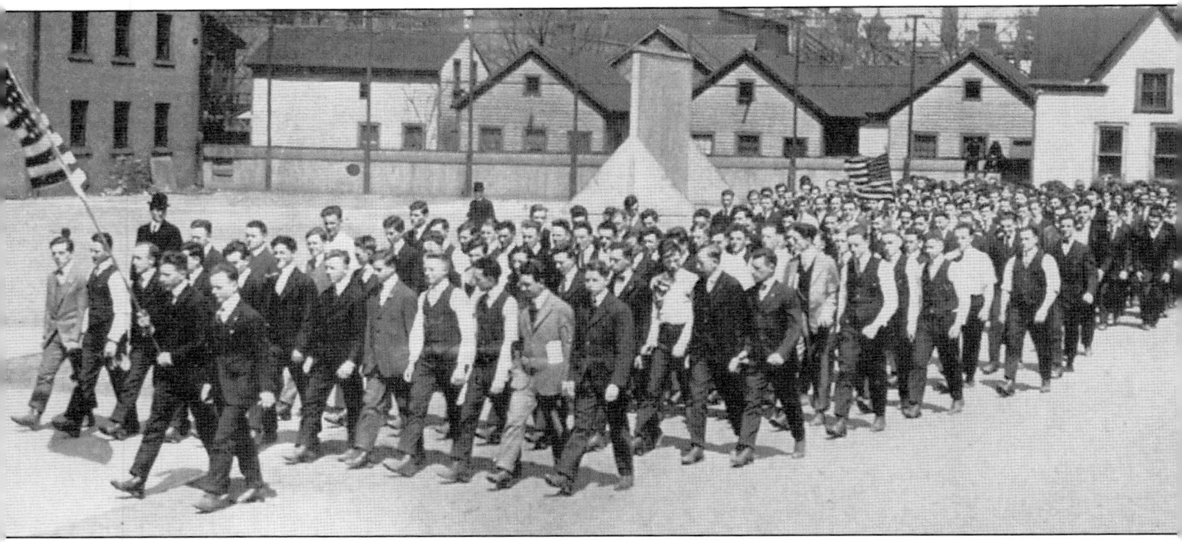

The college, sensitive to its German beginnings (during the war-induced anti-German hysteria) and to its Irish student body (the Irish generally opposed a war to aid England), formed a drill team on April 21, 1917, days after the United States declared war on Germany. Students also enthusiastically sold $145,500 worth of war bonds. In the summer of 1918, after the draft age had been lowered to 18, the federal government set up a Student Army Training Corps to defer active military service for college students. Saint Ignatius' corps of 130 (pictured) included both college and high school students. The War Department was supposed to pick up some of the expenses, but the war ended before the corps' uniforms could arrive. Three Ignatius graduates served as military chaplains, and many more served in the medical corps and in all the armed services. This display of patriotism was important for a college still trying to secure its place in American society.

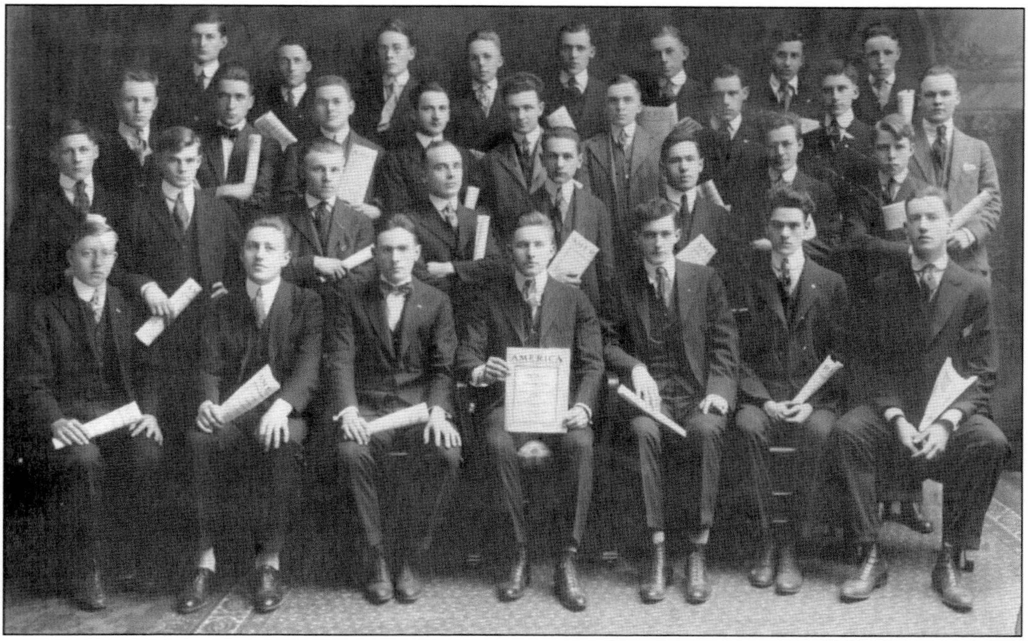

The freshman class of 1916–1917 posed with copies of *America: A Catholic Review of the Week*, a Jesuit journal that is still published today. It is not clear whether this was to illustrate their interest in current events or their loyalty to the United States. In any case, they look extraordinarily mature. (Courtesy of Saint Ignatius High School.)

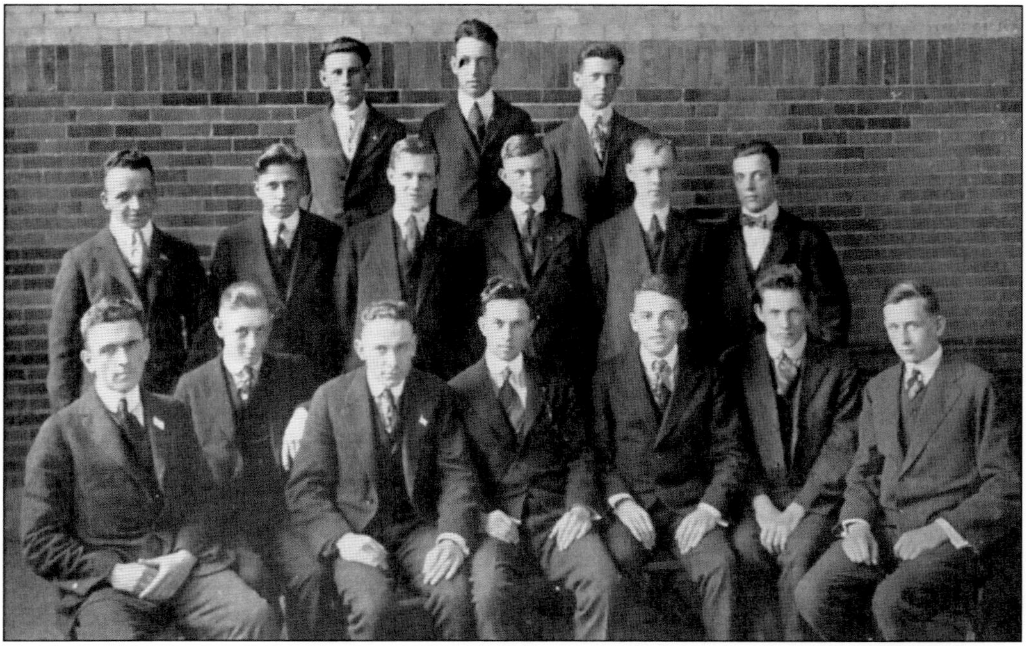

The 1916–1917 sophomore class pursued an arduous course of studies, including Latin and Greek, the sciences, and "the lives and works of some of the famous poets" in the students' second to last year of college (the college course at this point lasted only three years). The *Historical Review* also noted that six members of the class had already "left to pursue their vocation" in the seminary.

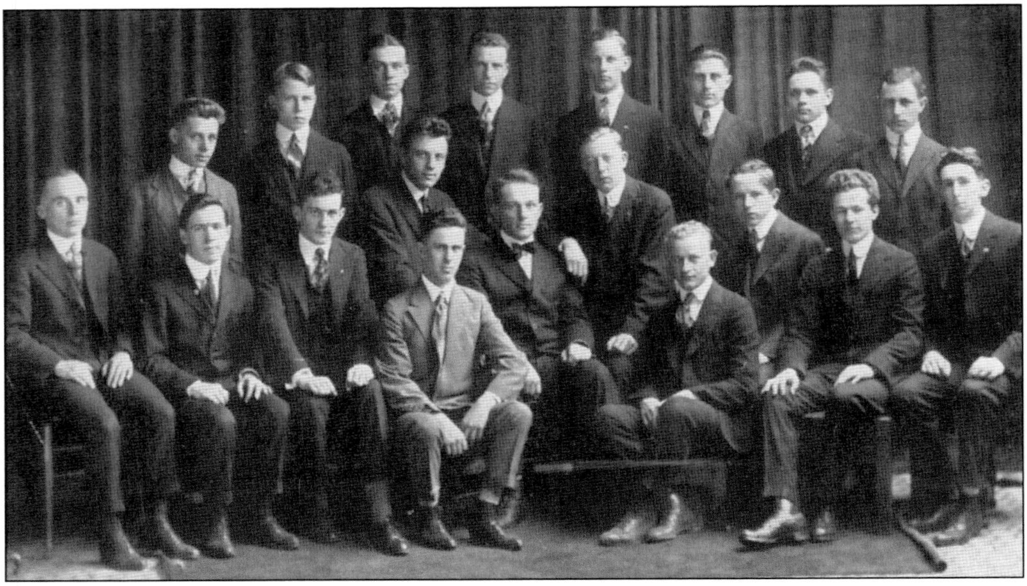

The members of the Scientific Academy, organized in 1915, were dedicated to promoting interest in the natural sciences. Also seeking to hone their public speaking skills, members used experiments and slides while giving lectures on campus and occasionally in public venues.

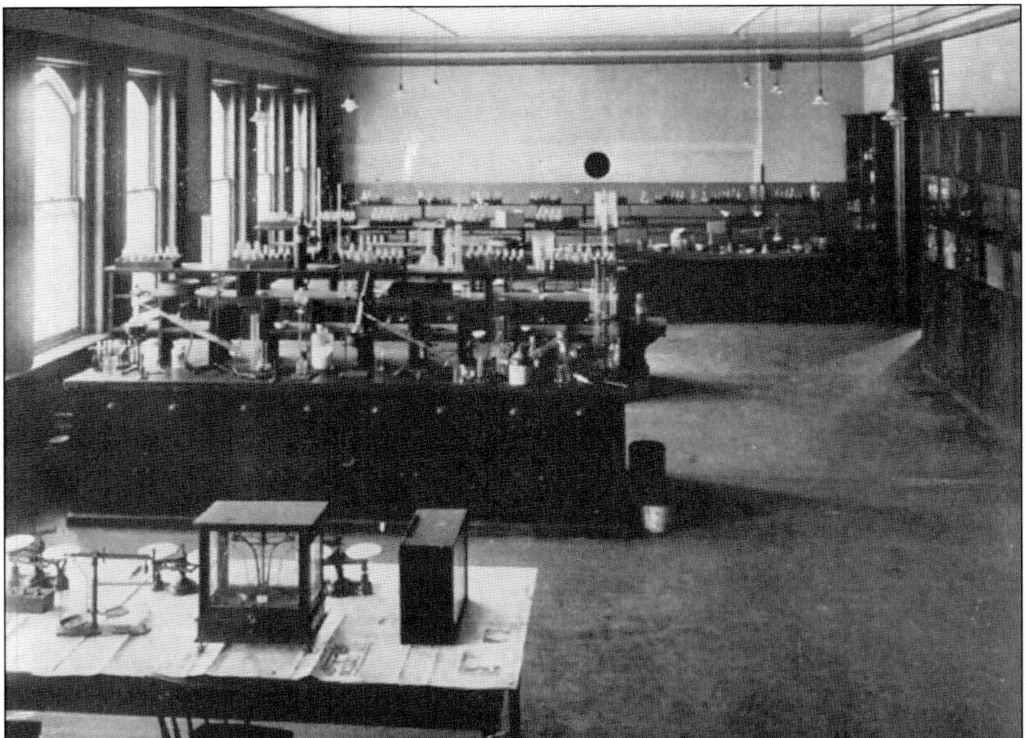

The equipment in the 1917 chemistry lab looks primitive. However, it testified to the importance of science in the curriculum not only for its practical applications, but because science was viewed as a necessary part of a Jesuit Catholic liberal arts education.

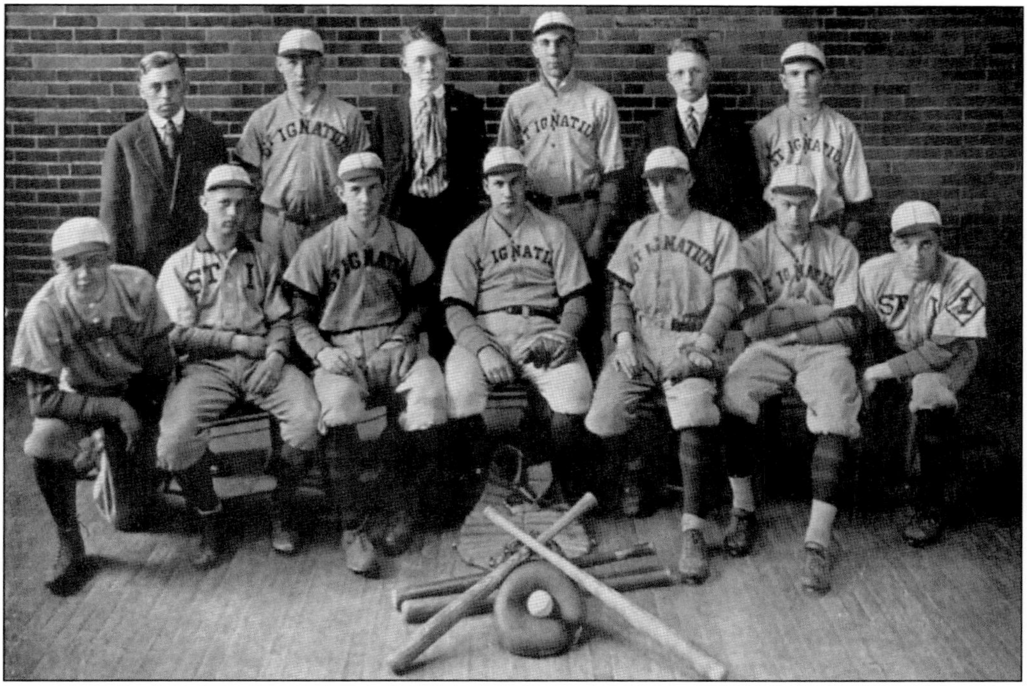

The varsity baseball team of 1917 had a disappointing season; their regular games were cancelled because of the war. Instead, they played practice games against neighboring colleges, including a winning no-hitter with 16 strikeouts. Baseball was discontinued in 1922 after the practice field was given to the football team.

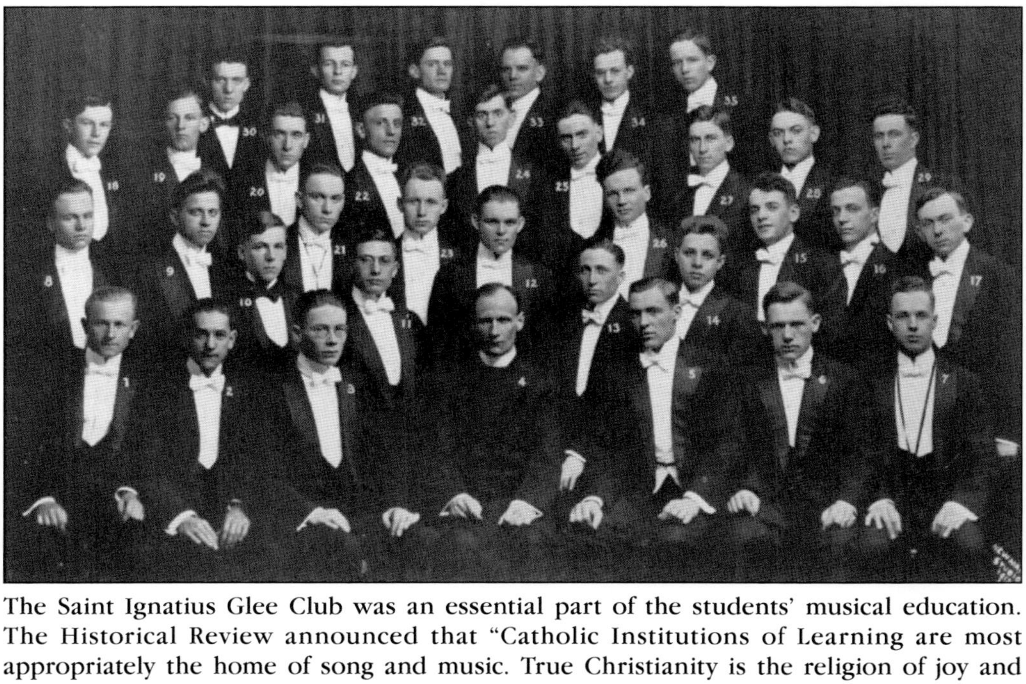

The Saint Ignatius Glee Club was an essential part of the students' musical education. The Historical Review announced that "Catholic Institutions of Learning are most appropriately the home of song and music. True Christianity is the religion of joy and happiness, so well expressed in these arts."

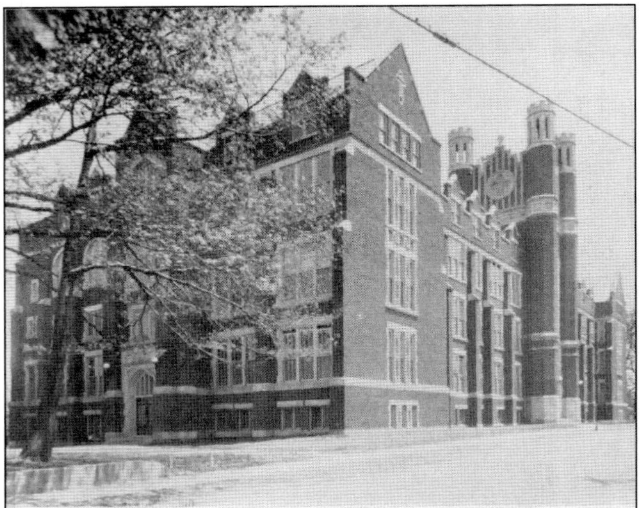

NOTRE DAME ACADEMY

1325 Ansel Road, Cleveland, O.

DAY SCHOOL

Conducted by the Sisters of Notre Dame

Kindergarten, Primary, Preparatory, Commercial, Academic Courses. Special Departments in Music, Art, Expression, Needlework and Domestic Science. Thorough Religious, Moral and Physical Training. Completely equipped Gymnasium. Modern, fireproof building. Location unsurpassed for convenience, healthfulness and beauty.

RECOGNIZED AS A STANDARD HIGH SCHOOL

Bulletin on request — Address, MOTHER SUPERIOR

This advertisement appeared in the *Historical Review.* Notre Dame Academy, founded in 1877 by the Sisters of Notre Dame, was intended for middle-class Catholic girls. It moved to Ansel Road in the Hough neighborhood in 1912, then to Chardon in 1963, then merged with the all-male Cathedral Latin High School in 1988. The Ansel Road building now houses Catholic social service agencies.

The Ursuline Sisters established the three schools mentioned in the advertisement below. The academy was a day school, and the other two were boarding schools. Ursuline Academy became Beaumont School when it moved to Cleveland Heights in 1942. Villa Angela and Saint Joseph's merged into a coeducational high school in 1990. The Ursulines also established Ursuline College in 1871.

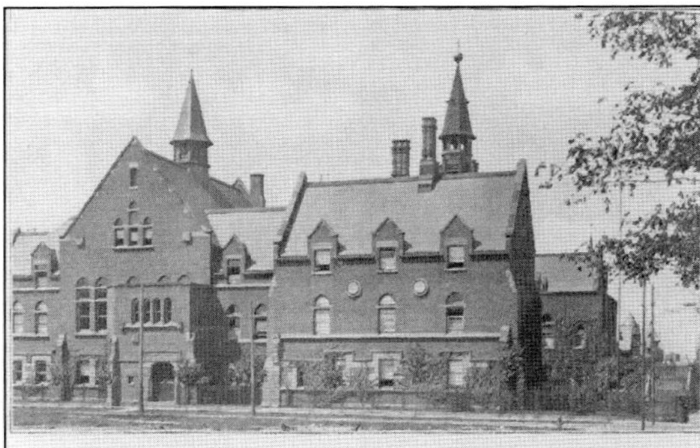

URSULINE ACADEMY

EAST 55th AND SCOVILL AVENUE

CLEVELAND, OHIO

DAY SCHOOL FOR YOUNG LADIES

AFFILIATED WITH THE CATHOLIC UNIVERSITY
WASHINGTON, D. C.

VILLA ANGELA

CLEVELAND, OHIO

Boarding Schools Conducted by the Ursuline Nuns

ST. MARY'S ACADEMY

For Girls and Young Ladies

Courses comprise College Preparatory, Academic, Commercial, Grammar, Intermediate and Primary Departments. Special advantages in French, German, Music, Art, Needlework, Domestic Science. Thorough Moral, Religious and Physical Training.

Location healthful and easy of access. Grounds extensive and beautiful.

ST. JOSEPH'S SEMINARY

adjoins Academy grounds

Boys are taken from the age of five to thirteen. Situation and equipment ideal. A thorough Grammar Grade Course, also Intermediate and Primary Departments. Religious, Moral and Physical Training, German, Music, Drawing, Military Drills, Gymnasium, etc.

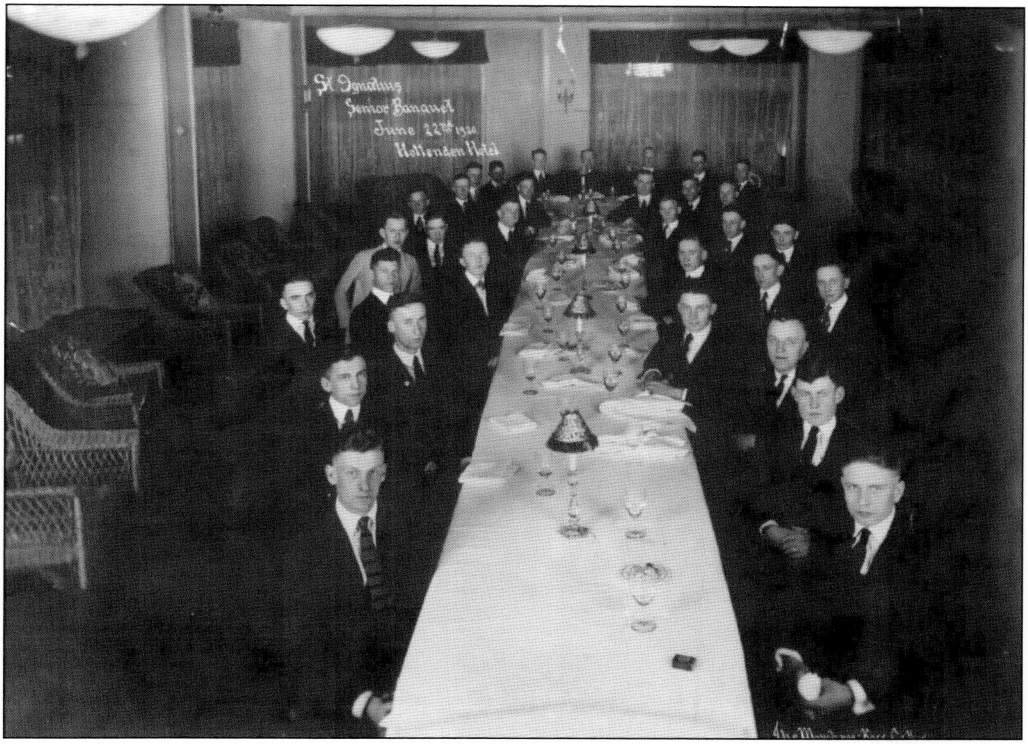

This formal stag affair was held in 1920 at the elegant Hollenden Hotel. That same year, the college began to sponsor dances—which were also held in elegant hotels—that aroused the ire of Bishop Joseph Schrembs because the dances lasted until too late in the evening and were not properly supervised. (Courtesy of Saint Ignatius High School.)

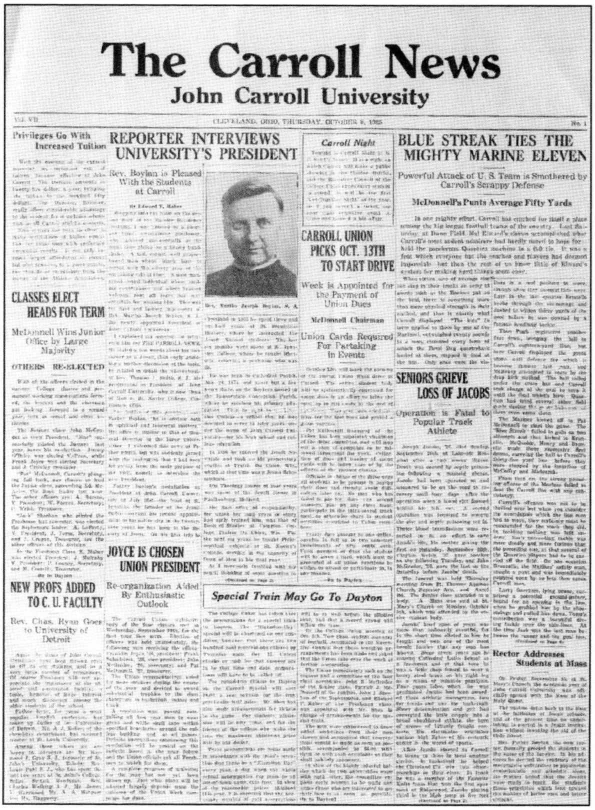

The Carroll News

John Carroll University

Privileges Go With Increased Tuition

REPORTER INTERVIEWS UNIVERSITY'S PRESIDENT

Rev. Boylan is Pleased With the Students at Carroll

Carroll Night

BLUE STREAK TIES THE MIGHTY MARINE ELEVEN

Powerful Attack of U. S. Team is Smothered by Carroll's Scrappy Defense

McDonnell's Punts Average Fifty Yards

CARROLL UNION PICKS OCT. 13TH TO START DRIVE

CLASSES ELECT HEADS FOR TERM

SENIORS GRIEVE LOSS OF JACOBS

JOYCE IS CHOSEN UNION PRESIDENT

NEW PROFS ADDED TO C. U. FACULTY

Special Train May Go To Dayton

Rector Addresses Students at Mass

The Carroll News, which began in 1925, was the successor to the *Ignatian*. The front page of this first edition featured an interview with the college president, Rev. Murtha Boylan, SJ, and an article describing a tied football game between the John Carroll Blue Streaks and the Quantico Marines.

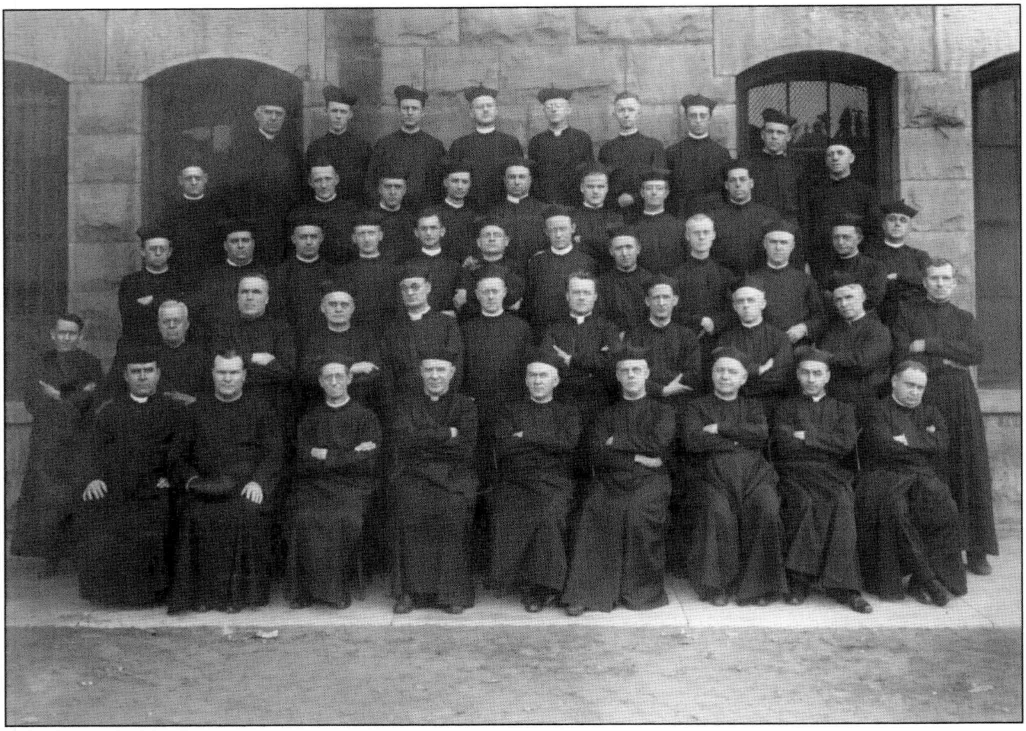

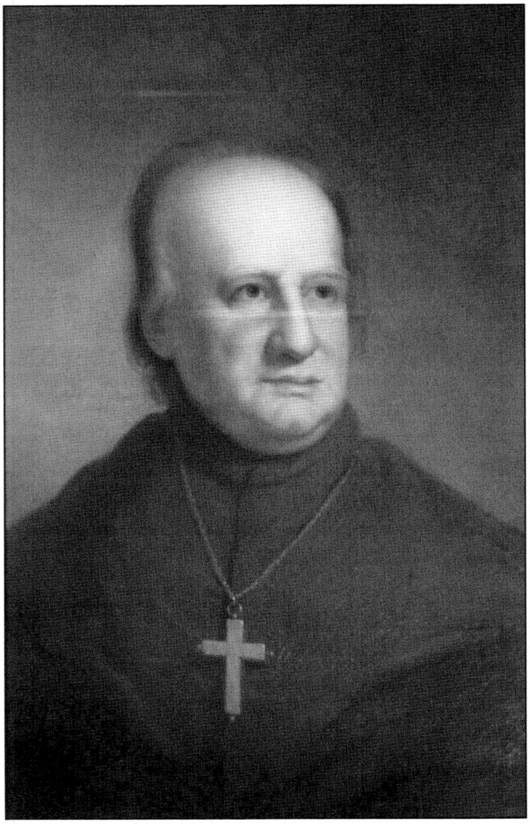

In 1920, the faculty of Saint Ignatius College and the two high schools was composed almost entirely of Jesuits. In addition to being expected to teach a wide range of subjects, they assisted in local parishes, which was necessary work because it brought in additional funds for the college. As the student body grew, more lay teachers were hired. In the 1920s, lay teachers were paid $100 a month for 10 months.

In the face of objections to the name "Cleveland University," the Jesuits decided to name the college after Archbishop John Carroll. He was a Jesuit, the first American bishop, and the founder of Georgetown University, the flagship of American Jesuit universities.

In 1926, the college amassed only two football victories, which were against the Quantico Marines and Adrian College; the team lost four games and tied one. Throughout the 1920s, the college did not play local teams, which negatively affected attendance at the games. When Saint Ignatius became John Carroll in 1923, its athletic teams gave up the name "Saints" and became the Blue Streaks.

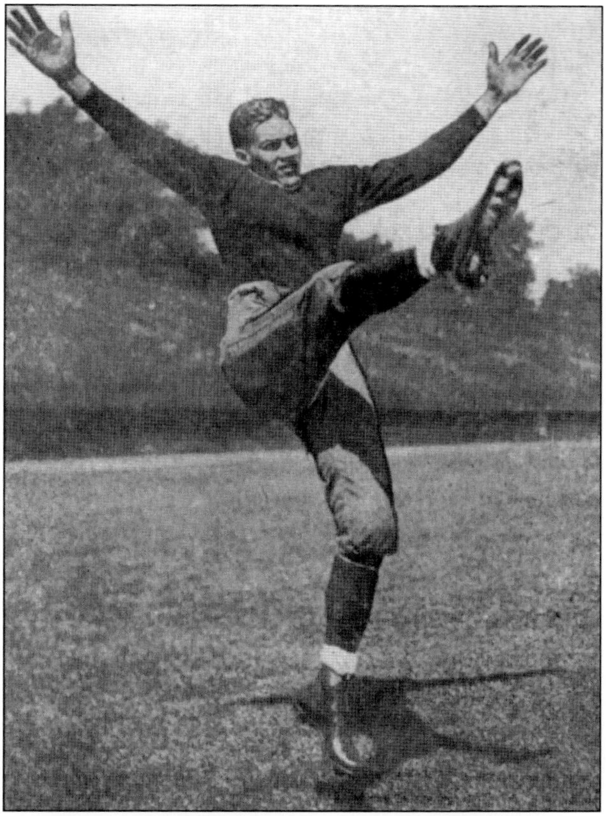

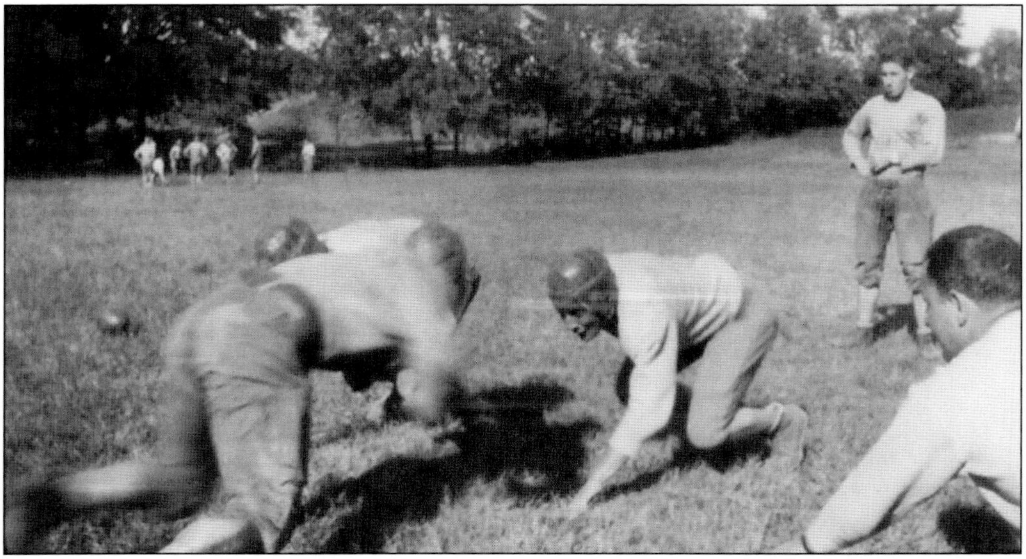

The John Carroll team played home games at League Park until 1926 and then at Luna Park, an amusement park where spectators could ride the roller coaster at halftime. The lack of athletic fields was an added incentive to move to the suburban campus. More importantly, the 1891 building was "crammed to the roof," according to a January 1930 article in the *Cleveland Plain Dealer* with the headline: "Patient Jesuits Await New Plant." The "patient Jesuits" would have to wait until 1935.

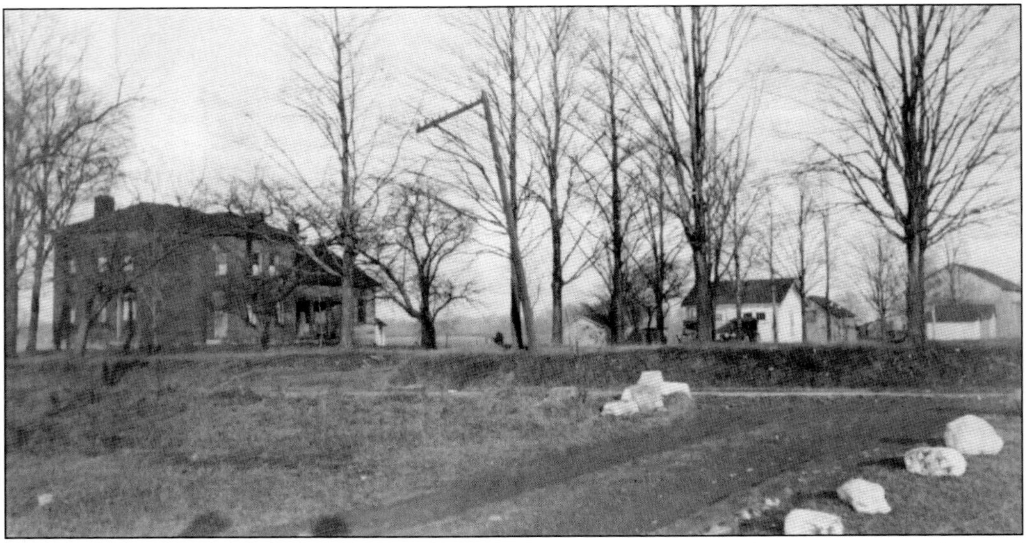

After looking at various locations on the east side, the Jesuits bought property in Idlewood Village, where there were fewer building restrictions than in Shaker Heights. This 1924 photograph, taken at the intersection of Cedar and Warrensville Center Roads (less than a mile from the proposed campus), shows how rural the village was. This became the site of the University Heights Golf Course; in 2011, this was the site of a Macy's department store. (Courtesy of Cleveland Heights–University Heights Library.)

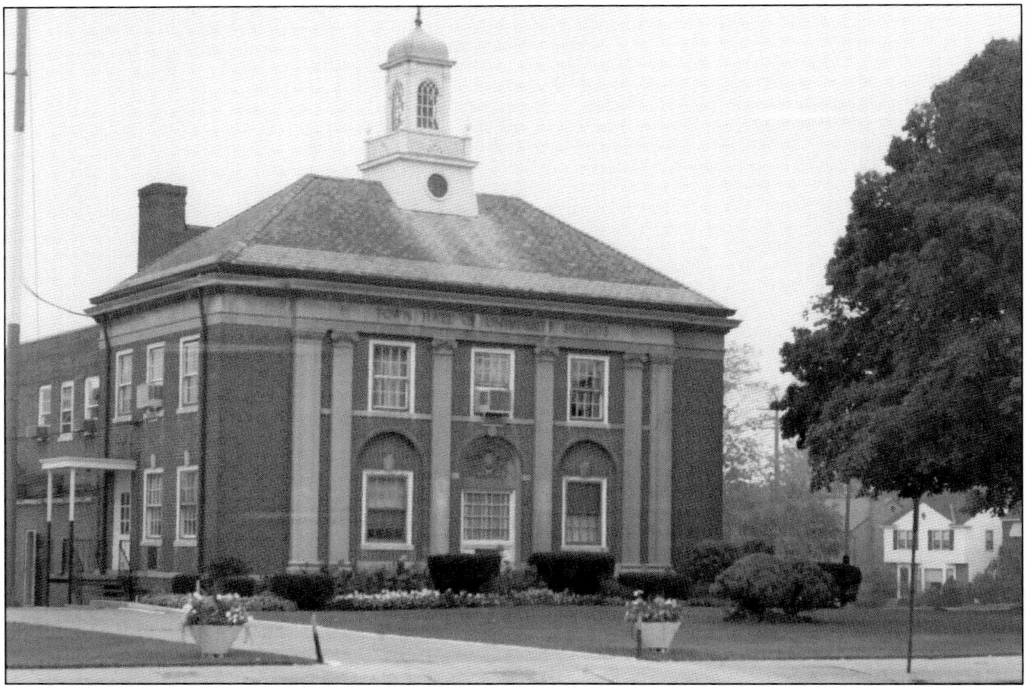

In 1925, the village of Idlewood incorporated as University Heights in anticipation of John Carroll's arrival, which was still six years away, and built this handsome Georgian city hall. As new homes were built around the university, the suburb's 1925 population of 500 rose to 2,237 in 1930 and to almost 6,000 in 1940. (Courtesy of Cleveland Heights–University Heights Library.)

Three

TRYING TIMES 1930–1960

Cleveland's heavy industry economy felt the Depression early and suffered it long until the demand for war materials put Clevelanders back to work. The return of prosperity encouraged more Clevelanders to leave the central city for distant suburbs such as the sparsely settled University Heights.

The Depression and World War II also presented challenges for the new university. Ground was broken for the University Heights campus in April 1931, but construction was halted from January 1932 until summer 1935 as the Jesuits struggled to secure a loan and collect outstanding pledges to pay the contractors. In October 1935, a half-completed campus greeted its first students.

After Pearl Harbor, John Carroll's student body dropped alarmingly, but in July 1943, young men from a Navy V-12 officer training program occupied John Carroll classrooms and moved into Rodman and Bernet Halls. The program graduated 787 men, paid faculty salaries, and helped to keep the university afloat.

Postwar prosperity brought another set of trials. By 1946, lay faculty outnumbered the Jesuits, and the laypersons became openly discontented with their salaries and heavy teaching loads: 15 hours per semester were required, but teachers sometimes taught 18 or more hours per semester to augment their incomes. Lay faculty also claimed that they had a limited role in university governance, pointing out that none served as administrators. In an effort to codify faculty responsibilities and roles at the university, the first faculty handbook was published in 1953.

Thanks to the GI Bill, many veterans returned to John Carroll to finish their educations; enrollment rose in 1960 to slightly over 4,000, a figure that included undergraduates, graduate students, and evening college students. New students necessitated new residence halls, a gymnasium, a science center, and a new library that was completed in 1961. In 1956, the university offered master's degrees in eight departments. John Carroll joined the Presidents' Athletic Conference in 1954, and the football and basketball teams enjoyed some significant victories.

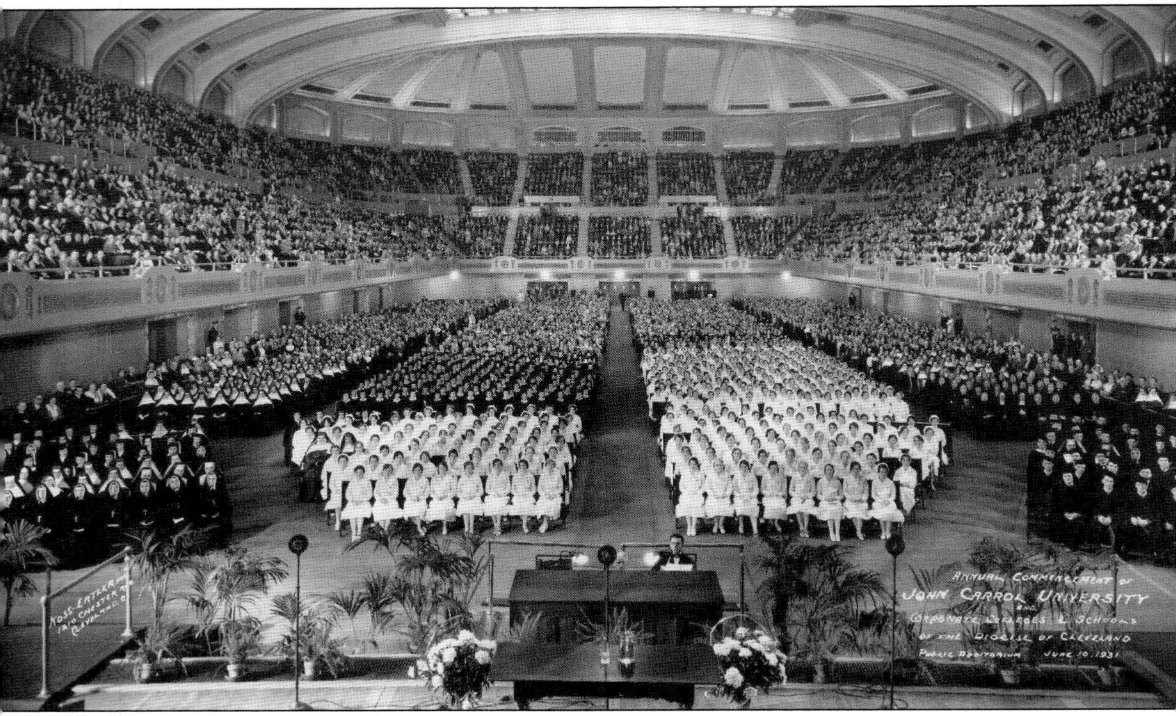

In 1931, Cleveland's Catholic institutions of higher learning held this joint graduation ceremony in the city's Public Auditorium. The ceremony was the product of the short-lived Corporate College Plan, inspired by Bishop Joseph Schrembs' desire for the seminarians and the nuns to receive college degrees. In addition to John Carroll, the loose affiliation included the Sisters' College (St. John's College), Notre Dame College, Ursuline College, St. Vincent Charity Hospital School of Nursing, St. Alexis Hospital School of Nursing, and the Seminary of Our Lady of the Lake. The plan only lasted until 1934, but these formally robed nuns, men in academic regalia, and newly uniformed nurses created an impressive spectacle.

Rev. Benedict Rodman, SJ, rector of the Jesuit Community and president of the university from 1928 to 1937, led the successful 1929 campaign to raise funds for the University Heights campus and steered the university through serious financial difficulties during much of the Depression before he became the pastor of the Church of the Gesu. Rodman Hall, which served as the Jesuit residence for years, was named in his honor.

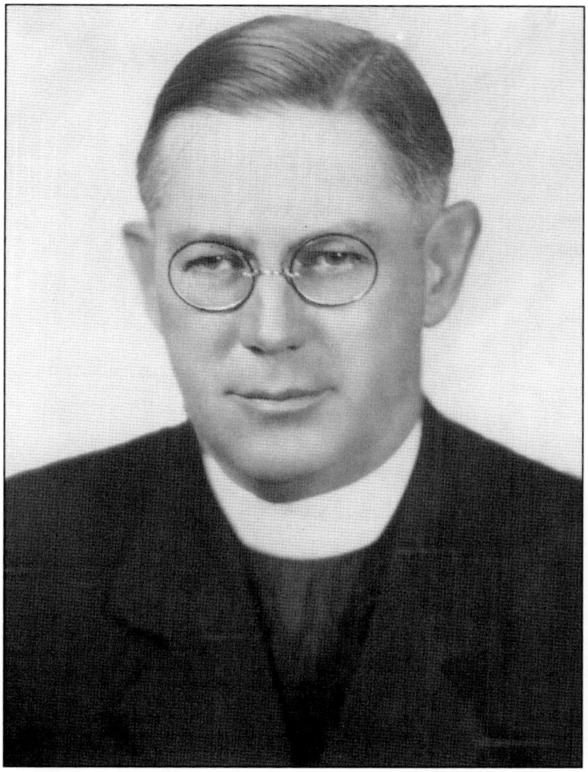

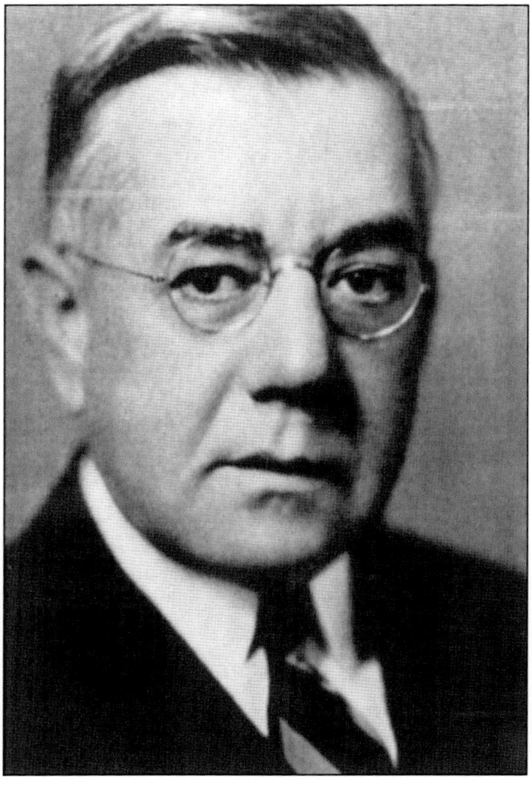

John J. Bernet, a self-made railroad tycoon, was the general chairman of the 1929 fundraising drive and set up a committee that included prominent Catholic and non-Catholic Clevelanders, some of whom—like Samuel Mather, Mantis J., and Oris P. Van Sweringen—made generous pledges. Bernet insisted that there be a residence hall on campus; subsequently, Bernet Hall was named after him.

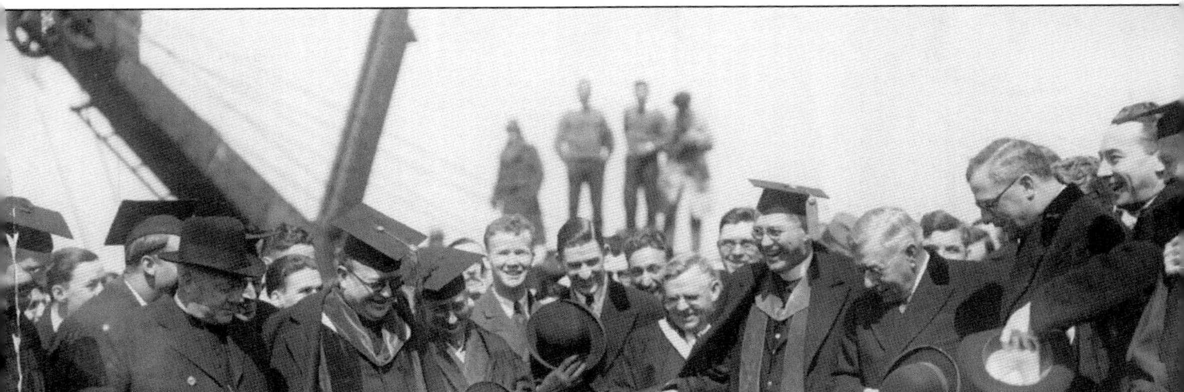

The ground-breaking ceremony for the new campus took place on April 7, 1931. Bishop Joseph Schrembs (center), who had enthusiastically supported the campaign, dug the first shovelful of earth. To his left stood Rev. Benedict Rodman, SJ, (in academic garb) and John J. Bernet. The campaign had reached its goal of $2,541,322 in pledges, but as the Depression worsened, they became harder and harder to collect. The ongoing Depression continued to plague the university and its benefactors, and administrators scrambled for the next three years to collect outstanding pledges and secure new loans; this forced them to halt construction in January 1932.

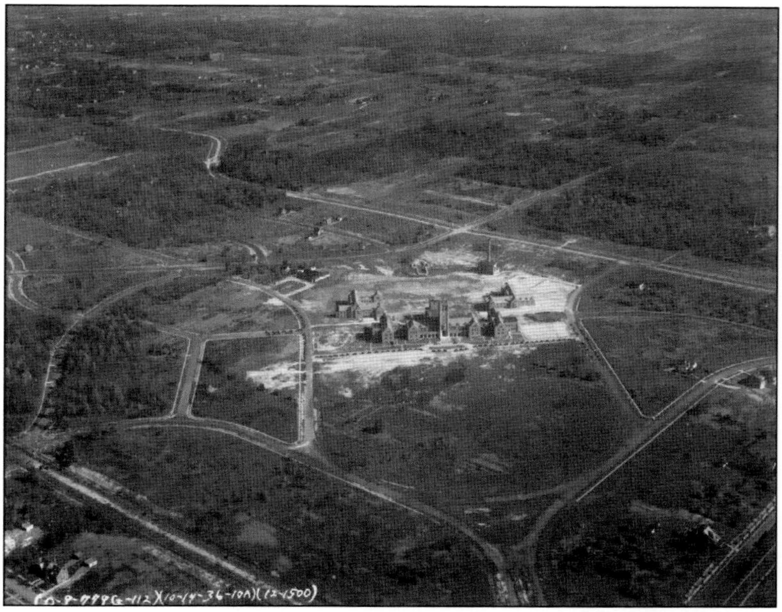

This aerial image shows the buildings still under construction, sitting almost alone in a still-rural setting. In the center is the administration building, flanked by the two science wings. On the right, Bernet Hall has been started, and Rodman Hall is on the left. The powerhouse is at upper right.

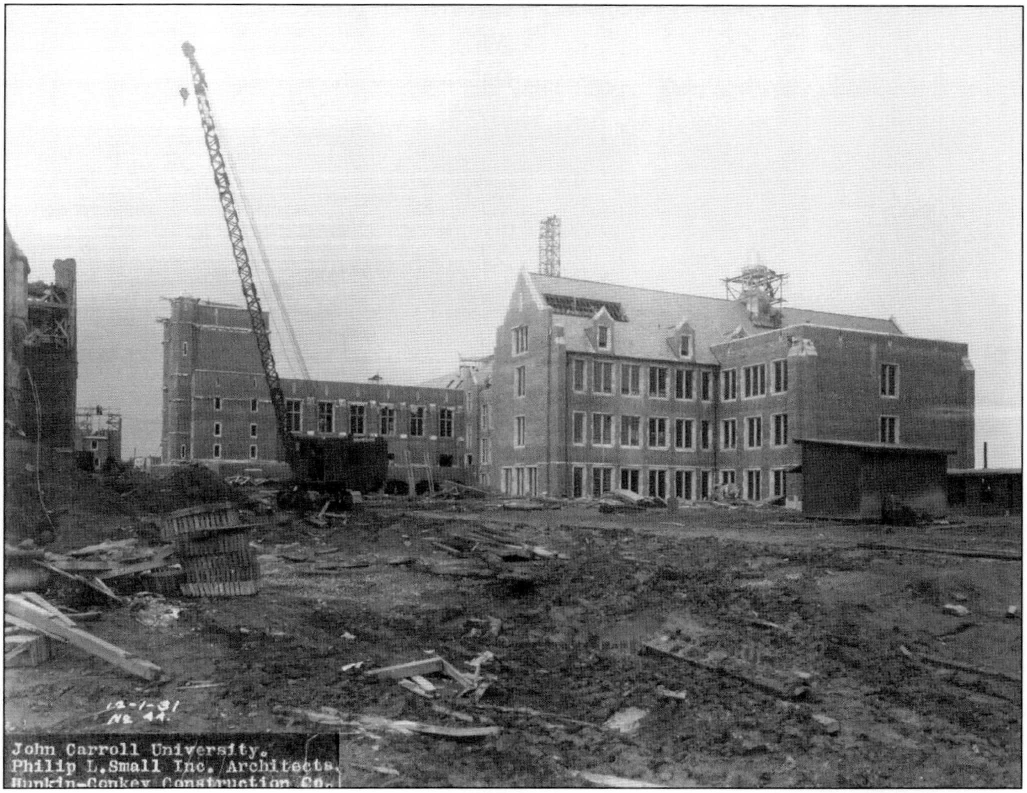

When construction stopped, the unfinished buildings had to be protected from the weather, and equipment and furnishings had to be protected from vandals. The university's architect, Philip Small, also designed Shaker Square, the Shaker Country Club, the Country Club in Pepper Pike, and buildings on the Case Institute of Technology and Western Reserve University campuses.

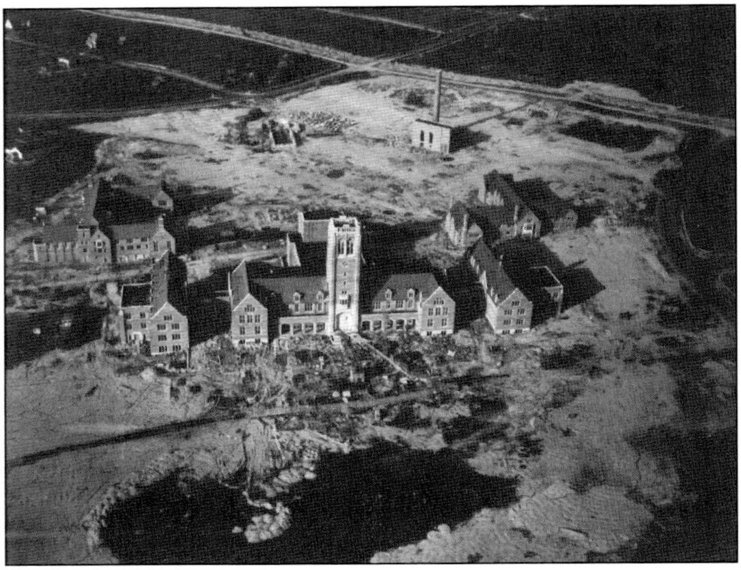

Construction resumed in the summer of 1935. This aerial view shows that much of the campus was still unfinished, but at least the buildings had roofs. The area in front of the administration building appears to be a sea of mud.

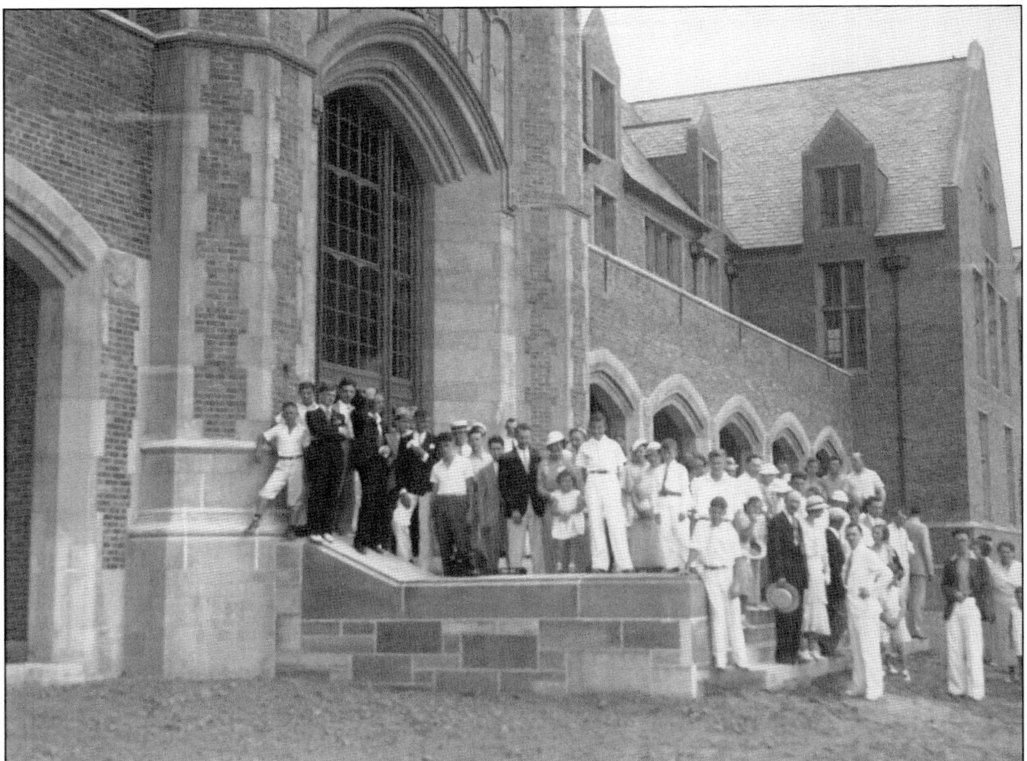

On John Carroll Day—July 2, 1935—10,000 people visited the new campus, which was still under construction. The event had been announced in the local newspapers and at Masses all over the diocese; many of the congregations had donated to the building drive.

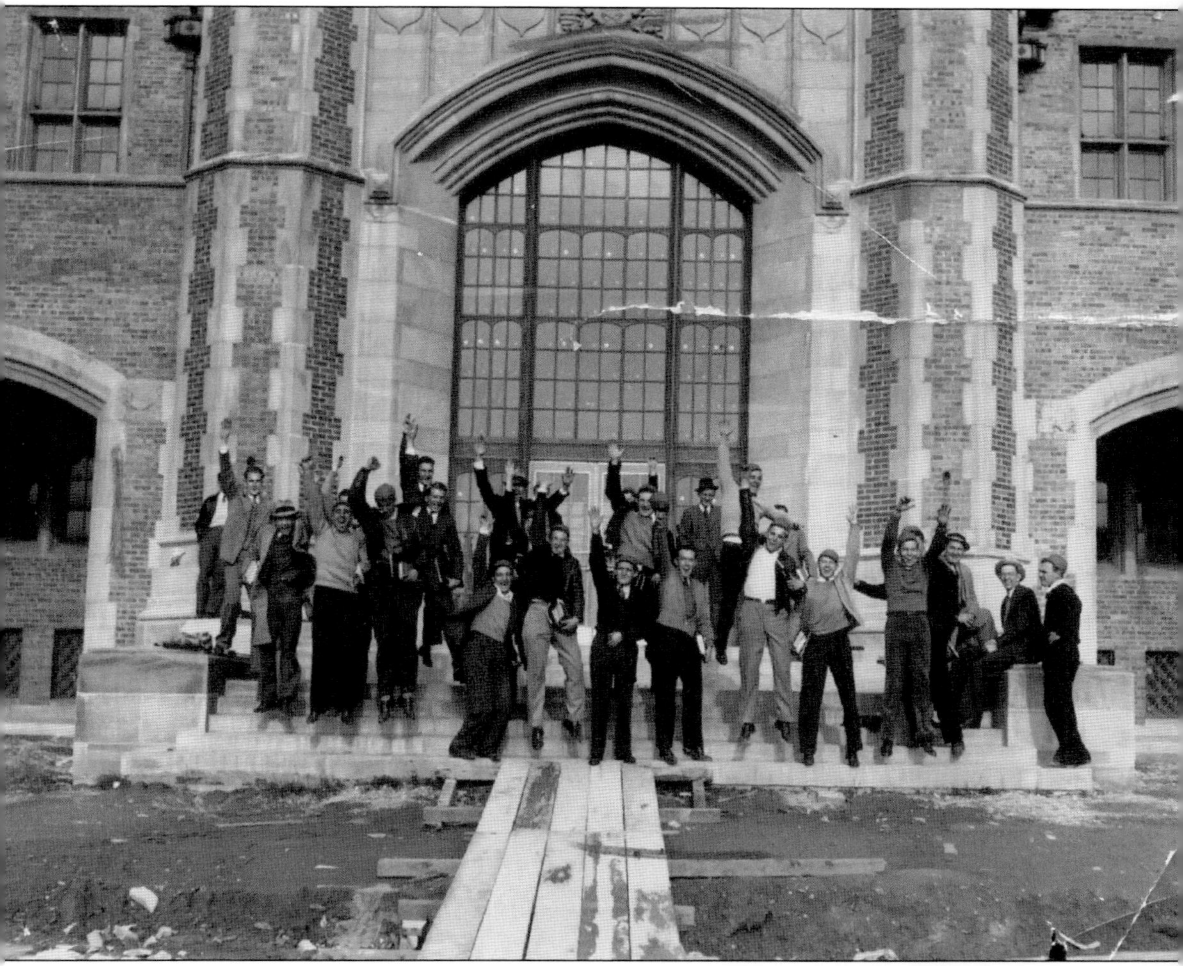

After a four-and-a-half-year wait, elated students cheered when their classes finally began in University Heights on October 7, 1935. The town's mayor officially welcomed its newest residents. Between classes, students and faculty dodged electricians and carpenters, who were still at work in the half-finished Administration Building. Resident students lived in private homes and ate in a local restaurant because Bernet Hall remained unfinished until Thanksgiving. The library was not ready until after Christmas. The Jesuits' long-held ambition to move east had been fulfilled. The entrance to the new building closely resembled the impressive entrance to the 1891 Saint Ignatius building. The university's enrollment remained stable through the 1930s, maintained by summer, evening, and Saturday students, most of whom were part-time and many of whom were women.

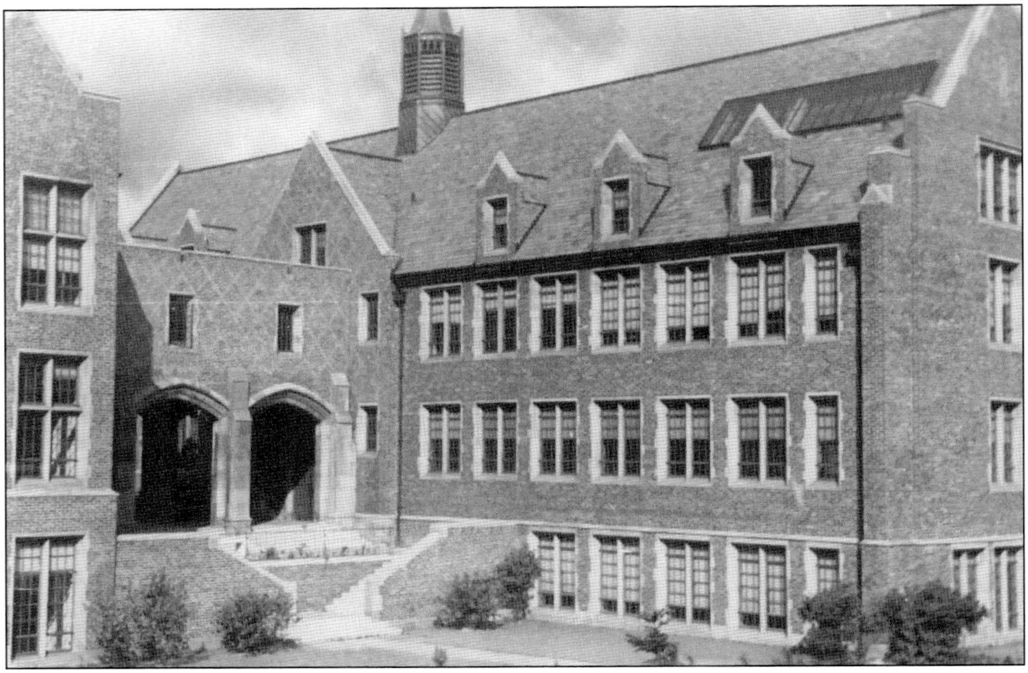

The Administration Building was connected through arcades to the biology and chemistry wings, which were designed in the Gothic style long associated with academic and sacred buildings. This view of the Chemistry Building displays a simplified version of that style, which was in the spirit of Depression-induced austerity.

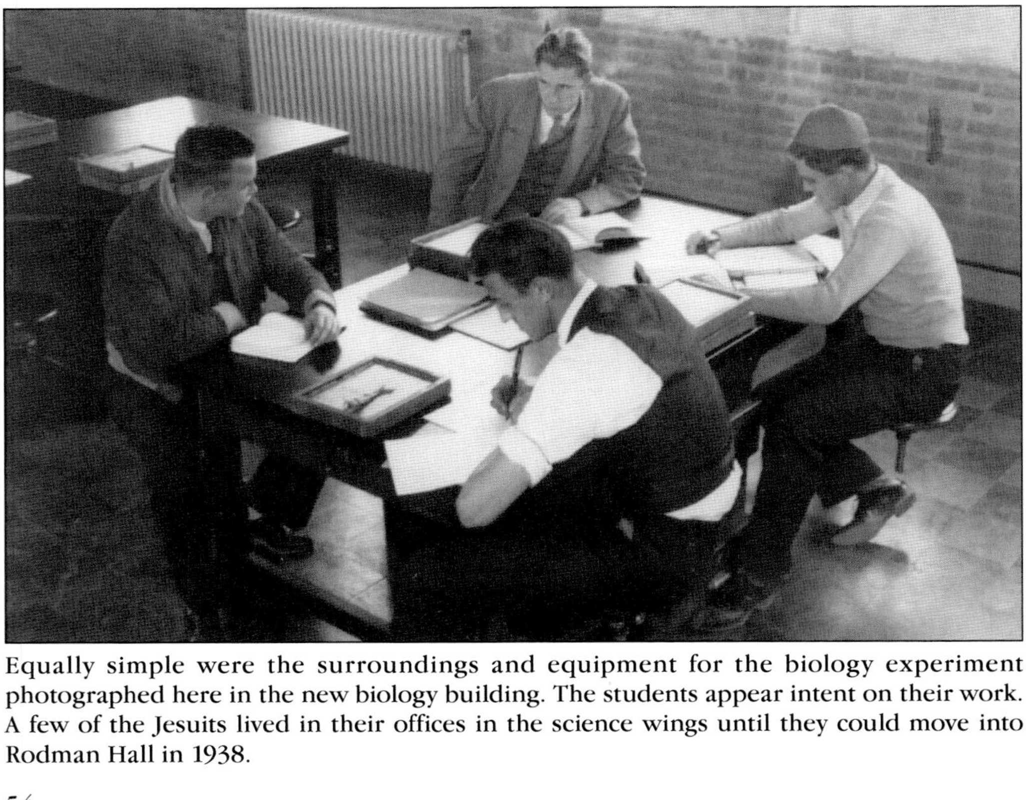

Equally simple were the surroundings and equipment for the biology experiment photographed here in the new biology building. The students appear intent on their work. A few of the Jesuits lived in their offices in the science wings until they could move into Rodman Hall in 1938.

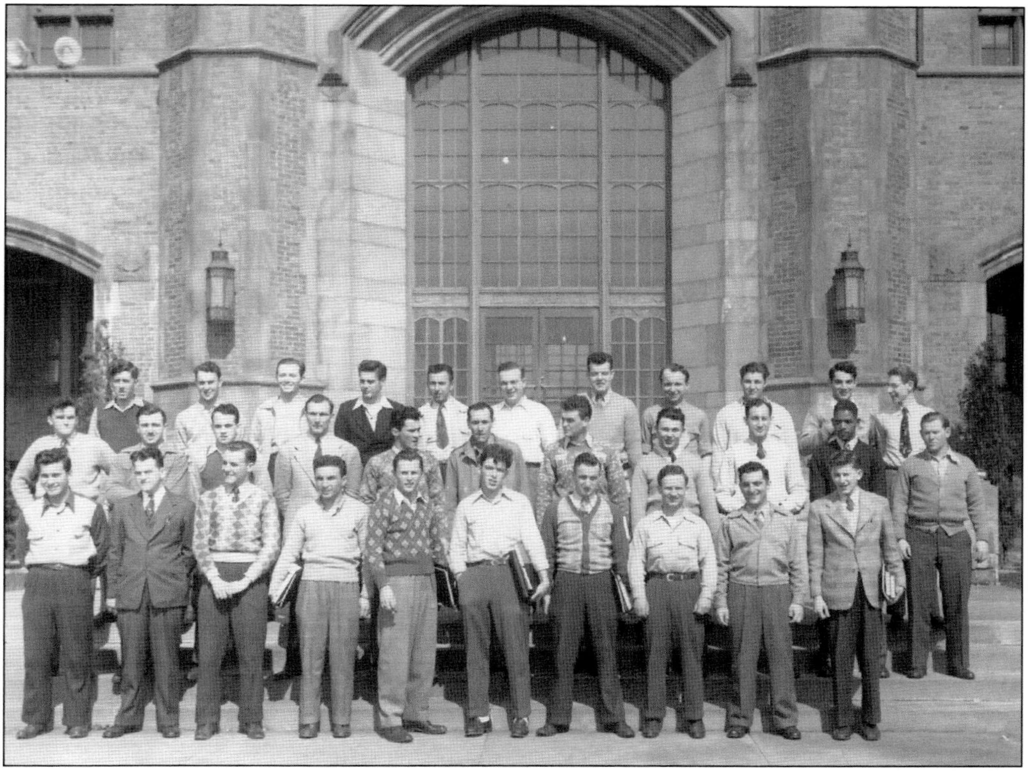

The establishment of the School of Business Administration in 1934 attracted new students. Men attended classes during the day and women could attend evening classes. Enrollment at the university reached 1,033 in 1939.

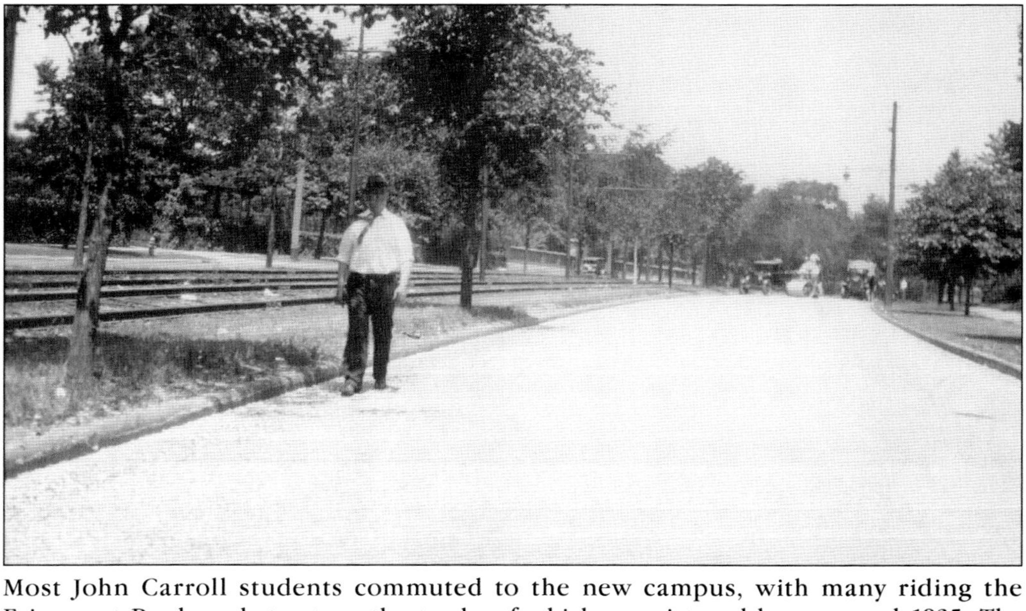

Most John Carroll students commuted to the new campus, with many riding the Fairmount Boulevard streetcar, the tracks of which are pictured here around 1935. The streetcar line ended just east of Taylor Road, where students were picked up by a John Carroll bus. (Courtesy of Cleveland State University Special Collections.)

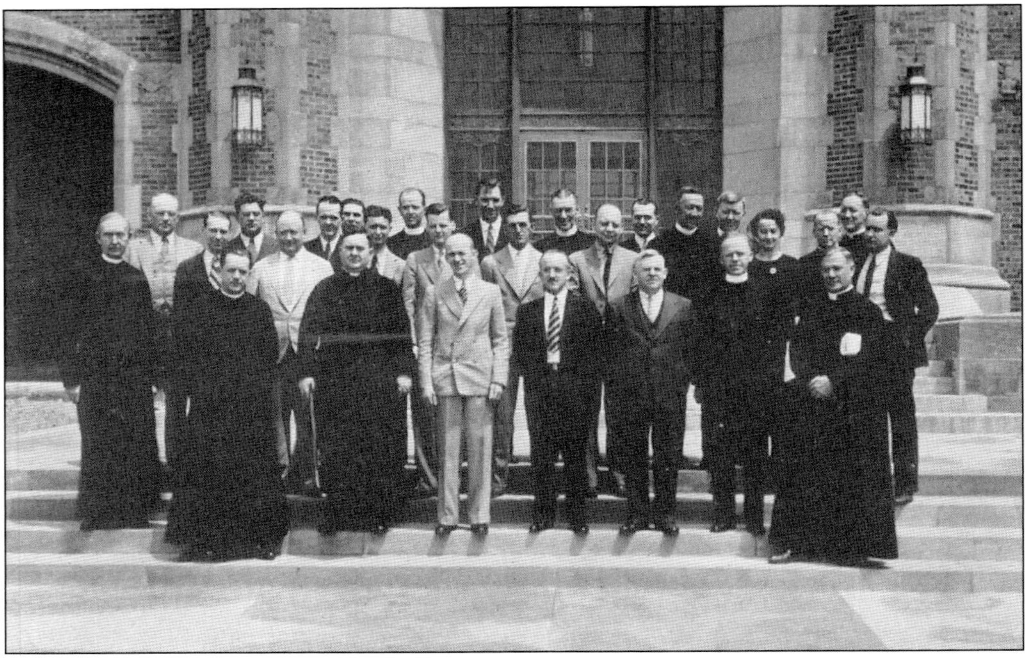

In 1936, there were 22 laymen on a faculty of 41 (not all faculty members appear in this photograph). The lay faculty took a 10 percent pay cut in 1932. Pay cuts were common for all teachers during the Depression. There were no fringe benefits for lay faculty, which was also common practice at colleges and universities.

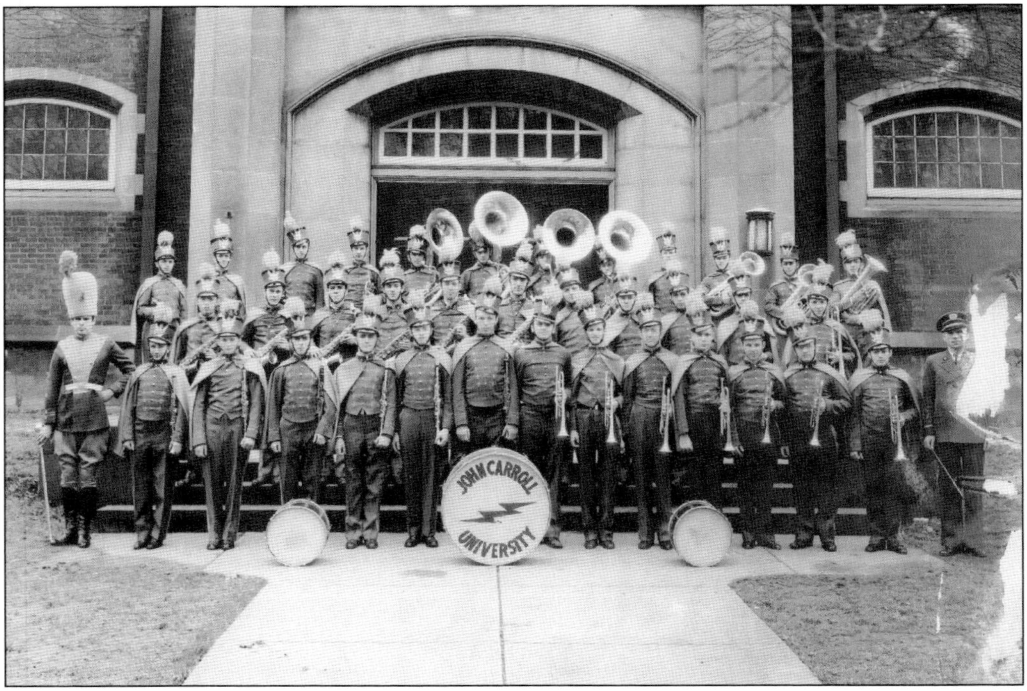

The orchestral music tradition established at Saint Ignatius was maintained at the new campus by the university marching band, arrayed in this 1937 photograph in military precision with uniforms and a drum major.

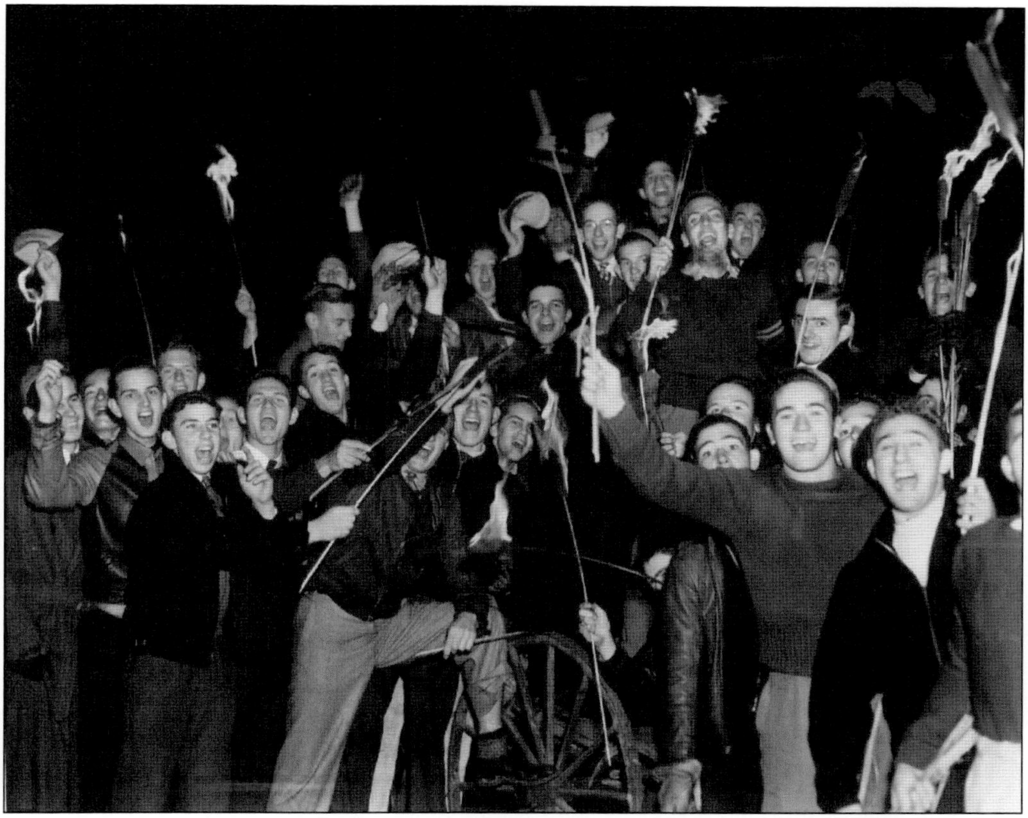

The bonfire on the evening before the annual homecoming football game became a John Carroll tradition that continues today. The bonfire was followed by a pep rally led by the head football coach. Festivities continued the next day with a parade and hopefully a victory over a rival team.

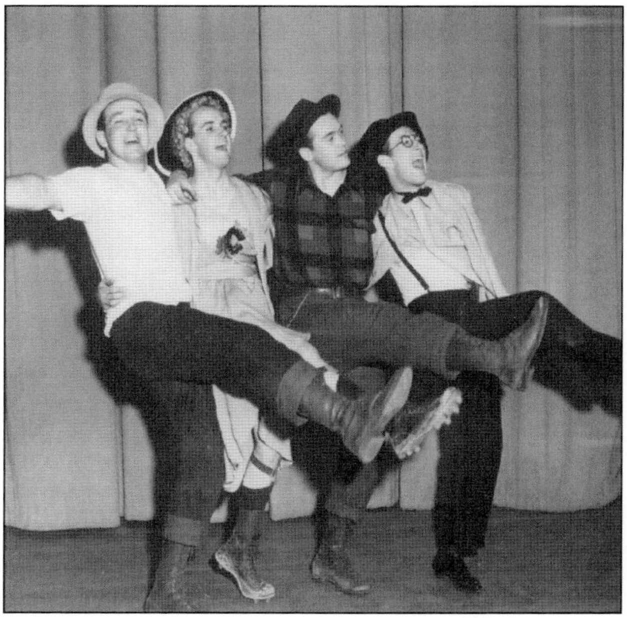

Stunt Night allowed students to poke fun at themselves, the faculty, and the university. Each class hoped to win the Stunt Night Trophy. Often verging on rowdiness, Stunt Night was discontinued in 1977.

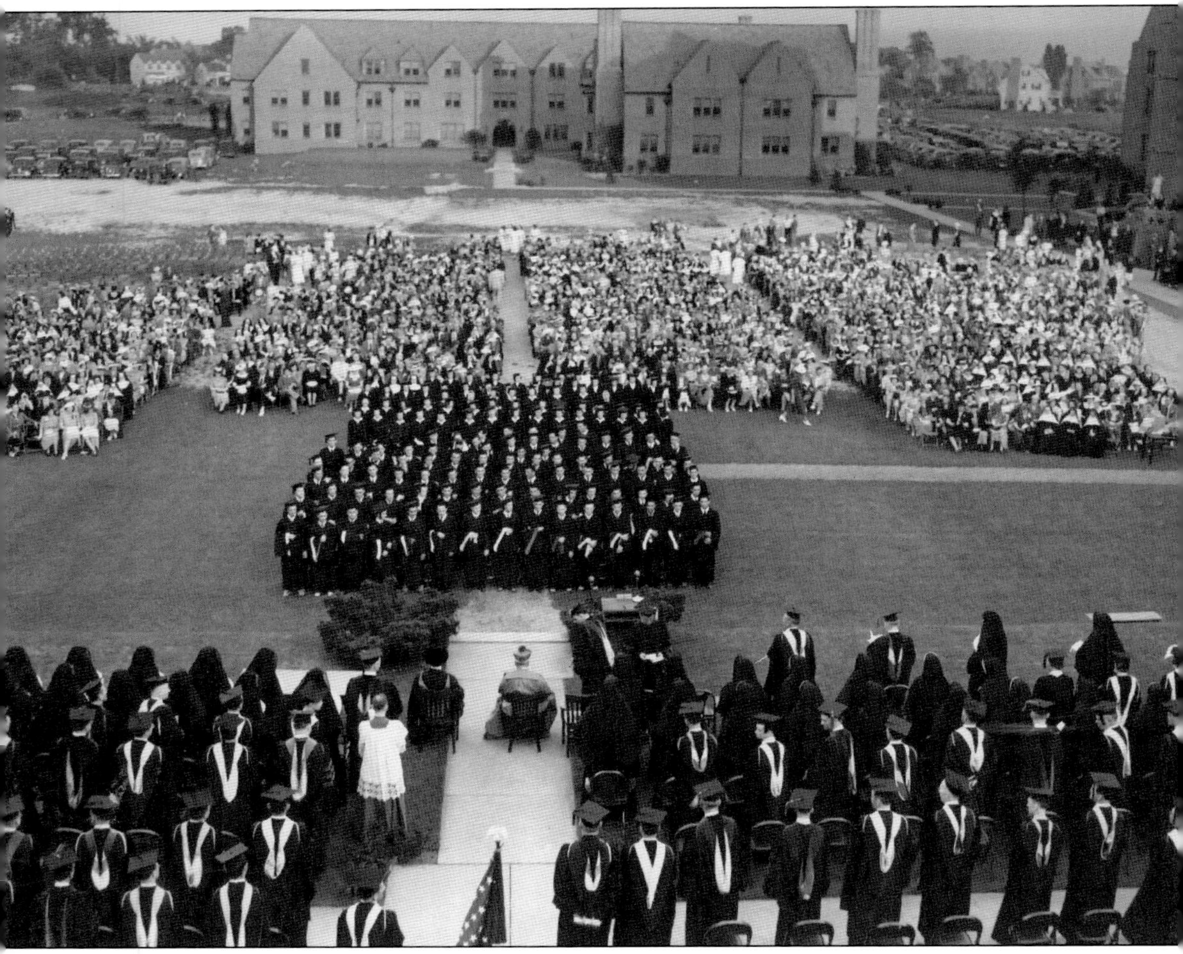

Since the move to University Heights, John Carroll commencement has been held outside (in cooperative weather) with graduates and their families facing the faculty, who were seated in front of Rodman Hall. On June 2, 1940, John Carroll, Ursuline, and Notre Dame College held this joint commencement. That year, 92 men graduated from John Carroll, the largest graduating class in the university's history up to that time. The *Cleveland Plain Dealer* listed the names of all graduates, each of whom received a bachelor of arts, bachelor of science, bachelor of philosophy, or bachelor of science in business administration from university president Rev. Edmund C. Horne, SJ. Bishop Joseph Schrembs awarded the degrees to the Ursuline and Notre Dame graduates. The commencement speaker was Rev. Aloysius Hogan, SJ, dean of the Graduate School of Georgetown University and former president of Fordham University. Bernet Hall appears at the top of the photograph, and the administration building is at right. The photograph shows only a few homes in the background.

The photograph is labeled "class of 1945." These young men—wearing their freshman beanies—were members of the small class that enrolled in the college in fall 1941 as the United States became increasingly drawn into World War II.

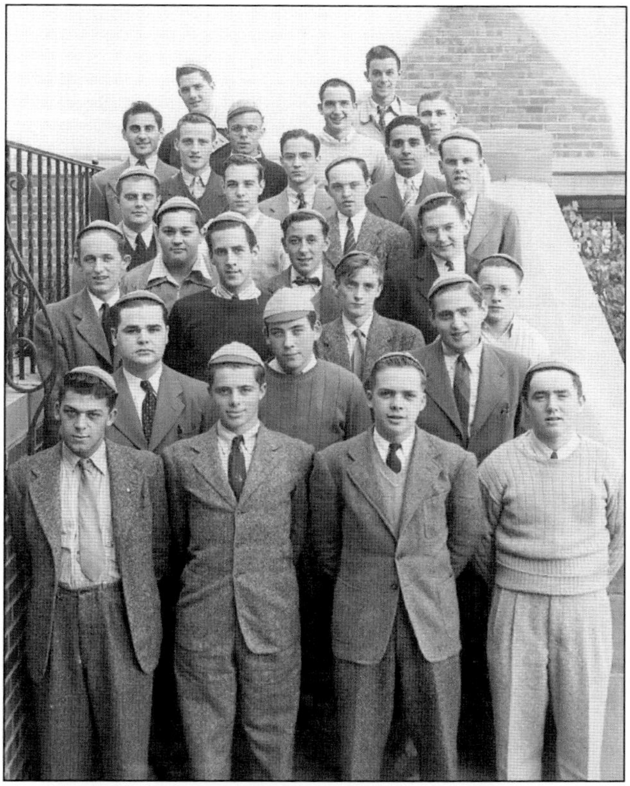

Enrollment nose-dived when the United States entered World War II and young men volunteered or were drafted to serve. The university administration made a successful effort to get this Navy V-12 officer training program at John Carroll. The V-12 programs provided liberal arts degrees for young men already in the Navy, in a college reserve unit, or for promising high school seniors who wanted to become naval officers.

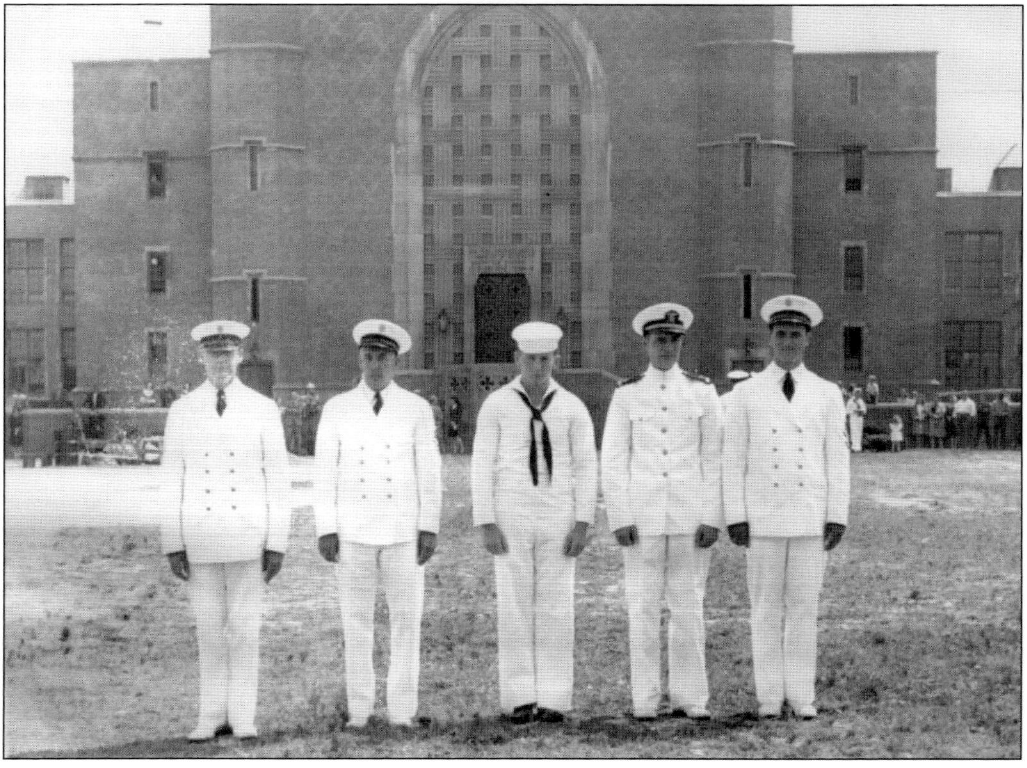

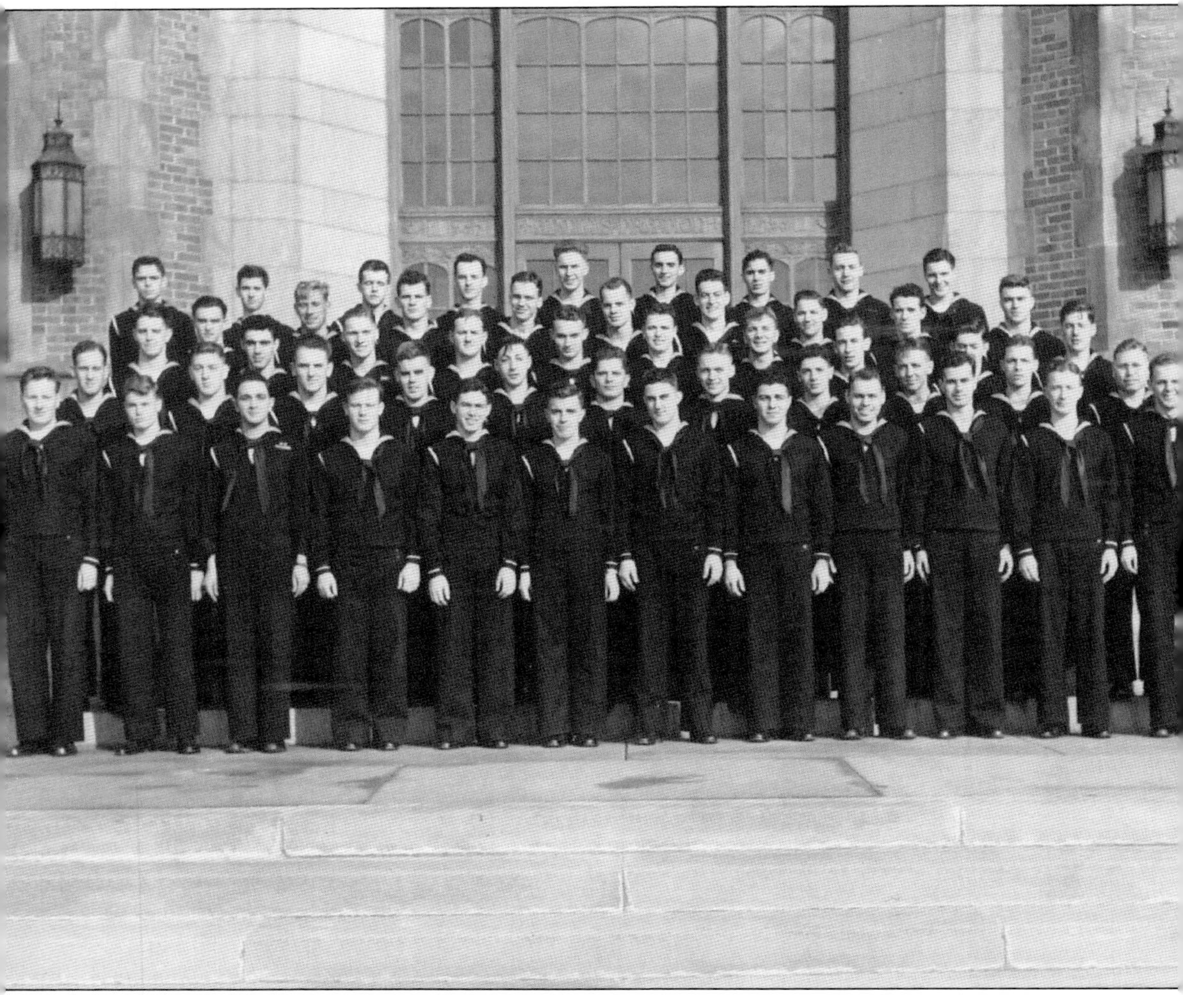

V-12 men took a minimum of 20 hours of lectures and labs each semester—with an emphasis on math, physics, history, engineering drawing, chemistry, and English—in classes taught by John Carroll faculty. Naval officers instructed the men in naval etiquette, physical education, and drill, as well as enforcing discipline. The school calendar was streamlined to meet the servicemen's needs. The seamen were housed in Bernet and Rodman Halls, which had been hastily rushed to completion. The men joined the university band, Glee Club, sports teams, and *The Carroll News*, even though they were only temporary students. V-12 units were educated at 131 American colleges, including Baldwin Wallace University, Case School of Applied Science, Denison University, and Oberlin College.

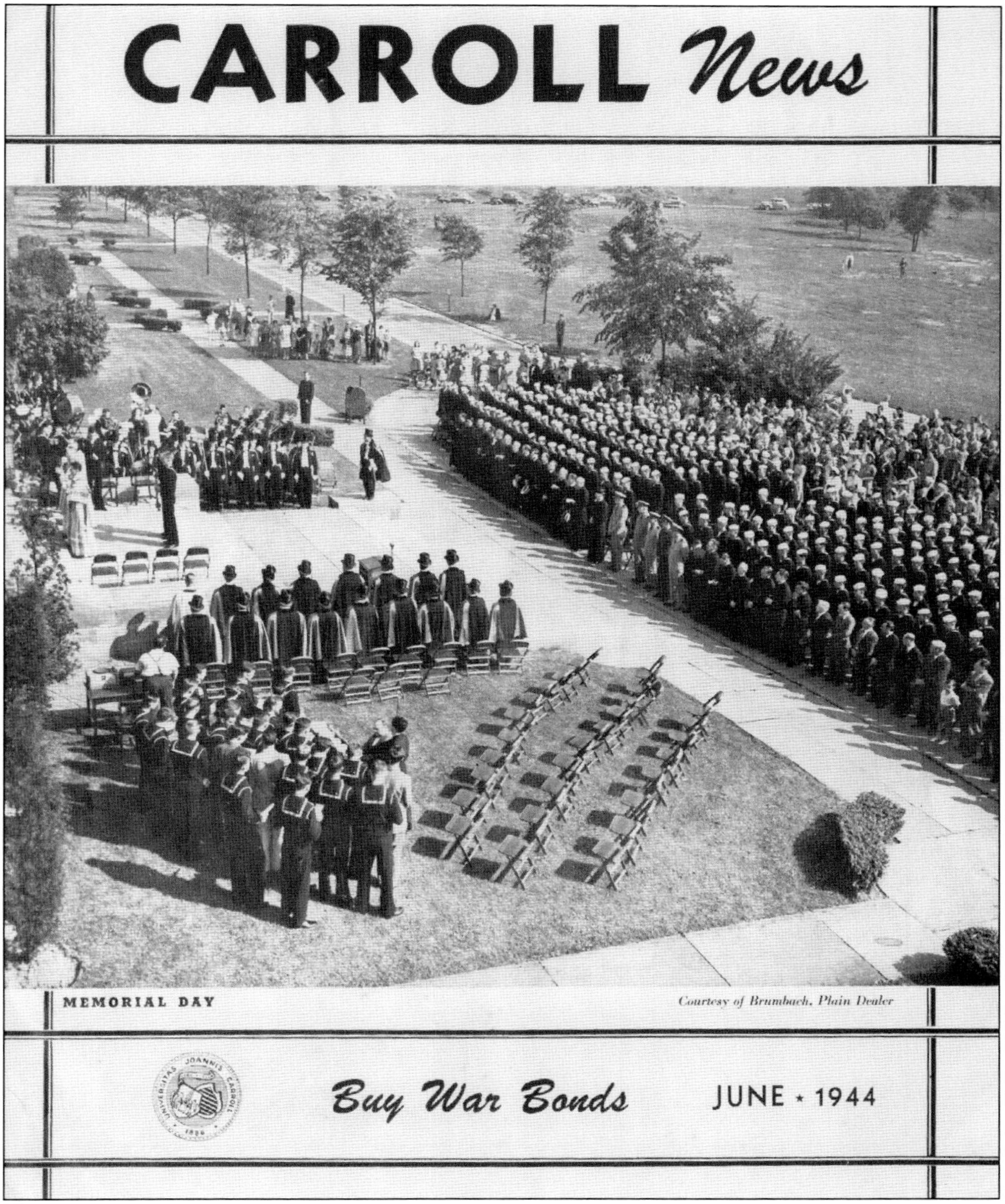

The Carroll News "Service Issue" reported on April 30, 1943, that 846 John Carroll men were serving in the US Army, Navy, and Coast Guard, and seven were chaplains. Eight John Carroll men had already died, including William L. Halloran, who was lost in the bombing of Pearl Harbor. In June 1944, this issue of *The Carroll News* commemorated Memorial Day; the university remembered its 1,300 men then serving in the armed forces and the 21 who had died. Clergy, visiting dignitaries, and John Carroll's V-12 sailors gathered in front of the Administration Building for the ceremony. Halloran, a journalist and an early volunteer in the US Navy, was Cleveland's first World War II casualty. In 1944, the USS *Halloran* was named in his honor, and in 1945, so was Cleveland's Halloran Park.

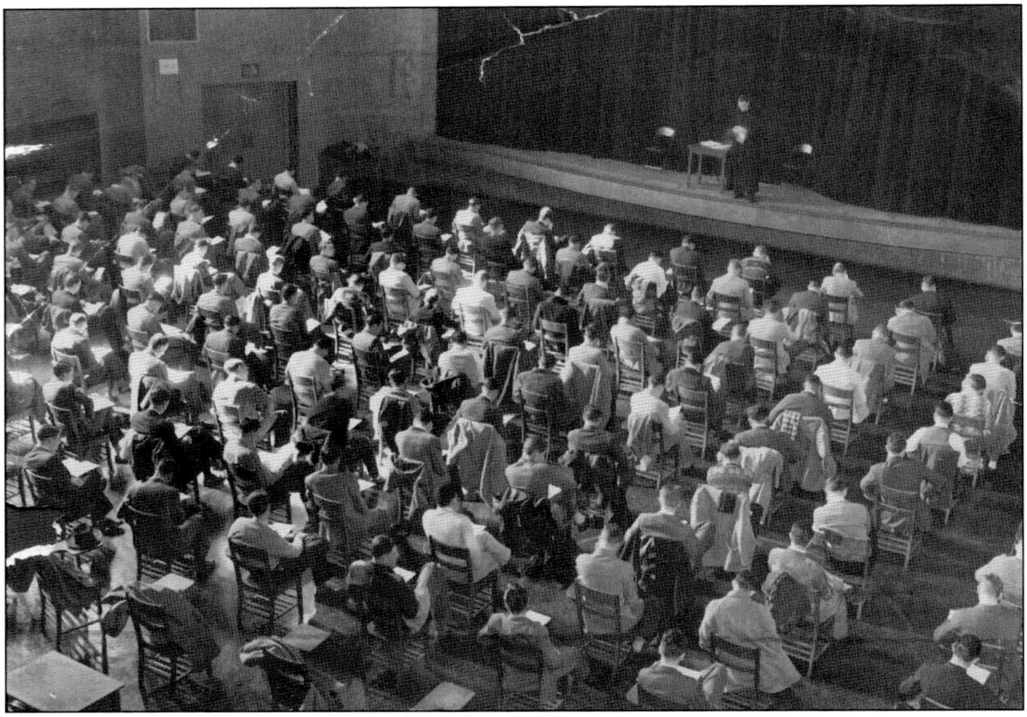

In March 1946, *The Carroll News* reported that enrollment had risen to 599 students for the spring 1946 semester—the largest enrollment since the start of World War II—and that four-fifths of them were returning veterans. Older and more mature than traditional undergraduates, many of them enrolled in business classes like the one pictured.

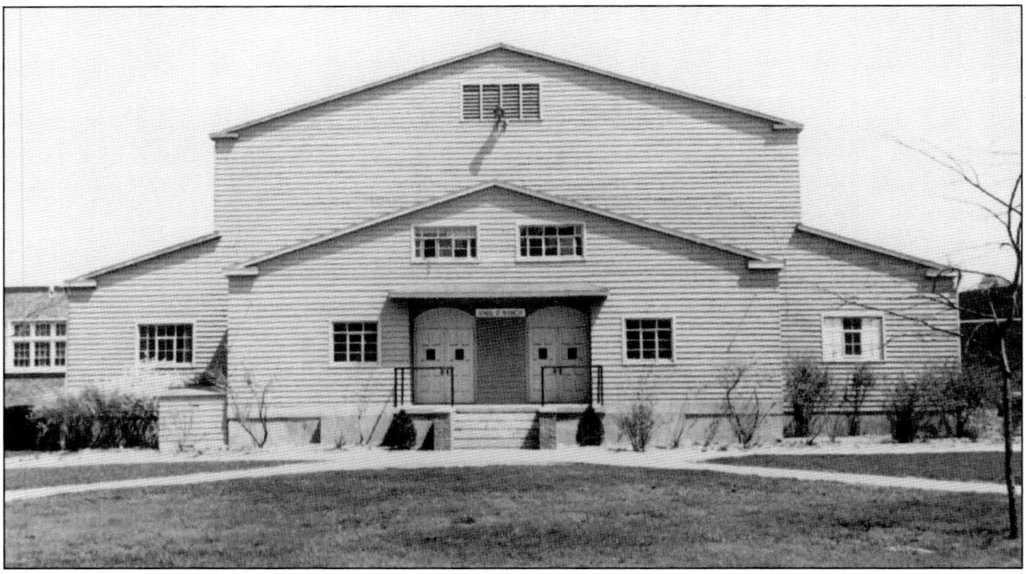

Most business classes were held in the Pink Barn, so-called because its frame exterior was painted a pale red to match the existing brick buildings. It also served as the gymnasium. In the original plan for the campus, this was to be the site of the Bishop's Chapel, which did not get built because of financial hardships during the Depression. This building is now the site of Saint Francis Chapel.

More students meant new residence halls. In this 1952 image, Archbishop Amleto Giovanni Cicognani, apostolic delegate to the United States, performs a solemn ritual at the dedication of Pacelli Hall, which (with special permission from Rome) was named after Pope Pius XII. Pacelli Hall was built with support from the local Italian American community. In 2012, the Cleveland Restoration Society honored the university for its historically sensitive restoration of this residence hall.

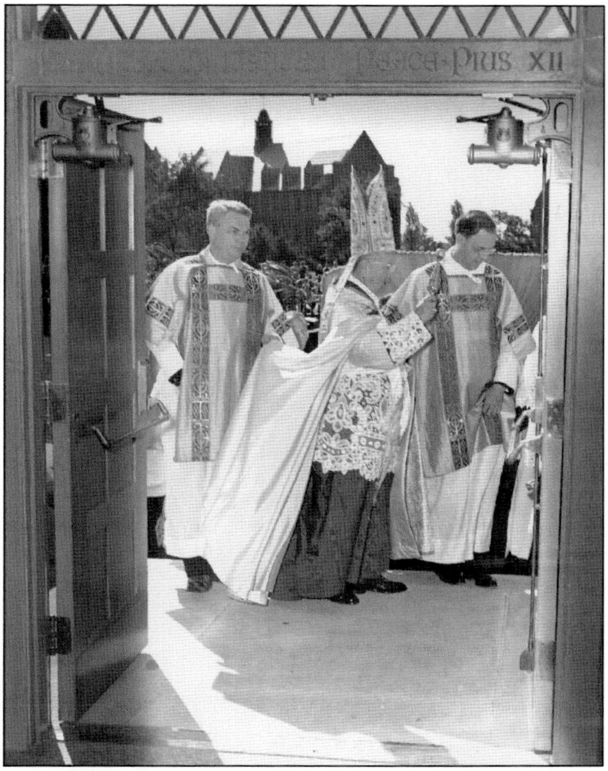

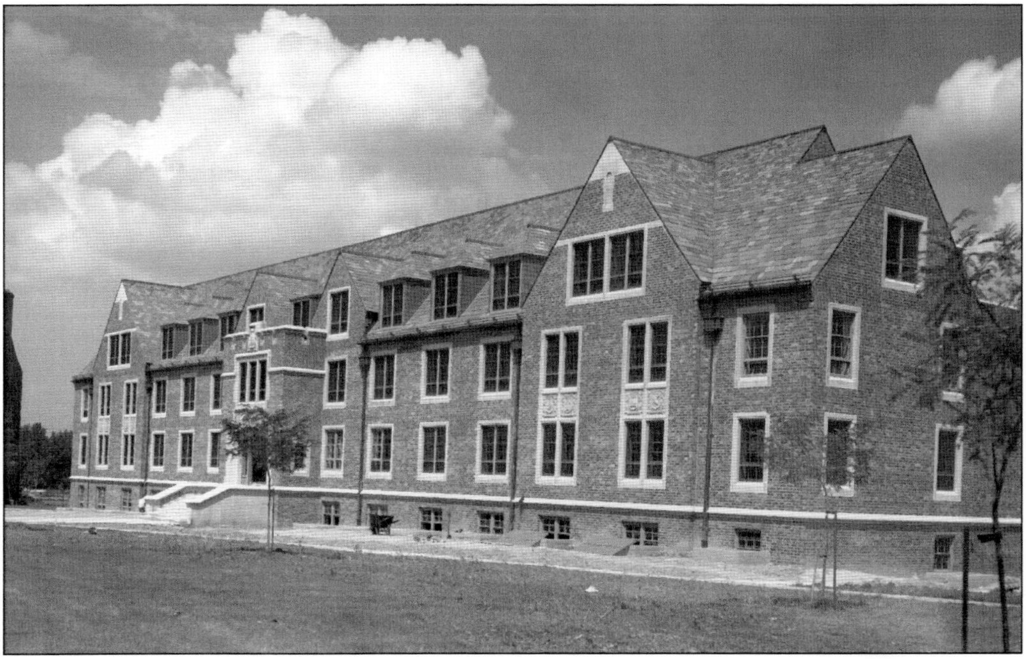

In 1955, Dolan Hall was completed with funds raised by Herbert Kennedy, Charles McCahill, and Thomas Dolan. Students who had been temporarily housed in Rodman Hall could move into the new residence halls, leaving Rodman Hall to the Jesuits, who had been living on the west side, in Bernet Hall, and occasionally in their offices.

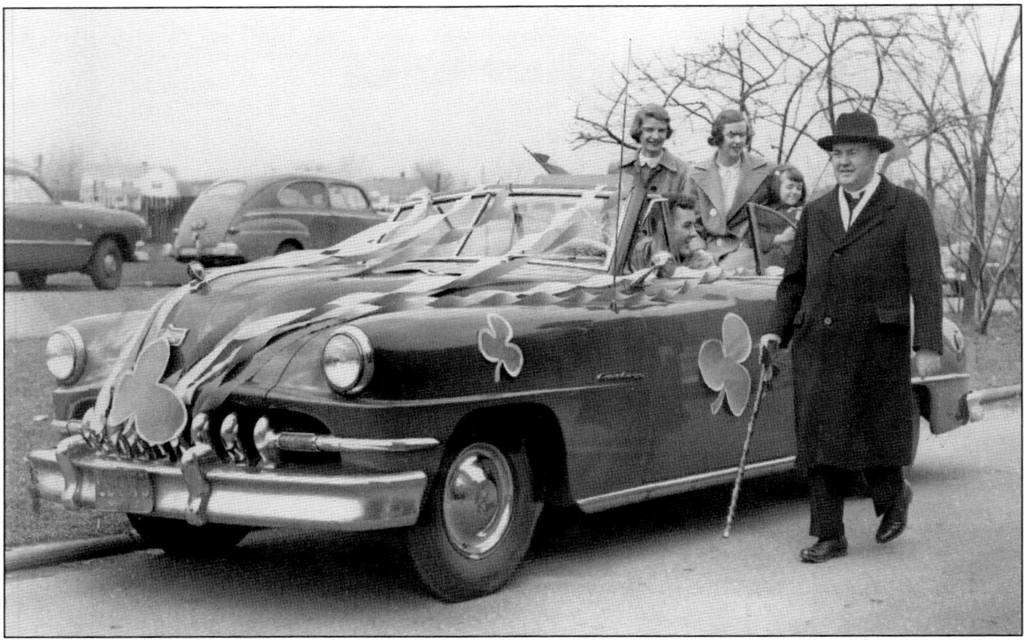

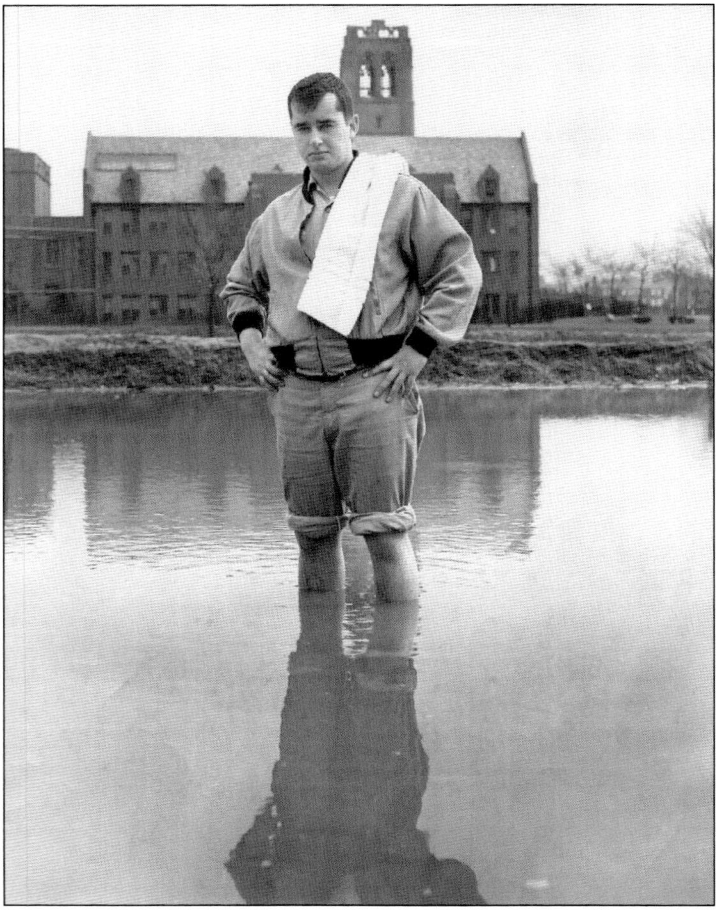

John Carroll has a long history of participation in Cleveland's St. Patrick's Day parade. In 1953, Rev. William J. Murphy, SJ, dean of men, practiced for his 20th St. Patrick's Day hike alongside a car full of university students and friends. Father Murphy paraded through rain, snow, fog, sleet, and occasionally sunshine. (Courtesy of Cleveland State University Special Collections.)

In 1953, the grounds around the administration building were still not landscaped. This student, George O'Callahan, had planned an ice-skating pond that did not freeze over in the winter and left this enormous puddle in the spring.

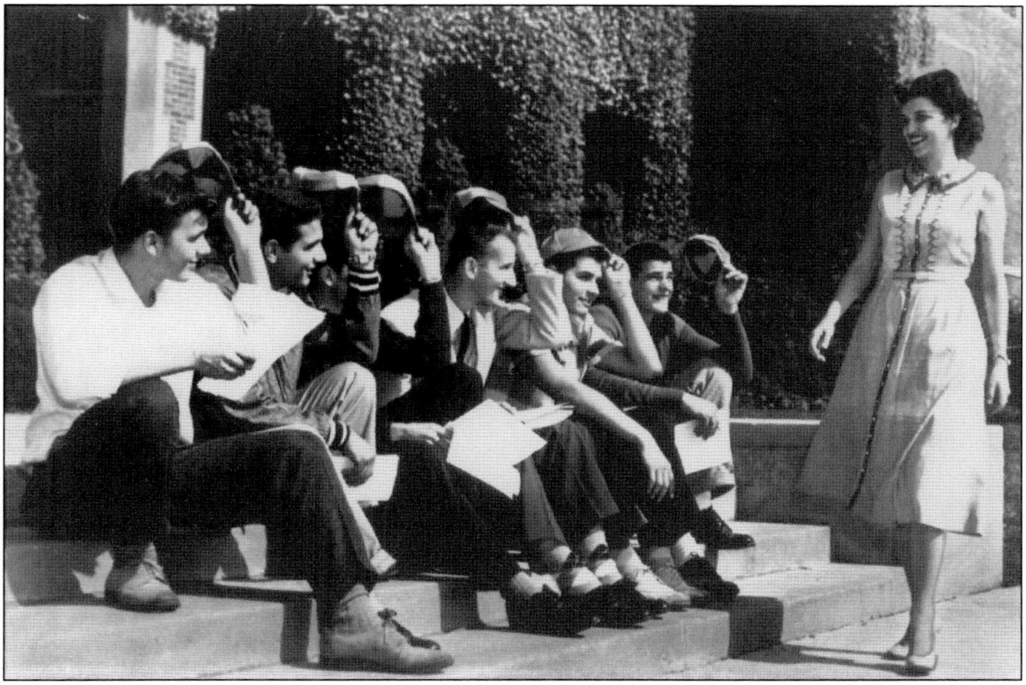

In 1956, John Carroll hired its first full-time female faculty member, Mary Neff, in the mathematics department. In this image, students politely tip their hats as Neff walks past them. At this point, the school had women working as part-time teachers and graduate assistants, and women could attend evening and graduate classes.

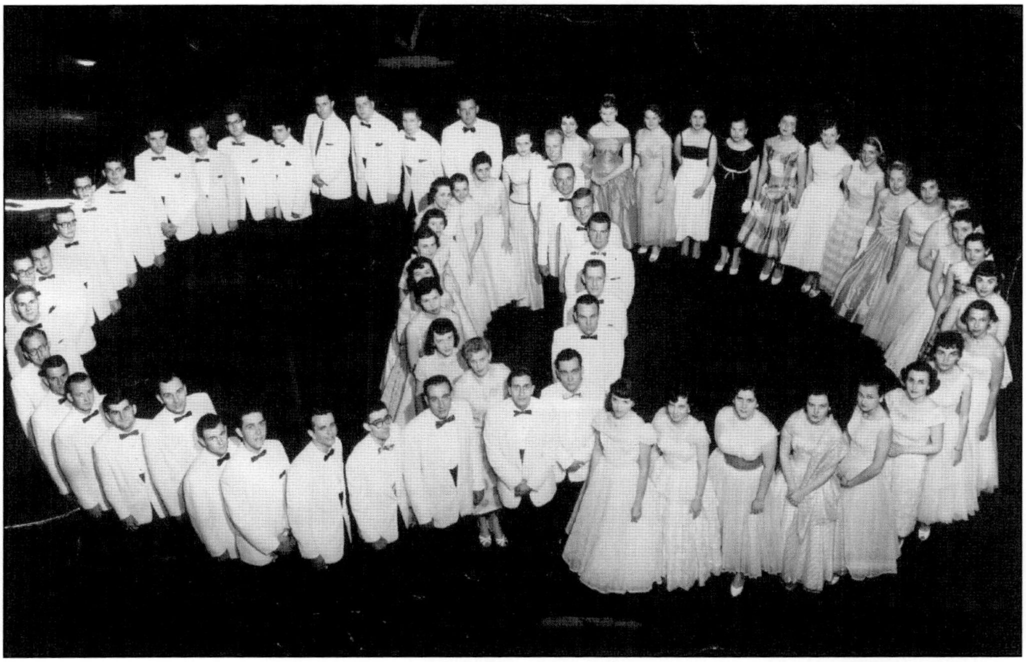

This Betrothal Ring of engaged couples became a John Carroll tradition in the postwar years. The young men and women received blessings before dancing at the "Betrothal Ball." In 1957, these 36 participating couples set a campus record.

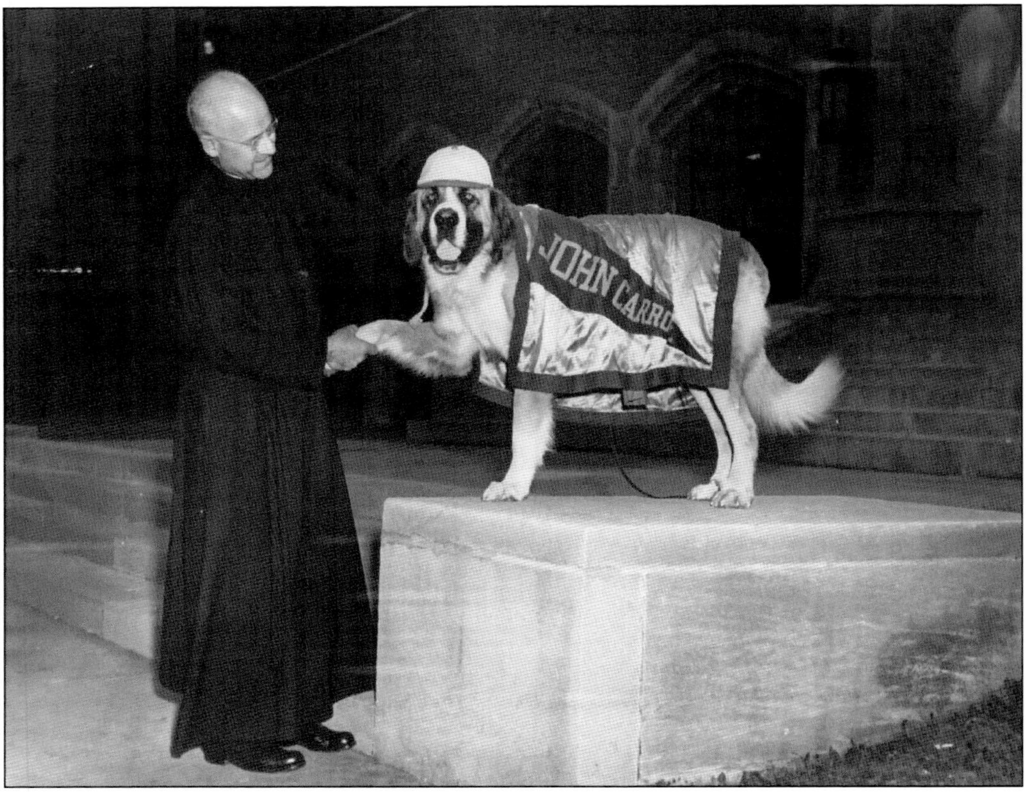

Rev. Frederick E. Welfle, SJ (pictured here with a mascot), president of the university from 1946 to 1956, inherited the physical and administrative difficulties and possibilities of the postwar period, including a building boom that included two new residence halls, a new gymnasium, and a student activities center. Welfle also instituted an advisory board of lay trustees and received the University Heights Citizen of the Year Award.

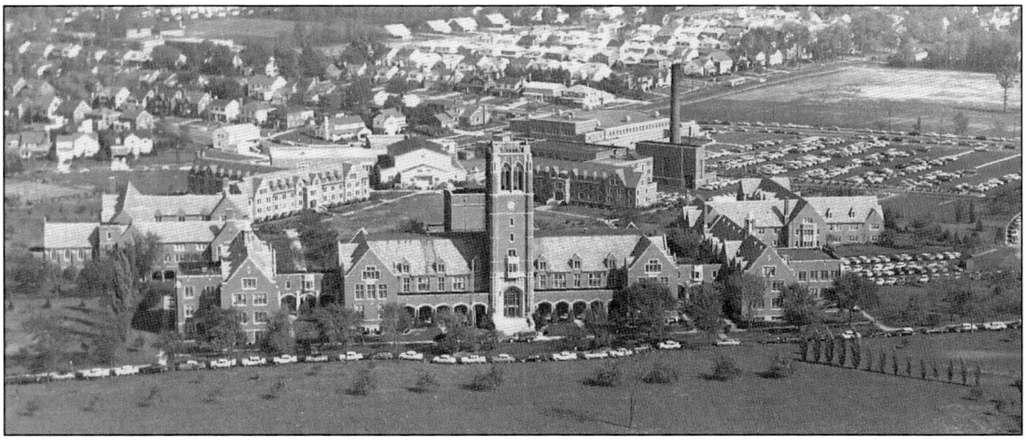

After Welfle's death in 1956, *The Carroll News* noted that he had guided the university "from infancy to adolescence." This mid-1950s aerial photograph illustrates how the campus took shape under his direction, especially when compared to how it looked in the early 1930s. University Heights grew into a town around the campus.

Four

The Winds of Change 1961–1986

During the decades between 1960 and 1990, the winds of change blew from the Vatican; from Vietnam; from Washington, DC; and from Northeast Ohio. John Carroll became a very different place; the university governance structure, the curriculum, the faculty, the physical plant, student life, and—most visibly—the student body changed.

Directives from the Second Vatican Council recognized the importance of laypersons and life in the secular world. In response, laypersons, both Catholic and non-Catholic, became members of the John Carroll University Board of Trustees in 1969. This change also made it easier for the university to receive federal funds, mostly for student aid. The university also had to show that it admitted non-Catholic students (it always had) and that theology courses were academic, not intended to convert students.

In 1968, for the first time, the university admitted women as full-time, degree-seeking undergraduates. Nuns and laywomen had attended John Carroll's evening and graduate classes since the 1920s. Nonetheless, the decision to officially go coed initially stirred controversy among faculty, students, and alumni.

More women joined a faculty increasingly made up of laypersons. In 1966, in response to a restive faculty, the faculty handbook incorporated the American Association of University Professors' 1940 Statement of Principles on Academic Freedom and Tenure.

In the mid-1960s, attendance at Mass and the annual retreat became optional for students. In May 1970, in the wake of the deaths of four students shot by members of the Ohio National Guard at nearby Kent State University, John Carroll students were angered but remained calm, and, like other educational institutions across the country, John Carroll closed before final exams. After confrontations with the administration, students celebrated relaxed rules for the residence halls, a more liberal dress code (coat and tie became optional), and a Student Bill of Rights in 1972. In 1973, the philosophy requirement was cut from five to three courses and the theology requirement from three to two.

To accommodate the growing numbers of students who wanted to live on campus, the administration built North and South Halls (later renamed Sutowski and Millor, respectively) and the Fritzsche Religious Center. By the early 1980s, John Carroll had made the transition from a streetcar college to a residential university. In 1986, the university celebrated its centennial with great fanfare.

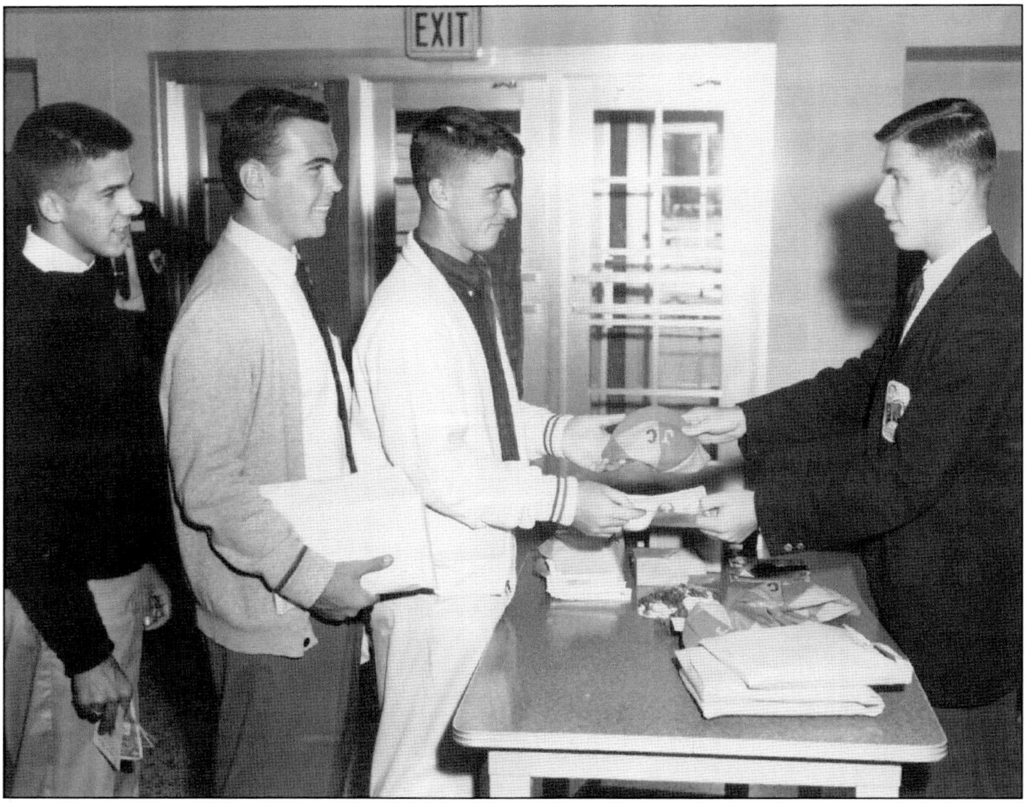

In 1960, John Carroll freshmen (all males) still wore beanies to indicate their status. Both the beanie tradition and the all-male undergraduate student body would change in the next decade.

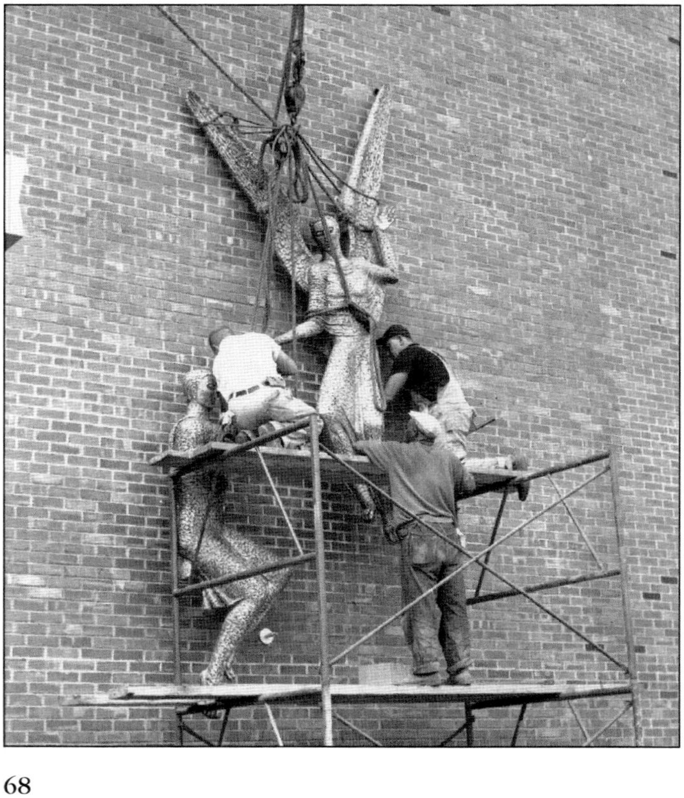

Grasselli Library, with this distinctive wall sculpture, opened in 1961. The library was a gift from the Grasselli family: Thomas, a student in Saint Ignatius College's first class; Josephine; Ida; and Aloise, who was married to William T. Cashman. The tower in the Administration Building was to be a memorial to the Grasselli children's mother, while the library was a memorial to their father.

In a scene reminiscent of the days of Rev. Frederick Odenbach, SJ, who flew instrument-bearing kites to record temperature and wind velocity, these students and Rev. Thomas Biecker, SJ, engaged in some kite-flying in the quadrangle on a windy spring day, probably more for fun than for gathering meteorological data.

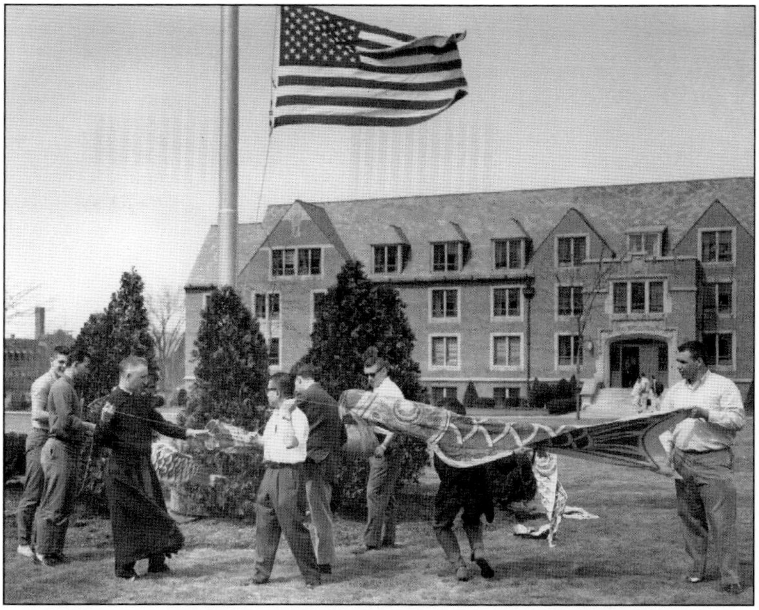

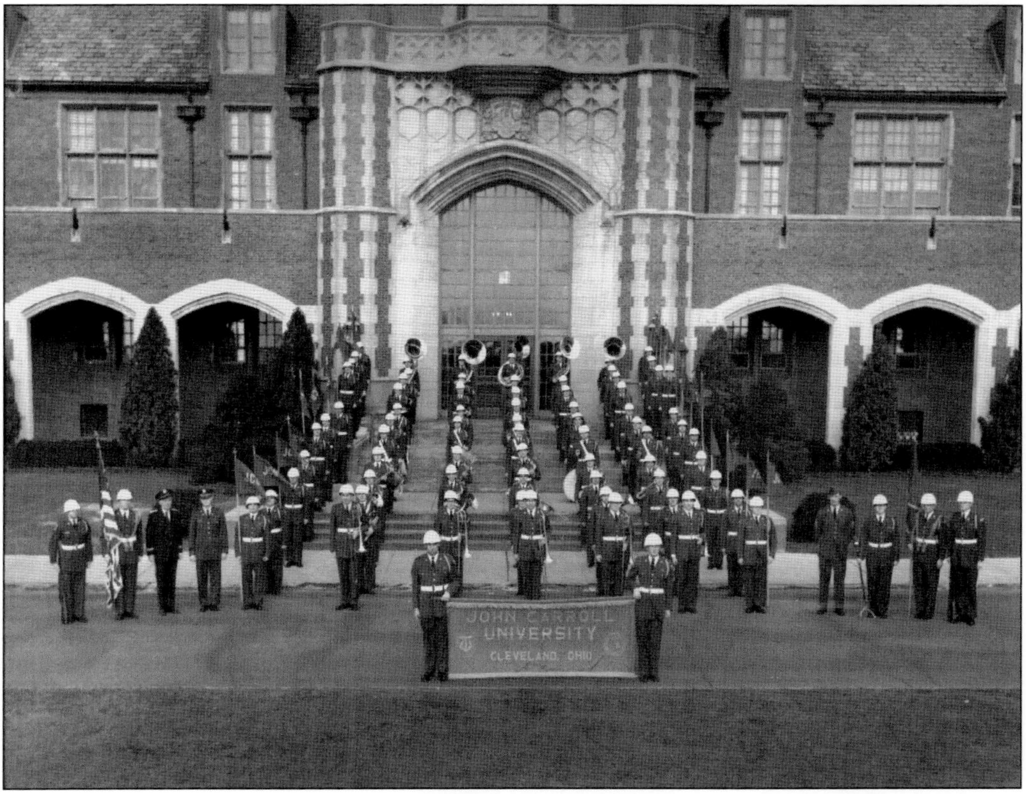

Fully deployed on the steps of the Administration Building, the ROTC marching band stands smartly at attention. John Carroll received an Army ROTC transportation unit in 1950. Enrollment in ROTC was mandatory for students until the fall of 1969; students and the local chapter of the American Association of University Professors had petitioned the university to make participation voluntary.

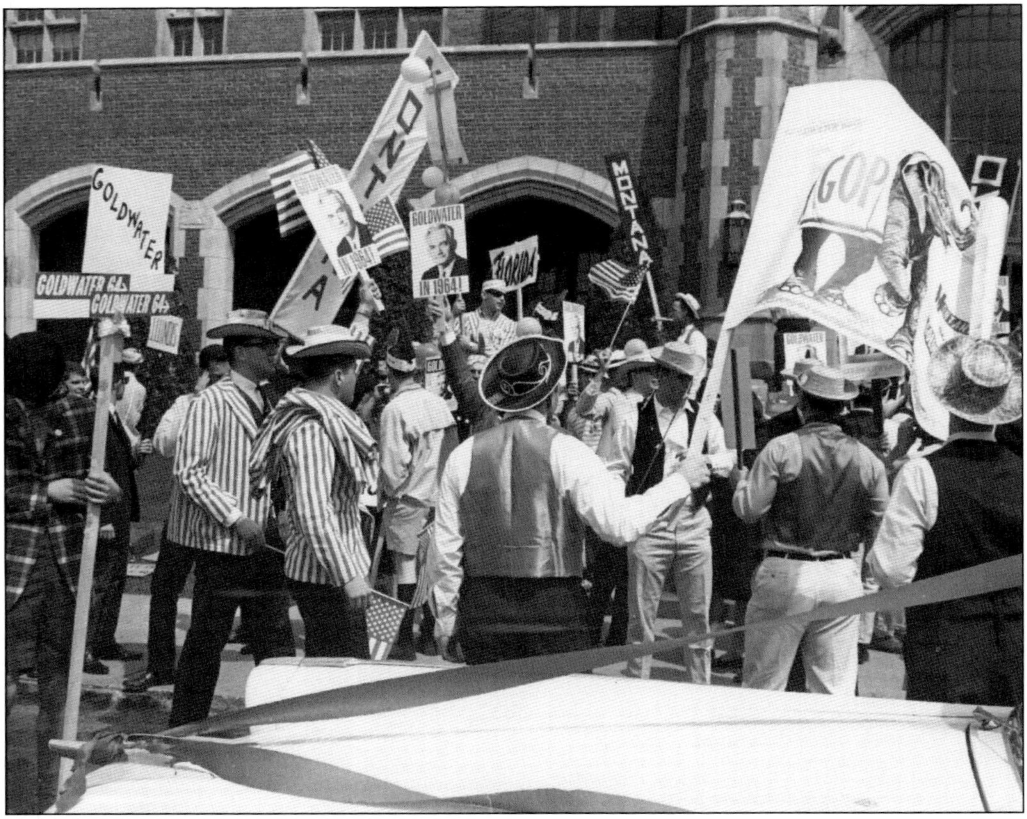

In 1964, John Carroll staged a mock Republican convention, and these students enthusiastically rallied in support of presidential candidate Barry Goldwater. In 1968, the university hosted a rally in support of presidential candidate Eugene McCarthy.

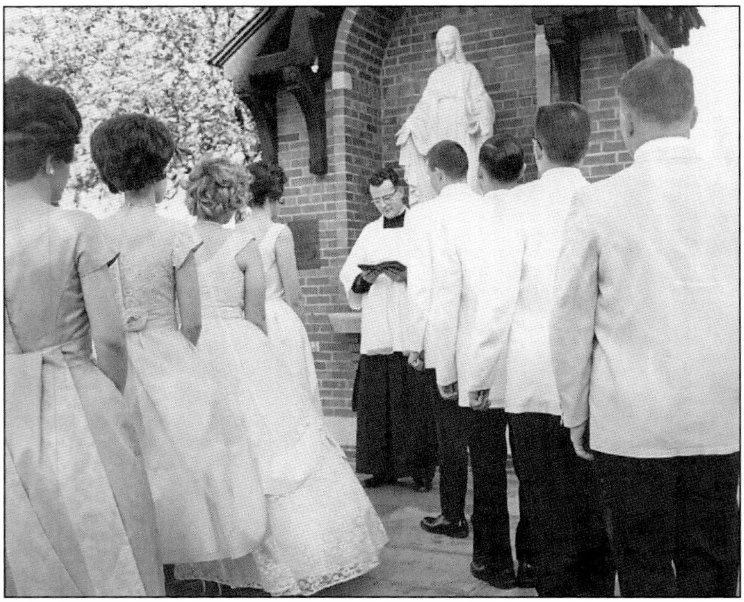

Betrothal ceremonies took place on the day before graduation in front of the shrine of Our Lady, Mother of Grace (also known as the Beaudry Shrine, named for John Carroll graduate Bob Beaudry, who was killed in a plane crash in 1951). This photograph is dated 1965.

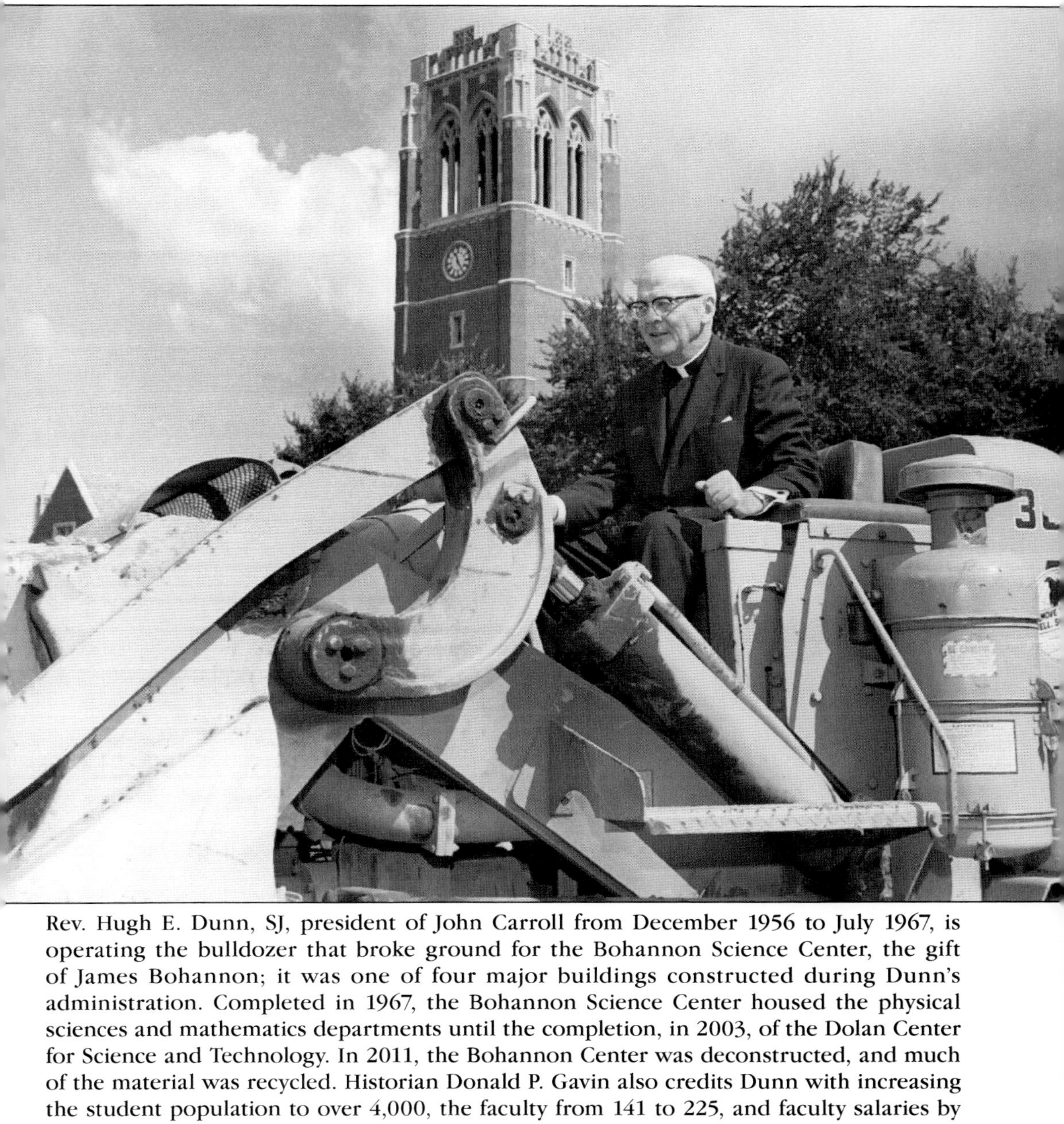

Rev. Hugh E. Dunn, SJ, president of John Carroll from December 1956 to July 1967, is operating the bulldozer that broke ground for the Bohannon Science Center, the gift of James Bohannon; it was one of four major buildings constructed during Dunn's administration. Completed in 1967, the Bohannon Science Center housed the physical sciences and mathematics departments until the completion, in 2003, of the Dolan Center for Science and Technology. In 2011, the Bohannon Center was deconstructed, and much of the material was recycled. Historian Donald P. Gavin also credits Dunn with increasing the student population to over 4,000, the faculty from 141 to 225, and faculty salaries by 100 percent.

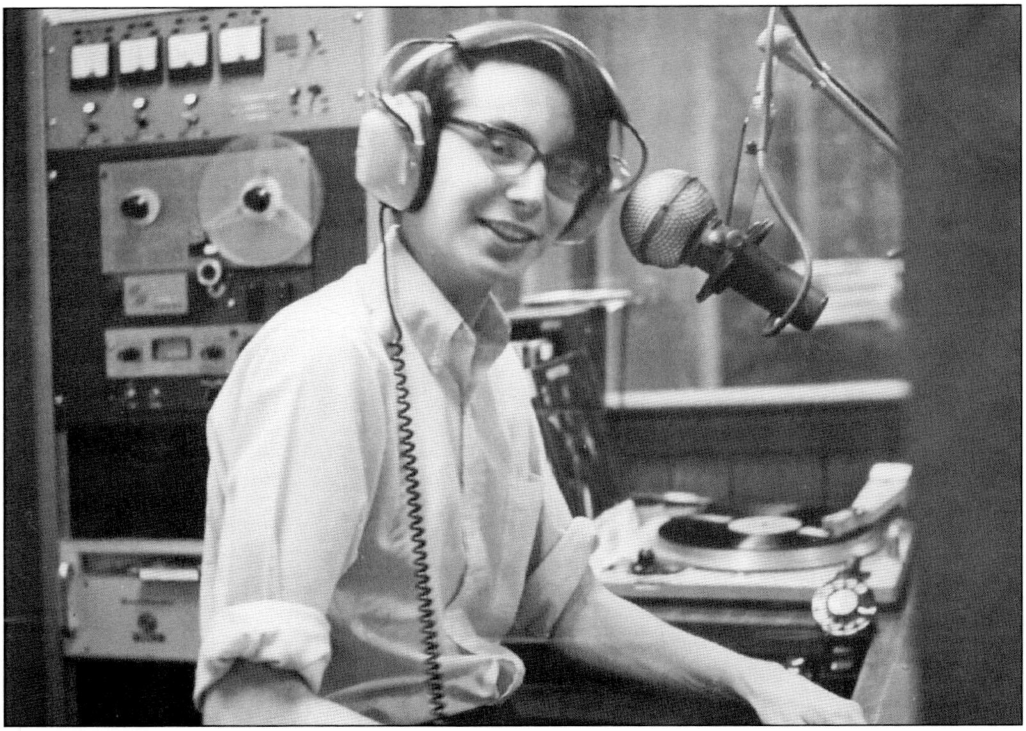

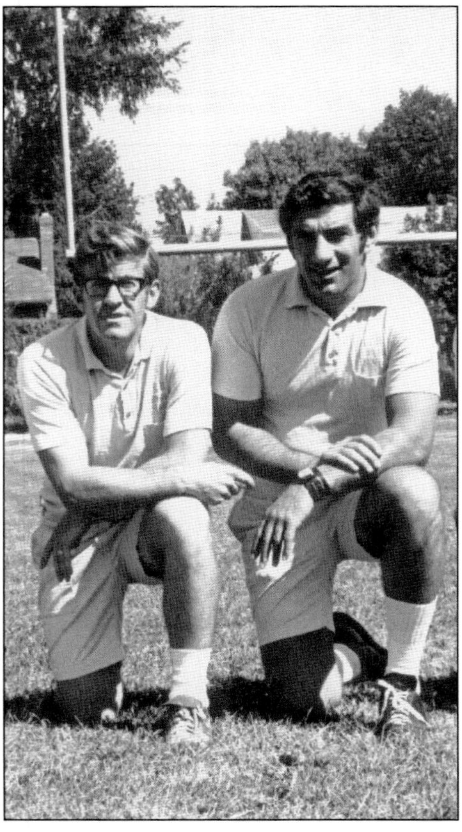

In 1966, the FCC licensed an FM radio station for educational purposes at John Carroll. In 1968, WJCU began operations with financial support from the university and the Student Union.

These two coaches started their JCU careers in the 1960s—Jerry Schweikert (left) in 1960 and Tony DeCarlo in 1966. Both coached winning teams in the Presidents' Athletic Conference in football, baseball, and wrestling. DeCarlo's 1975 wrestlers won the NCAA Division III championship. Both men have John Carroll athletic facilities named for them.

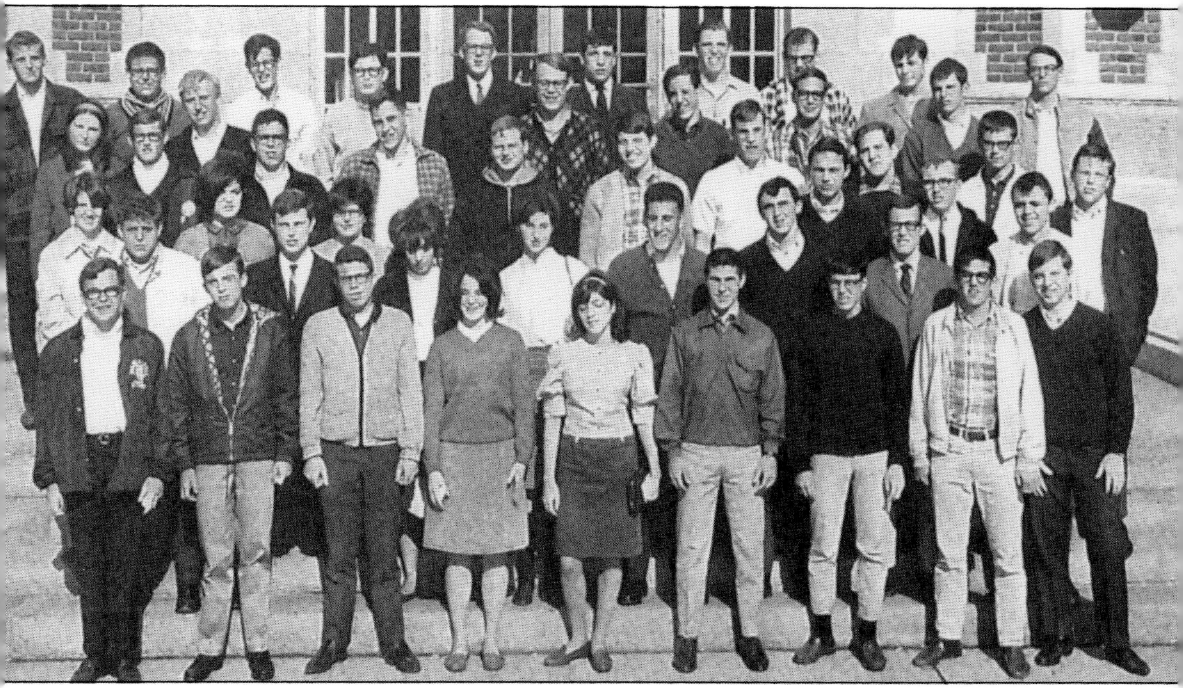

This photograph of John Carroll sophomores, which appeared in the *Carillon* in 1967 (a full year before women were officially admitted as full-time undergraduate students), reflected the fact that women were already John Carroll students. Many female undergraduate students enrolled in the evening division but took their classes during the day. Some alumni, faculty, and students opposed coeducation, fearful that it would irretrievably change the character of the university; others supported it for the same reason. The school's official explanation for the change was that female students would expand and improve the student body.

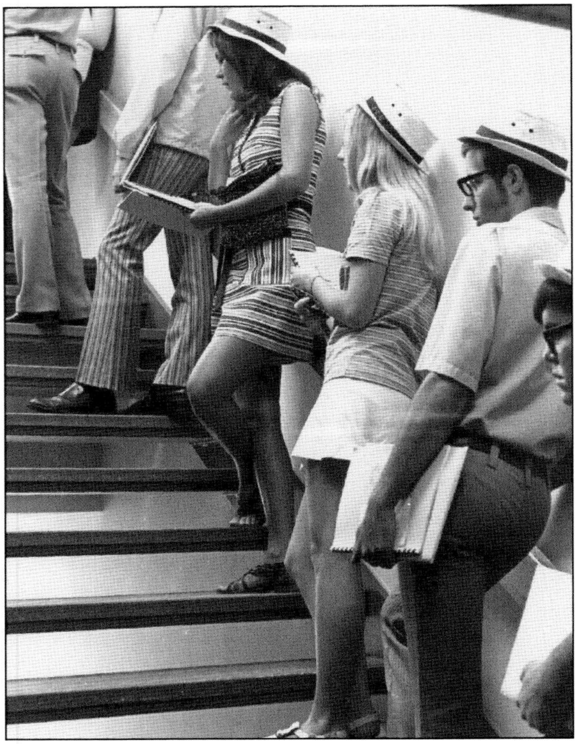

After 1968, women—finally and officially full-time freshmen at the university—donned the "duffers" that had replaced the freshman beanies. Since the 1920s, nuns had attended Saturday sessions at John Carroll; laywomen had attended the evening and graduate classes since the 1930s, and dozens of women had already received John Carroll diplomas.

By the time they were officially allowed to be full-time undergraduates, women already participated in campus activities such as this women's choir. In 1967, the *Carroll Quarterly* had its first female editor, and in 1968, so did *The Carroll News.*

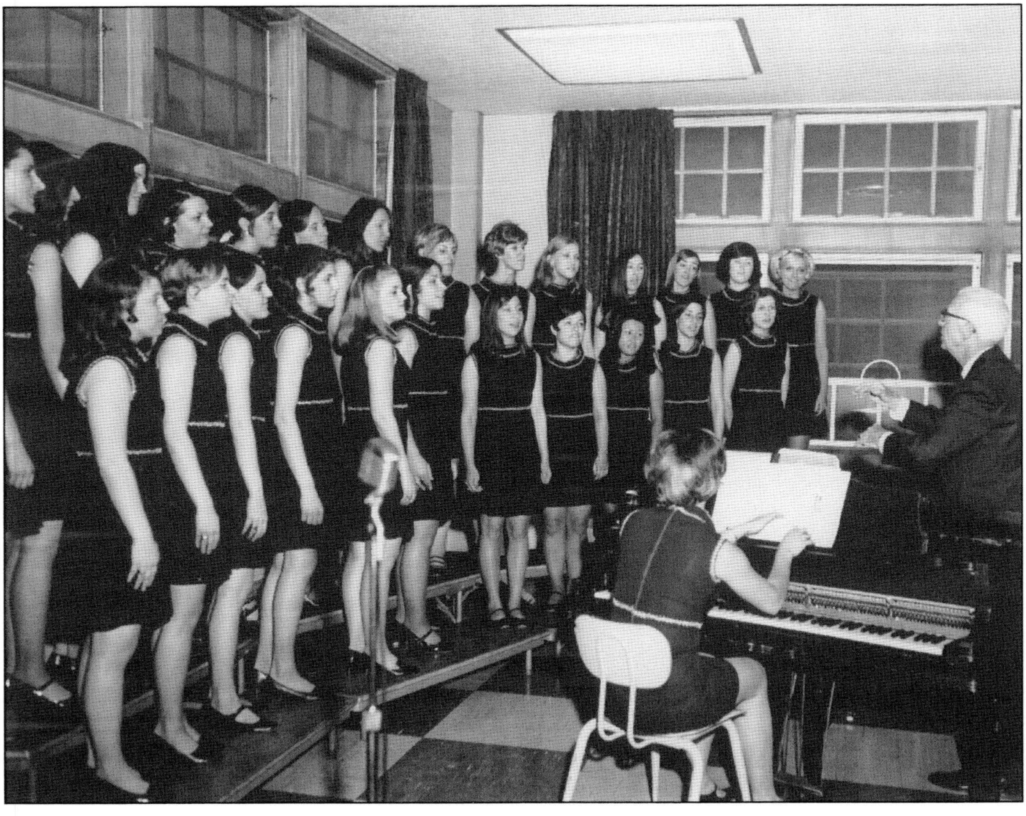

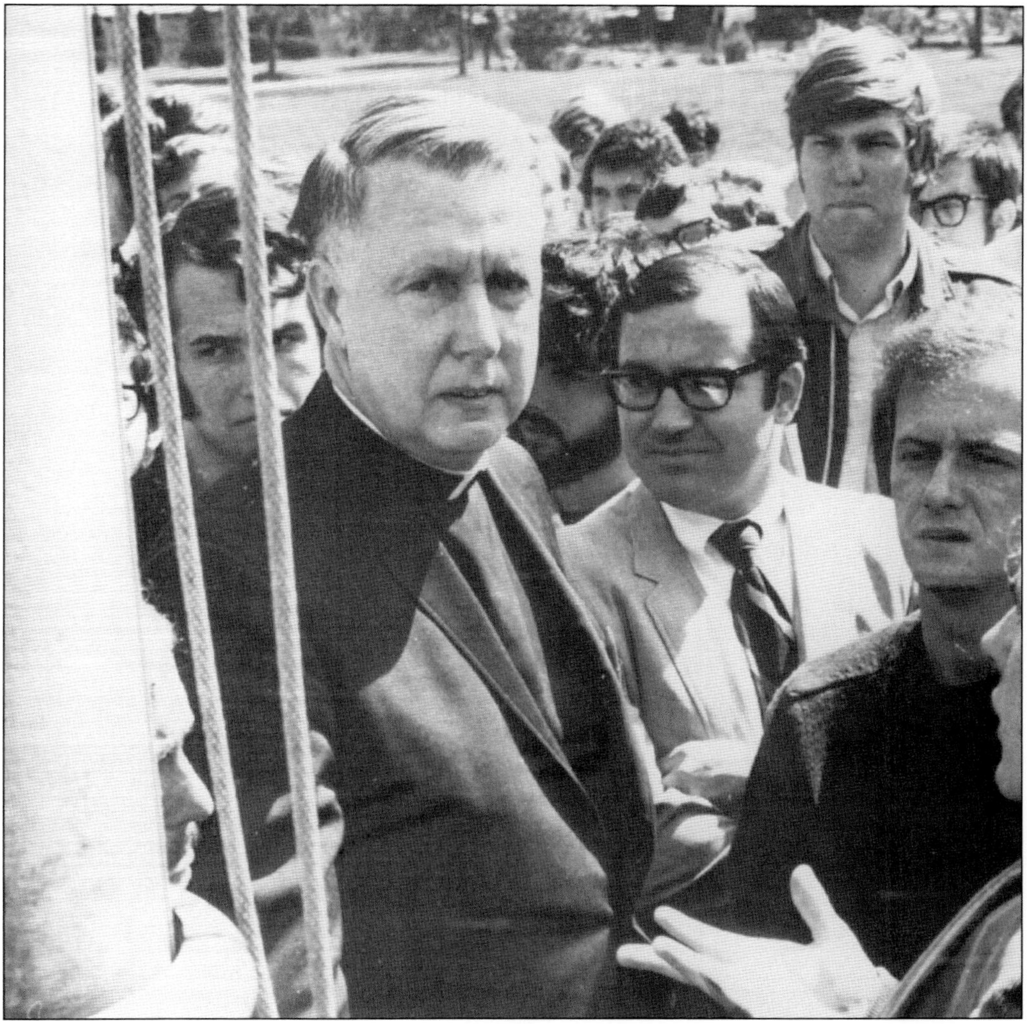

Rev. Joseph O. Schell, SJ, president of the university from 1967 to 1970, found himself embroiled in several controversial issues: coeducation, the establishment of a lay board of trustees, and—throughout the spring of 1970—growing student unrest. After members of the Ohio National Guard shot and killed four Kent State students on May 4, 1970, the John Carroll faculty passed a resolution commending the students for their nonviolence, but the university closed before final exams. Interspersed throughout the 1970 *Carillon* are photographs of campus protests and this poem: "While some died in Vietnam, in Cambodia, in the streets, and on campuses, others protested their deaths; some of us did, too. Some of us sought peace through threats, through confrontation, and through violence. Some sought peace through kindness, through understanding, and through love." Known for his closeness to the students, Schell found himself besieged by them, as seen in this photograph. He chose to resign from the presidency in late spring 1970 but served the university for 58 years as a professor of philosophy, spiritual counselor to generations of students, and founder of the John Carroll University Campus Ministry.

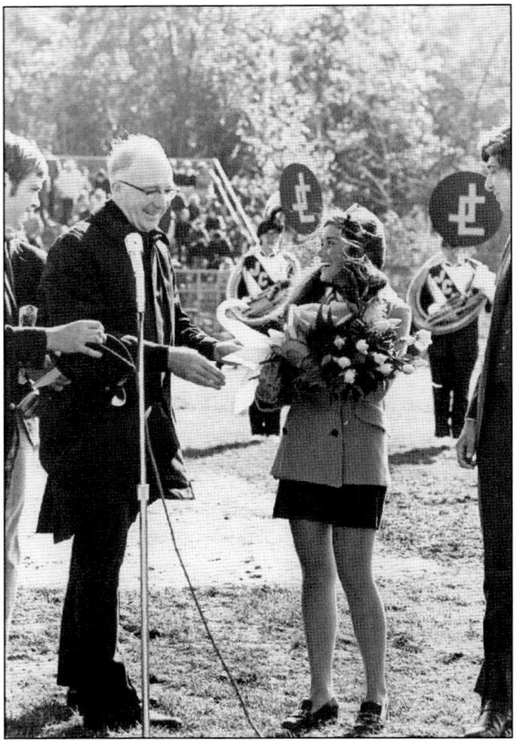

Rev. Joseph Schell was succeeded by Rev. Henry F. Birkenhauer, SJ, who served as president of John Carroll until 1980. Father Birkenhauer became dean of the Graduate School when it was established in 1956. He was the assistant to Schell and a nationally known seismologist. Here, he presides over homecoming festivities.

The Fritzsche Religious Center, named for longtime trustee Allan Fritzsche, opened in 1971. These musicians, their clothes, and their hair are definitely of that era. The center was created by renovating the old Pink Barn, the former site of the business school and gymnasium, and facing it with brick.

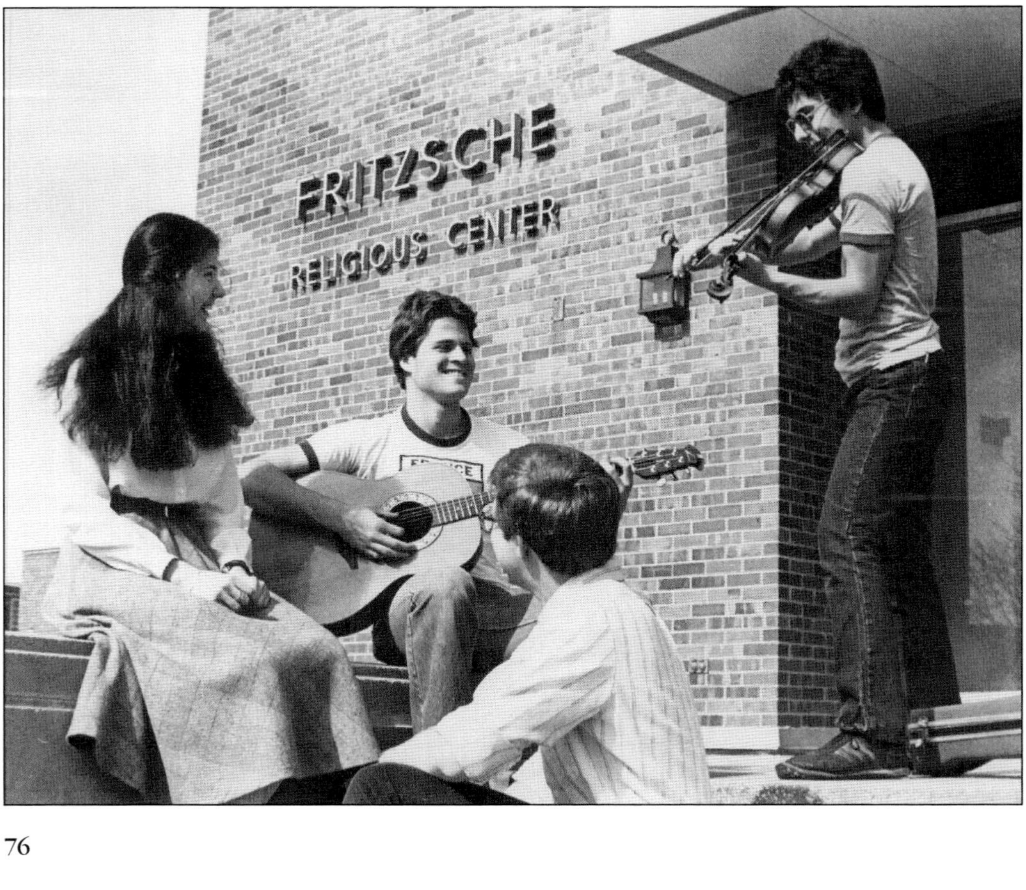

In the 1970s, many other female faculty members followed Mary Neff. Dr. Jacqueline Schmidt joined the communications department (now the Tim Russert Department of Communication and Theatre Arts). At that time, female faculty members and graduate assistants tended to cluster in the humanities.

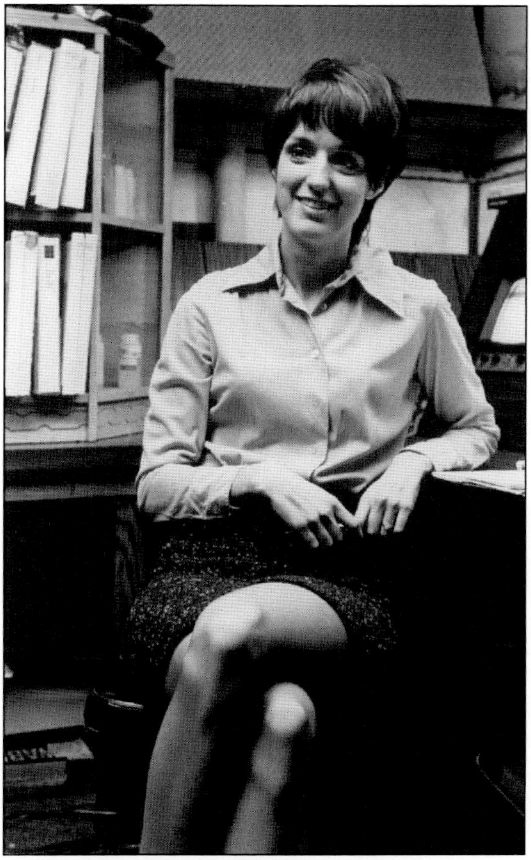

Dr. Mary Ann Flannery, SC, also joined the communications department. In 2011, 114 laymen, 84 laywomen, and four Jesuits made up John Carroll's full-time faculty. Female faculty members at John Carroll, as elsewhere, have sought pay equity with their male peers.

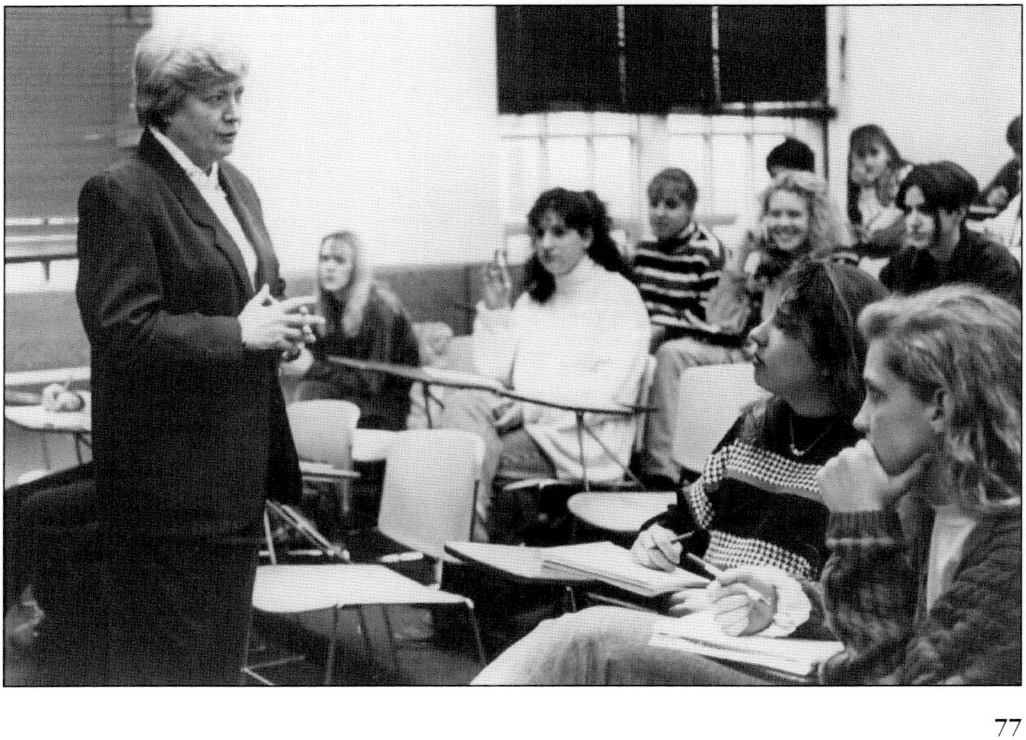

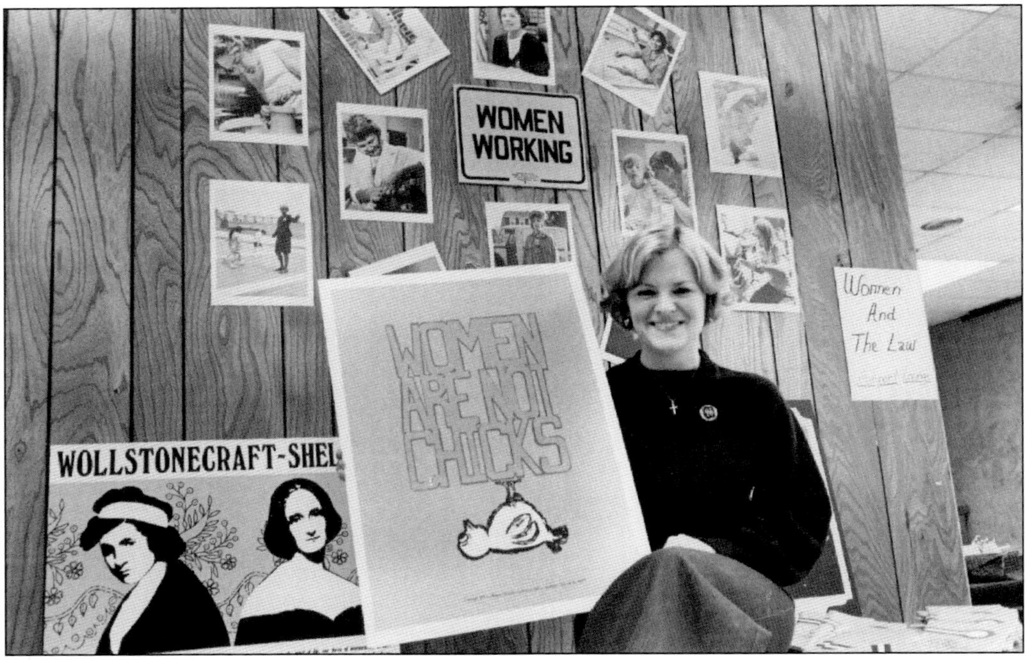

Feminism flourished at John Carroll in the 1970s. Surrounded by posters of feminist icons like Mary Wollstonecraft and photographs of working women, this student reminded her peers that "women are not chicks." In the mid-1970s, the university added an interdisciplinary concentration, Perspectives on Sex and Gender.

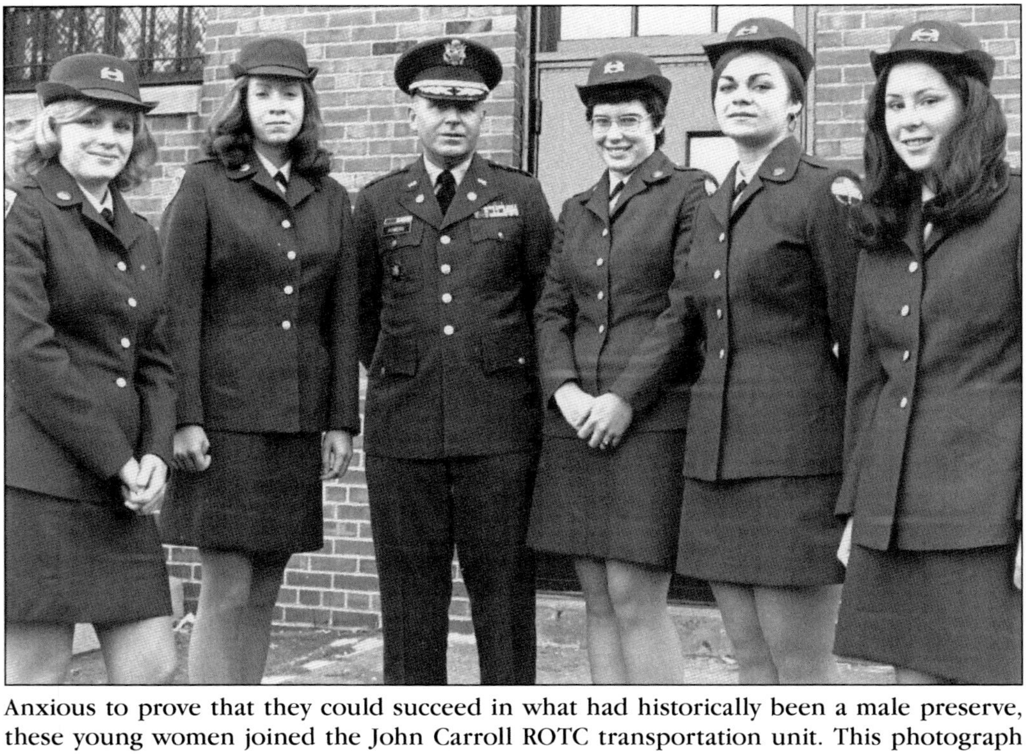

Anxious to prove that they could succeed in what had historically been a male preserve, these young women joined the John Carroll ROTC transportation unit. This photograph appeared in the *Catholic Universe Bulletin* in 1973.

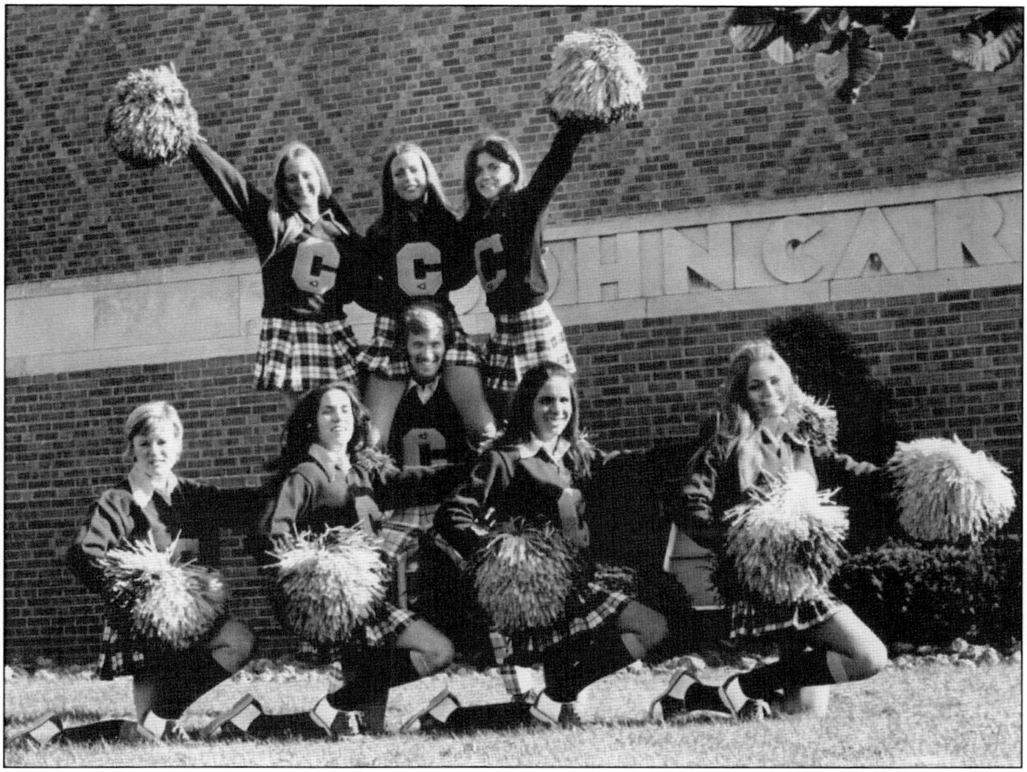

Cheerleaders played a more traditional role in the limelight. John Carroll first added female cheerleaders in 1948.

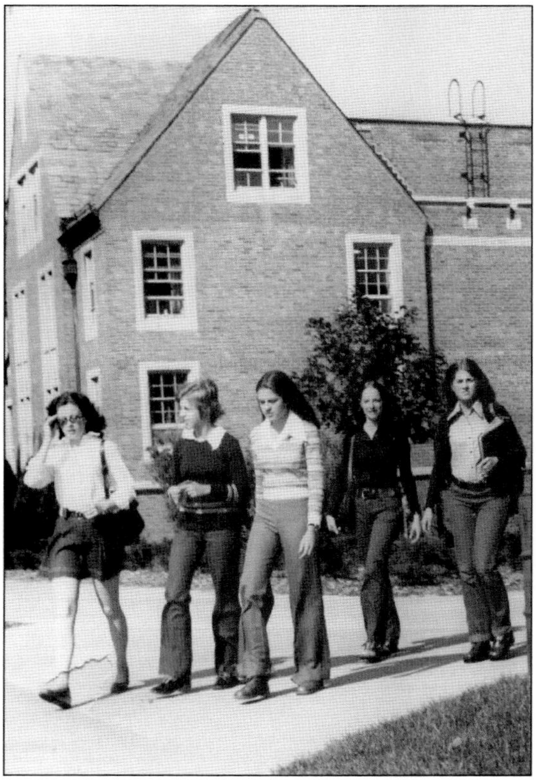

In the fall of 1968, 48 women registered in the College of Arts and Sciences moved into a self-contained floor in Murphy Hall. Women quickly became a common sight on campus.

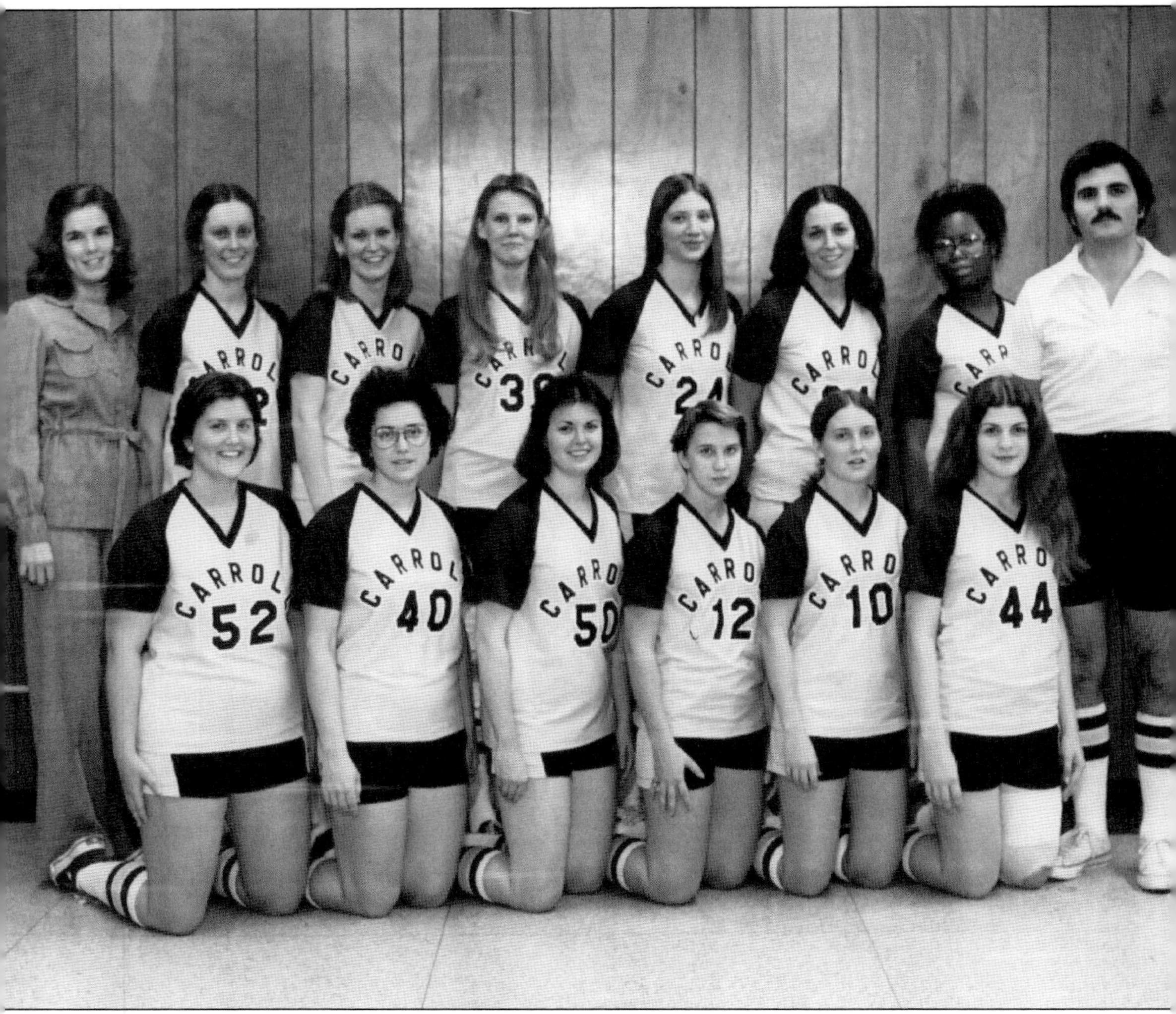

Women entered JCU intercollegiate athletics in 1970, but only in volleyball and basketball. This is the 1977 women's basketball team. Initially, there was no budget for uniforms or transportation, and the women practiced only when the men were finished with the courts. Dr. Kathleen Manning, a 1972 graduate, was the first coordinator of women's athletics at John Carroll. Spurred by Title IX of the 1972 Education Amendments, which barred sex discrimination in educational programs receiving federal funds, John Carroll soon provided other athletic opportunities for women. In 1975, a women's swimming and diving program was started, followed by a tennis program the next year; in 1984, softball and cross-country; in 1985, track and field; in 1989, soccer; and in 1999, golf. In the 1989–1990 school year, John Carroll women joined the Ohio Athletic Conference, where they have competed successfully ever since. By 2011, 26 individual female athletes—plus the 15-member 1993 women's volleyball team—had entered the John Carroll Athletic Hall of Fame.

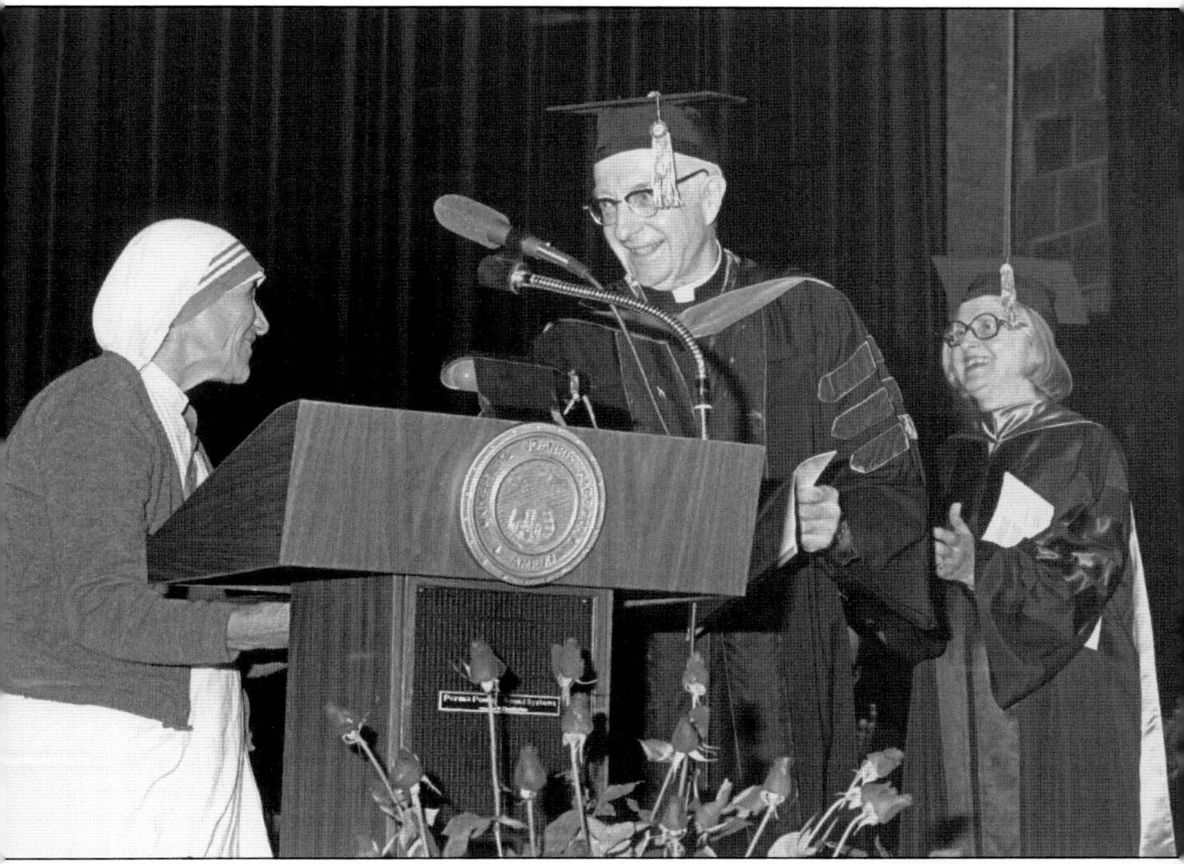

Mother Teresa (left) received an honorary Doctorate of Humane Service degree at John Carroll in April 1978. Rev. Henry F. Birkenhauer, SJ, presented the degree. Sally Griswold, a 1976 graduate and honorary trustee, stands to the right of Birkenhauer. The university also hosted several distinguished commencement speakers during these 1960s, 1970s, and 1980s, including US senators Edmund S. Muskie, Fred R. Harris, Lowell P. Weicker Jr., and Mark O. Hatfield, and US congressman Philip M. Crane. Other speakers included prominent educators Rev. Robert J. Henle, SJ, former president of Georgetown University; Rev. John J. Powell, SJ, former professor of theology at Loyola University of Chicago; and Rev. William J. Byron, SJ, former president of the Catholic University of America.

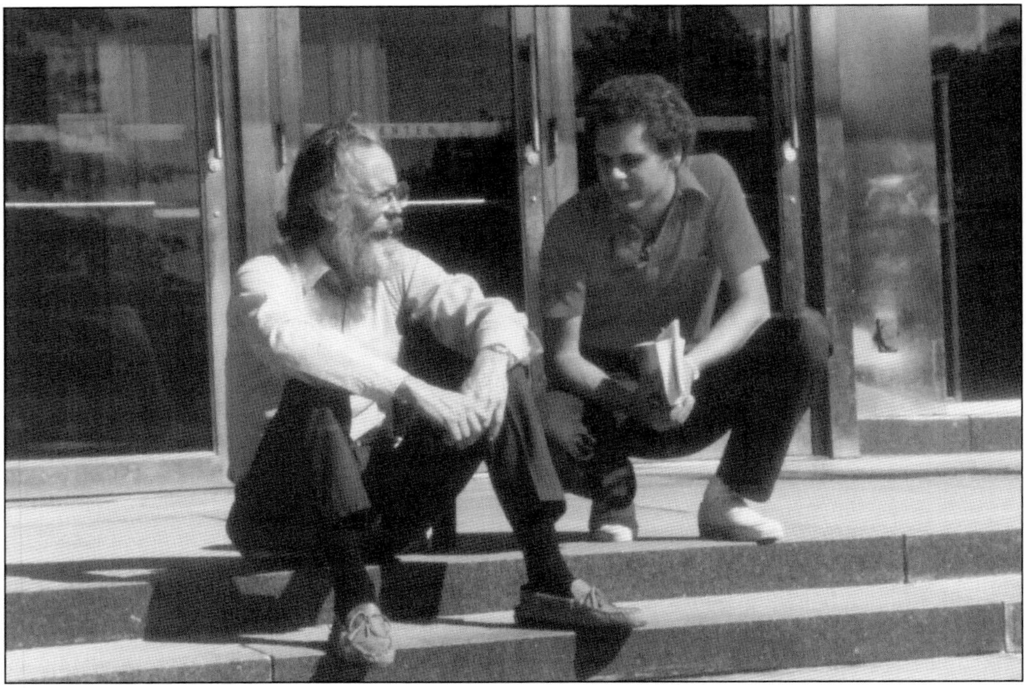

The disruption and changes of the late 1960s and early 1970s encouraged efforts to foster a sense of community on campus. This took several forms, including strengthening bonds between students and faculty. Here, Dr. James Magner (left) of the English department chats with an unidentified student.

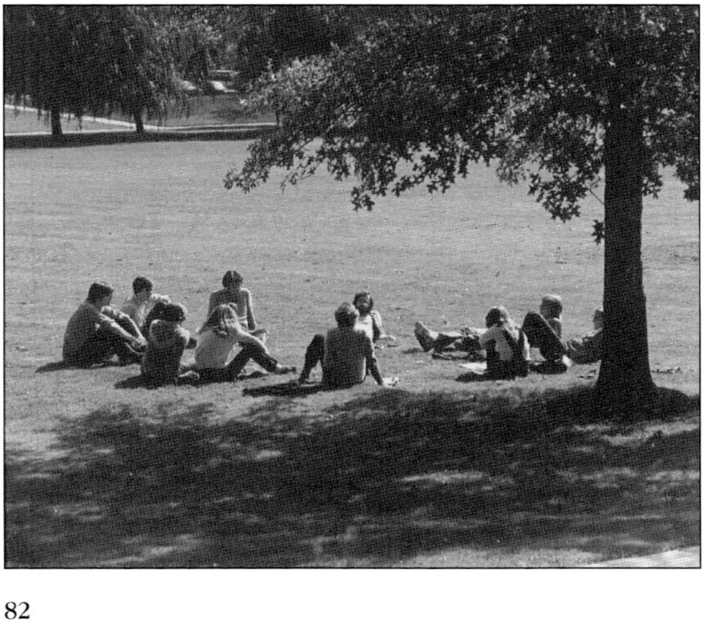

After long Cleveland winters, some spring days are just too beautiful to stay inside the classroom. The green lawns beckon and teachers move their students outside. This lawn was in front of the Grasselli Library. From 2001 to 2011, the lawn served as a temporary parking lot; in 2011, it was restored as the Richard M. & Yvonne F. Hamlin Quadrangle, recognizing the generosity of Dick Hamlin (class of 1949) and his wife, Yvonne.

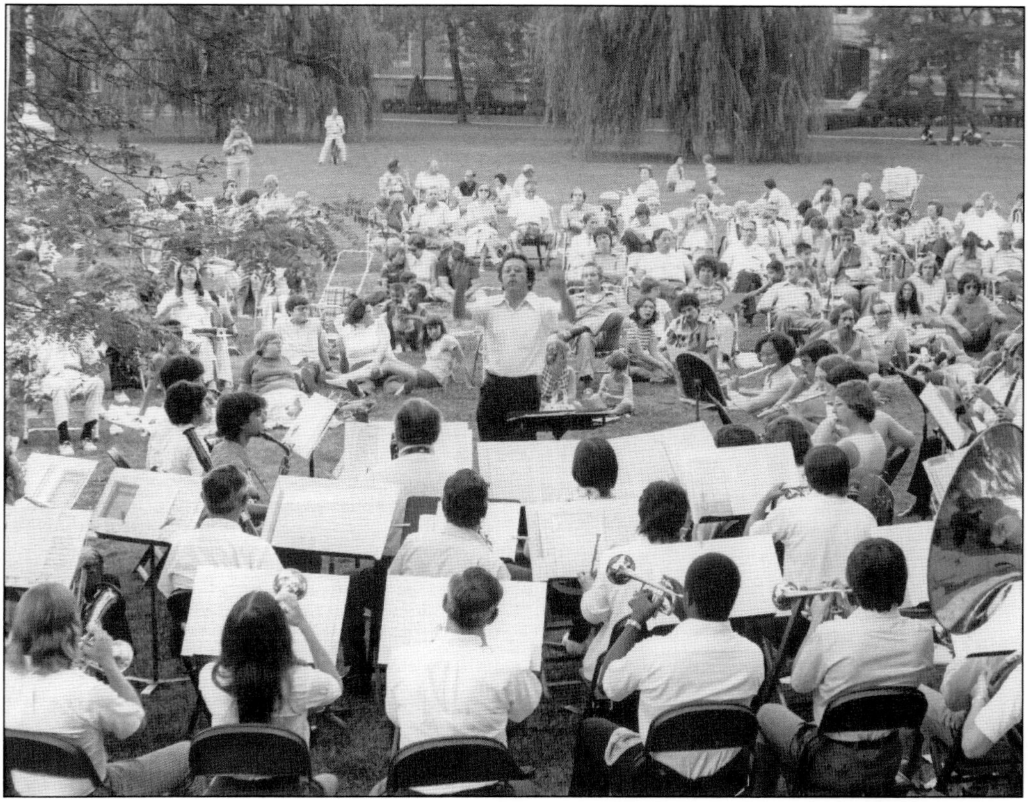

In the half-century after its 1935 arrival in University Heights, John Carroll came to play an important part in the city. Here, faculty member Dr. Harvey Sisler conducts the summer community band during a free concert on the campus quadrangle. (Courtesy of Cleveland Heights–University Heights Library.)

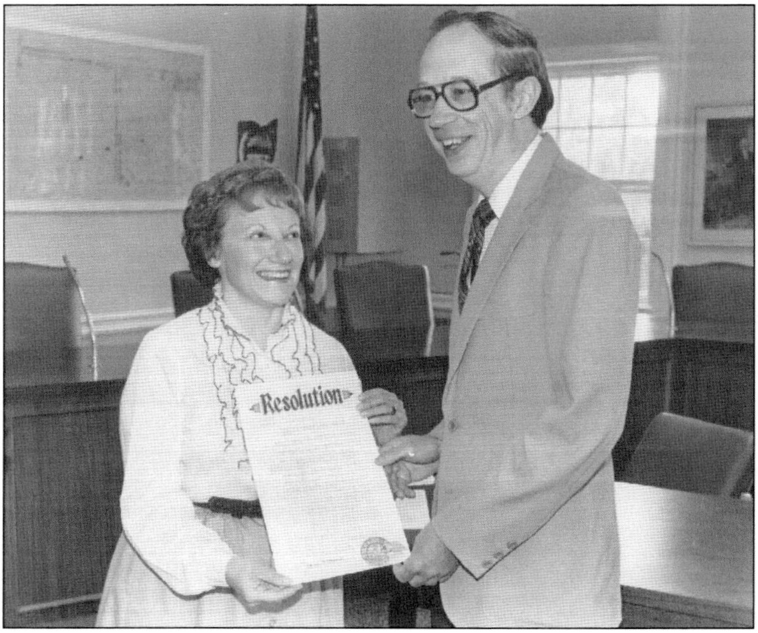

In 1983, University Heights mayor Beryl Rothschild (left) presented the university's Distinguished Faculty Award to Dr. Joseph Miller of the communications department. This symbolized the close relationship between the city and the university. (Courtesy of Cleveland Heights–University Heights Library.)

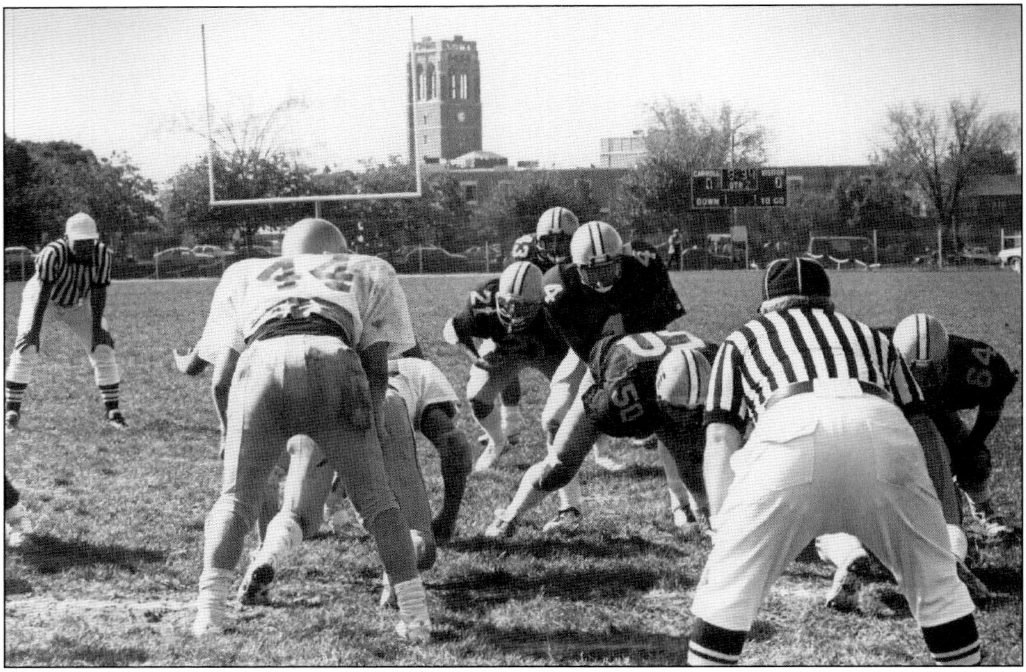

In October 1983, a homecoming crowd of 2,700 watched the JCU Blue Streaks beat Allegheny College in a close game (final score: 16–14) on Wasmer Field, now also the site of the Don Shula Stadium. Since 1974, the university has competed at the Division III level in the NCAA.

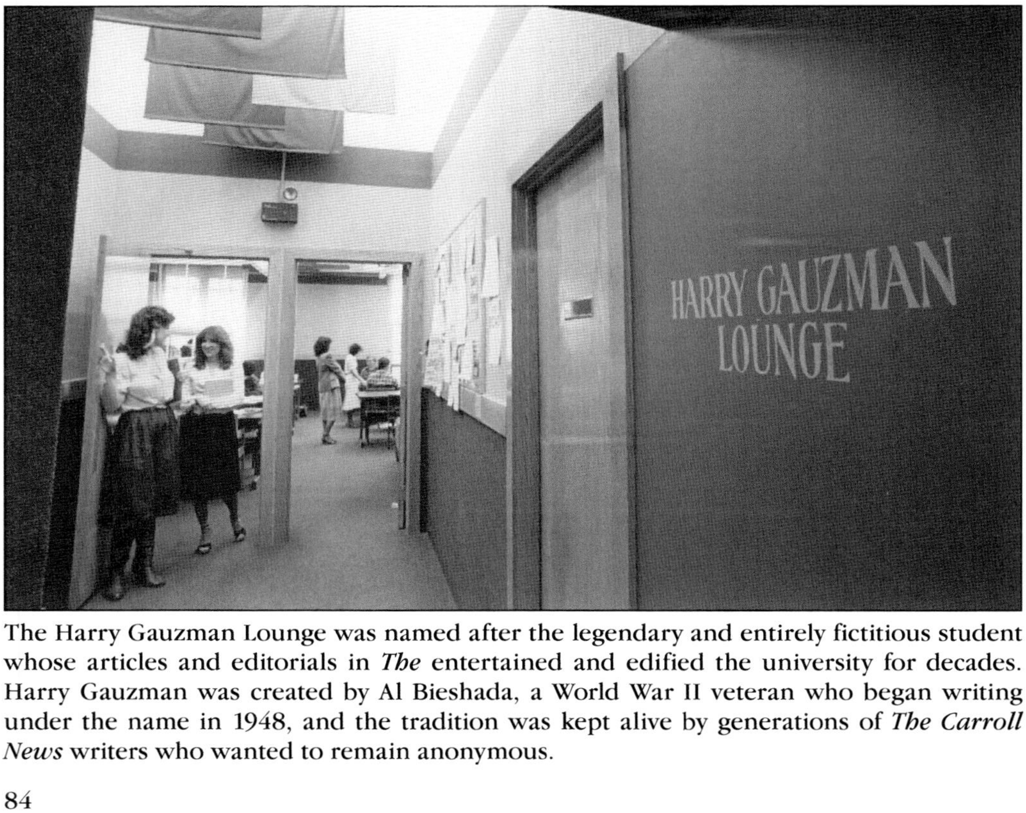

The Harry Gauzman Lounge was named after the legendary and entirely fictitious student whose articles and editorials in *The* entertained and edified the university for decades. Harry Gauzman was created by Al Bieshada, a World War II veteran who began writing under the name in 1948, and the tradition was kept alive by generations of *The Carroll News* writers who wanted to remain anonymous.

Rev. William J. Millor, SJ, held many posts at the university: chairman of the classics department, headmaster of the residence halls, dean of the Graduate School, executive dean, and academic vice president. He was referred to as "the Duke," a reference to his formal clothing and/or his imperious manner. The South Hall residence was renamed Millor Hall in 1982.

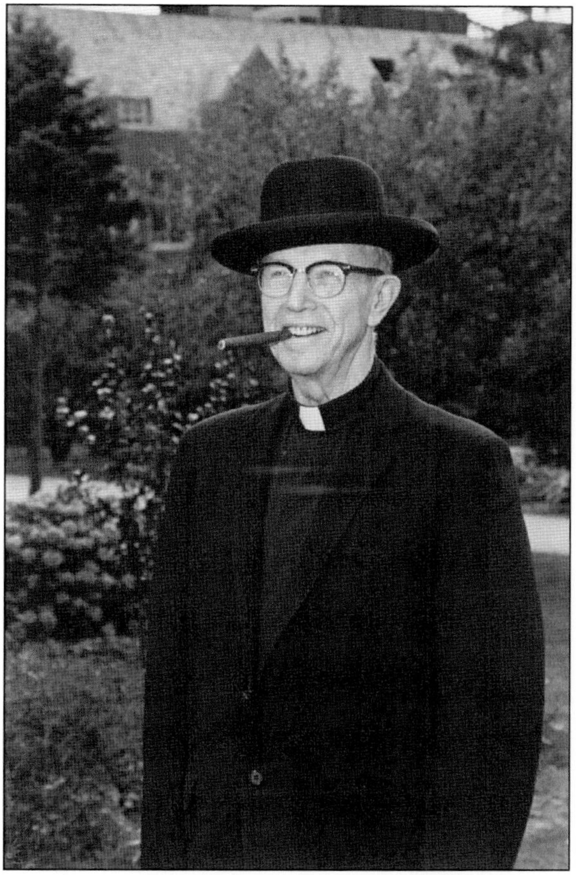

This photograph of the John Carroll Jesuits was taken in the mid-1980s. Rev. Thomas P. O'Malley, SJ, university president from 1980 to 1988, is fourth from the right in the first row, and his successor, Rev. Michael J. Lavelle, SJ, is sixth from right in the first row. Although the number of Jesuits in John Carroll classrooms had diminished, they still held most of the university's administrative positions.

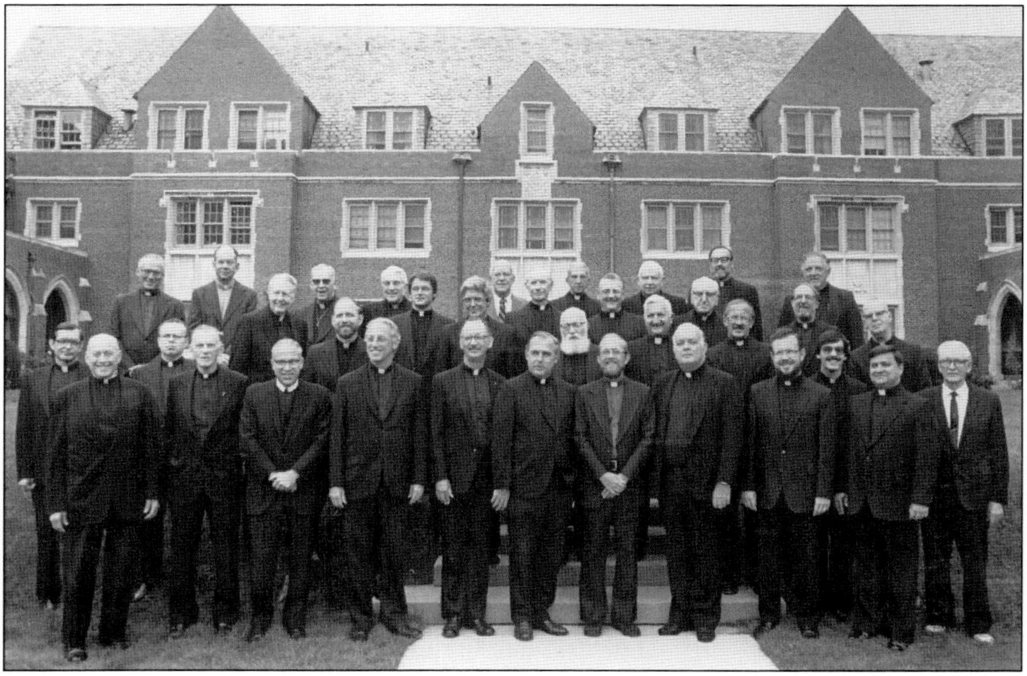

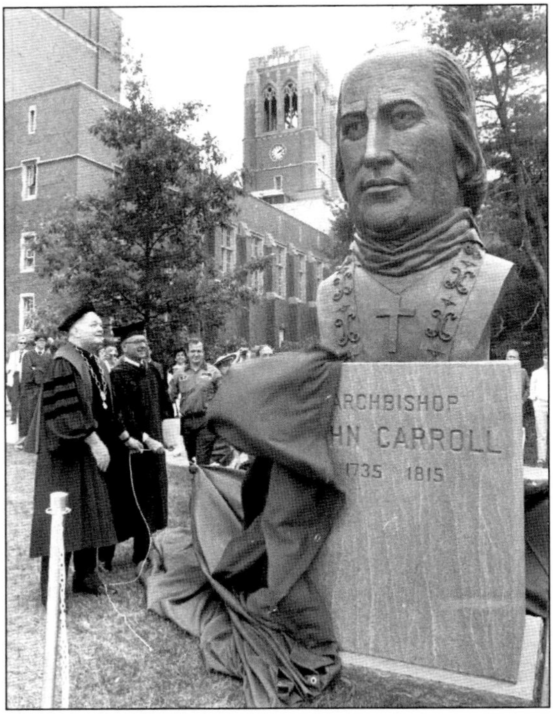

John Carroll celebrated its centennial throughout 1985 and 1986. Centennial events included the unveiling by Pres. Thomas P. O'Malley of this bust of Archbishop John Carroll. The bust, created by sculptor William McVey, had been covered since it arrived on campus, so there was some apprehension that mischief might have been done to it. The unveiling revealed that the bust was unharmed.

The university awarded a number of centennial medals to members of the university and the community. President O'Malley (left) awarded this medal to Dr. Donald P. Gavin (class of 1933), a longtime John Carroll faculty member and administrator and the author of *John Carroll University: A Century of Service*, the definitive history of the university.

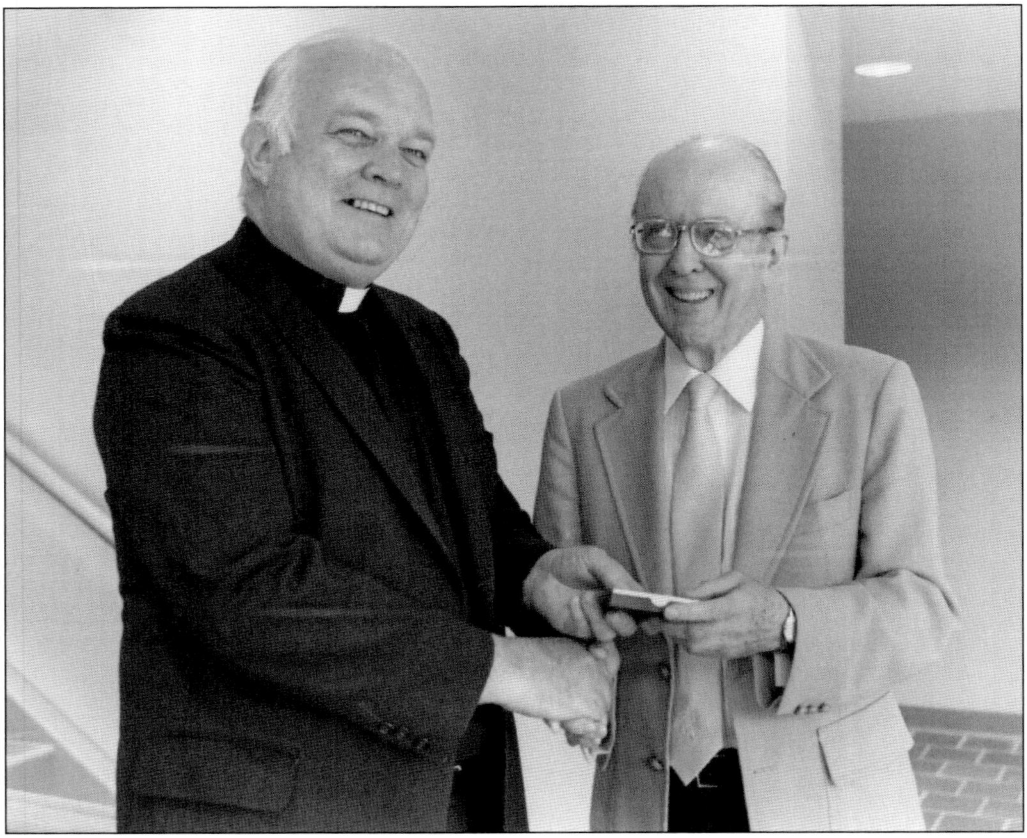

Dr. Kathleen Barber, chair of the Department of Political Science, presented this medal to her predecessor, Rev. Paul Woelfl, SJ.

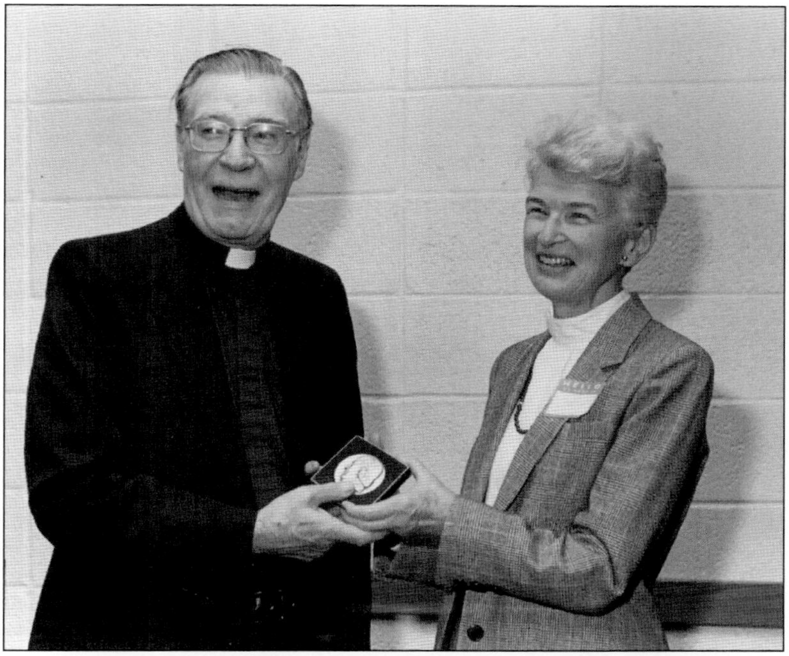

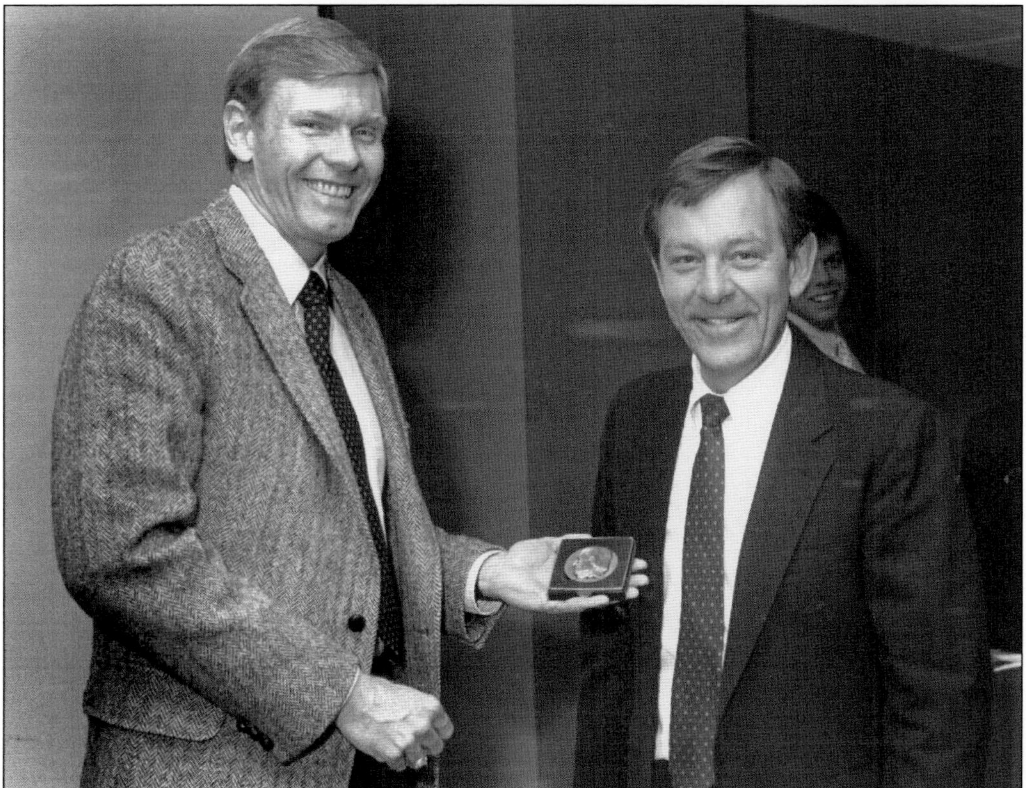

Dr. David Robson (left), chair of the Department of History, awarded a centennial medal to Cleveland mayor George Voinovich. Voinovich served as governor of Ohio from 1991 to 1998, then as a US senator from 1999 until 2011.

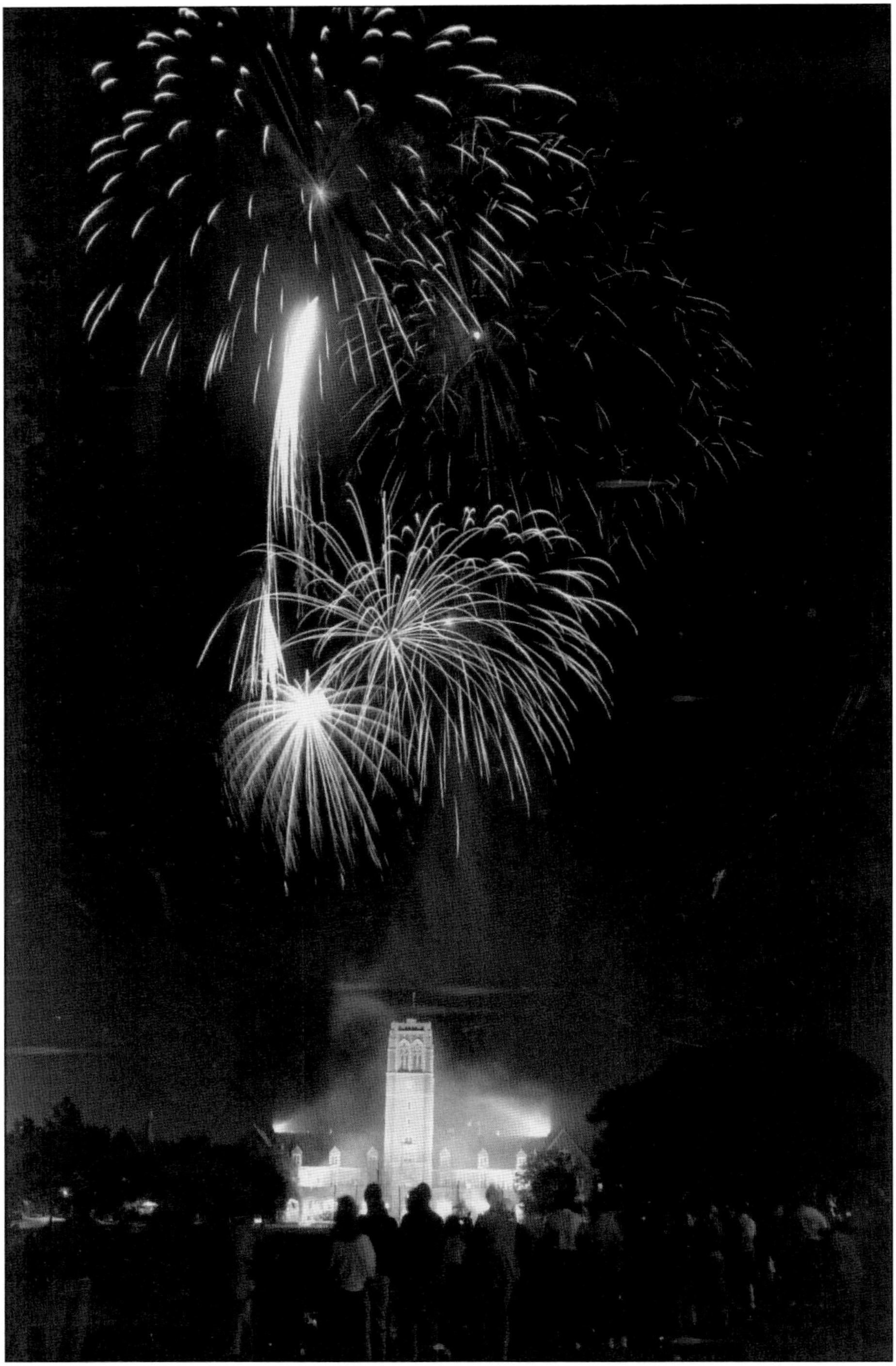

The yearlong centennial celebration ended in 1986 with concerts on the lawn and a fireworks display that lit up the summer skies, marking the end of three decades of tumultuous changes that reshaped John Carroll and celebrating the university's achievements during a difficult century. John Carroll looked optimistically toward its next century.

Five

Entering the Mainstream 1987–2011

Clevelanders, including Catholics, continued the exodus that had accelerated in the post–World War II era. Although this necessitated the closing of many Catholic churches in the city, for parishioners, this exodus signaled further incorporation into the fabric of American life.

By the beginning of the 21st century, John Carroll had entered the mainstream of American higher education, winning regional and national recognition. Its faculty, athletic teams, student newspaper, debate team, and undergraduates also garnered national acclaim.

The university's campus and physical plant expanded to compete for new students and to maintain national status. The school's administrators bought nearby homes, apartments, and a shopping center, which troubled some University Heights neighbors. This expansion, combined with regional job losses and population decline and the national economic downturn of 2008, required more need-based aid and resulted in reduced net tuition, creating financial difficulties for the university. Strategic budget cuts and belt-tightening became necessary.

In 2011, slightly more than half of John Carroll undergraduates (58 percent) were Catholic; others were Protestant, Jewish, Muslim, Buddhist, and undeclared. Almost 13 percent of undergraduates were nonwhite, and male students slightly outnumbered women. The university president remained a Jesuit, but laypersons, male and female, occupied most administrative positions.

As John Carroll raised its expectations, broadened its horizons, and cultivated a more inclusive student body and administration, it also sought to reemphasize and celebrate its Jesuit Catholic identity. It stressed its Ignatian heritage and spirituality and established an Institute of Catholic Studies, as well as adding a vice president for University Mission and Identity and a chair in Catholic Systematic Theology.

Service to the community and the world, sponsored by Campus Ministry and the Center for Service and Social Action, became an essential part of the school's identity. In 2012, the university received national recognition when it was named to the President's Higher Education Community Service Honor Roll for the fifth time for students' thousands of hours of community service. The John Carroll Access Initiative, combined with federal and state grants, allowed academically qualified, low-income students to enroll at the university at a minimal cost.

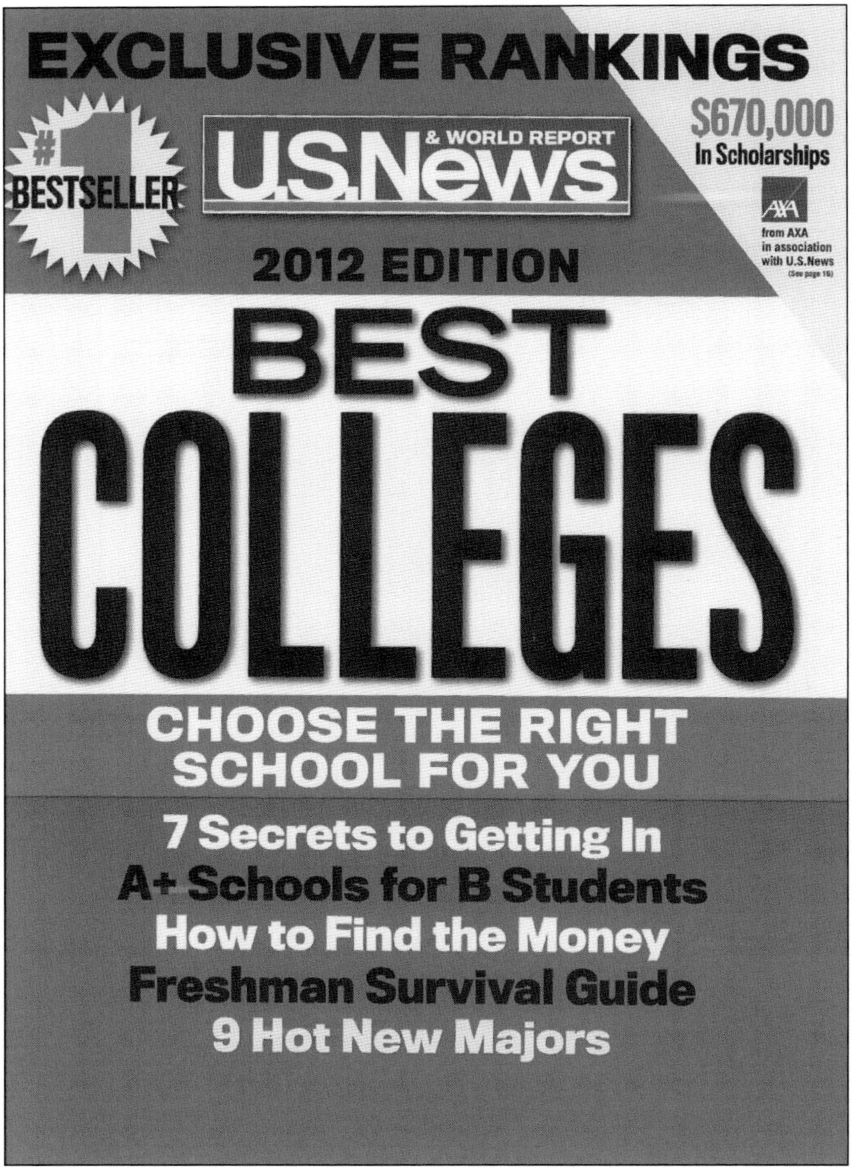

For 23 consecutive years, John Carroll has ranked among the top 10 universities in the Midwest that grant master's degrees, according to the 2012 edition of "America's Best Colleges" (published in 2011) by *US News and World Report*; the university also ranked first in its "Commitment to Undergraduate Teaching" and fourth in "Great Schools, Great Prices." *Barron's* ranked it as a "Best Buy," and the *Princeton Review* said that it was "one of the best colleges in the Midwest." John Carroll graduates 66 percent of its students in four years, better than the 56 percent graduation rate at other private schools nationwide and 52 percent at other private schools in Ohio. In 2010, the Ohio Board of Regents and the Woodrow Wilson National Fellowship Foundation selected the university as a site —one of only four in Ohio—for a distinguished Teaching Fellows Program that will grant students a master's degree and licensure to teach the sciences in "high-need" schools. John Carroll faculty members have been named Fulbright scholars; students have earned Truman scholarships and Fulbright student scholarships.

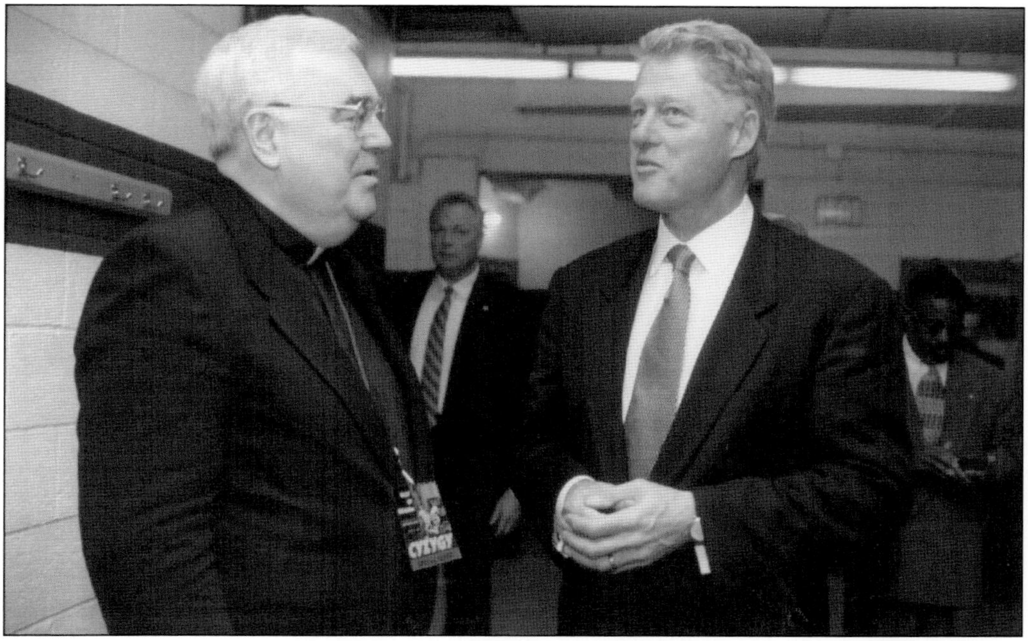

In June 1998, Pres. Bill Clinton, pictured with John Carroll president Rev. Edward Glynn, SJ, spoke to City Year Cleveland volunteers on the John Carroll campus. Other recent distinguished visitors include Supreme Court Justice Samuel Alito Jr.; poet Rita Dove; anti–death penalty advocate Sister Helen Prejean, CSJ; former Secretary of Defense Robert S. McNamara; and consumer activist Ralph Nader.

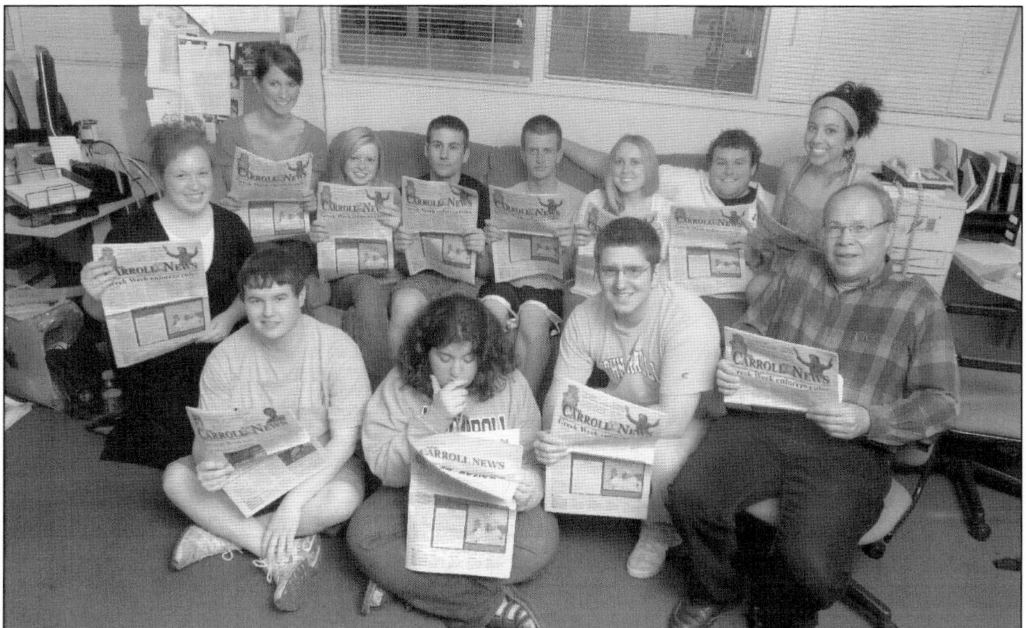

The Carroll News, which dates back to 1925, also has a distinguished present: in 2010, it was named Ohio's "Best College Non-Daily Newspaper" for the third consecutive year by the Ohio chapter of the Society of Professional Journalists. Since 1998, the newspaper has won more than seven dozen national and regional awards.

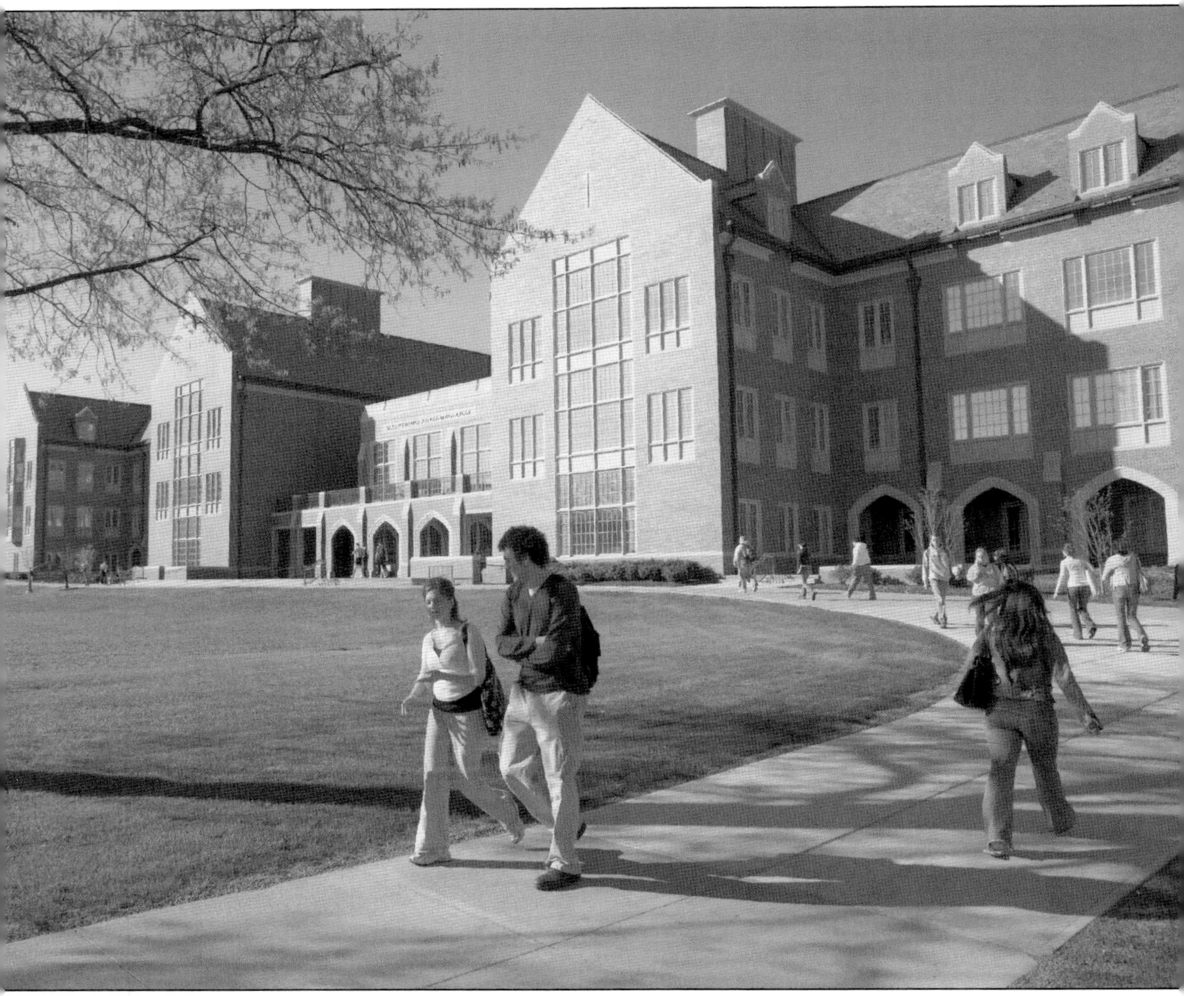

These were also years of ambitious building and renovation, with the completion of two new residence halls; a new dining facility; the O'Malley Center addition to the Administration Building; the Breen Learning Center addition to Grasselli Library, a gift from Mary Jane (who earned a bachelor's degree at John Carroll in 1991 and went on to complete graduate school there in 1996) and John G. Breen, a 1956 graduate; and the renovated Boler School of Business, a gift from Mary Jo and John M. Boler, a 1956 graduate. The most spectacular new building was the Dolan Center for Science and Technology (pictured) at the westernmost edge of the campus, a gift from Charles and Helen Dolan and other John Carroll alumni and friends. Its design echoed the Gothic style of the Administration Building. The Dolan Center houses offices, classrooms, and laboratories for biology, chemistry, mathematics, computer science, physics, psychology, art history, and humanities, as well as an auditorium and atrium used for large public gatherings.

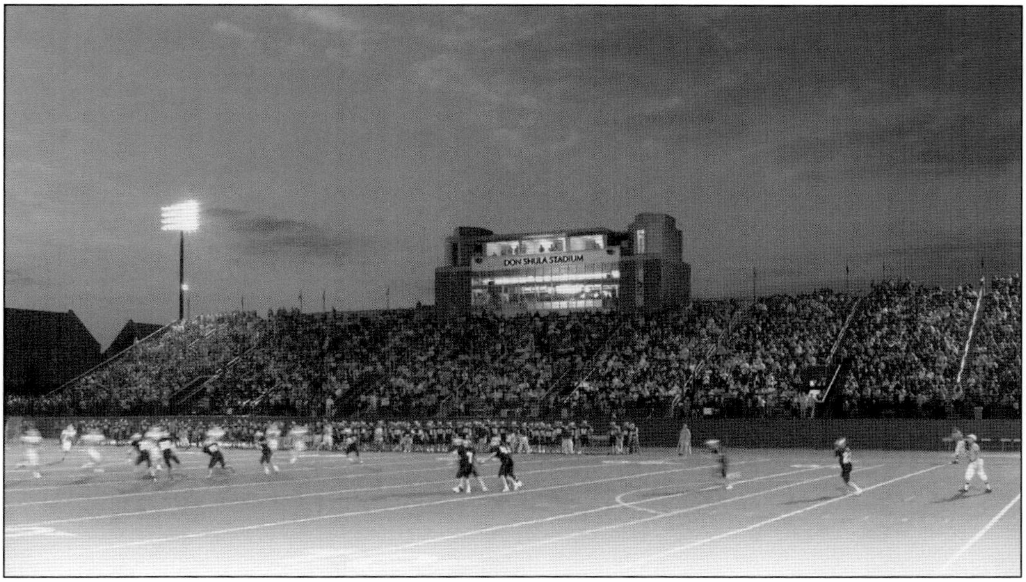

John Carroll's most recent capital campaign, which concluded in 2004, raised over $100 million and enabled the university to build the Dolan Center for Science and Technology; the Don Shula Stadium at Wasmer Field (pictured), named for winning professional football coach, JCU benefactor, and alumnus Don Shula (class of 1951); and the Tony DeCarlo Varsity Center, named for longtime head coach, athletic director, and fundraiser Tony DeCarlo (class of 1966).

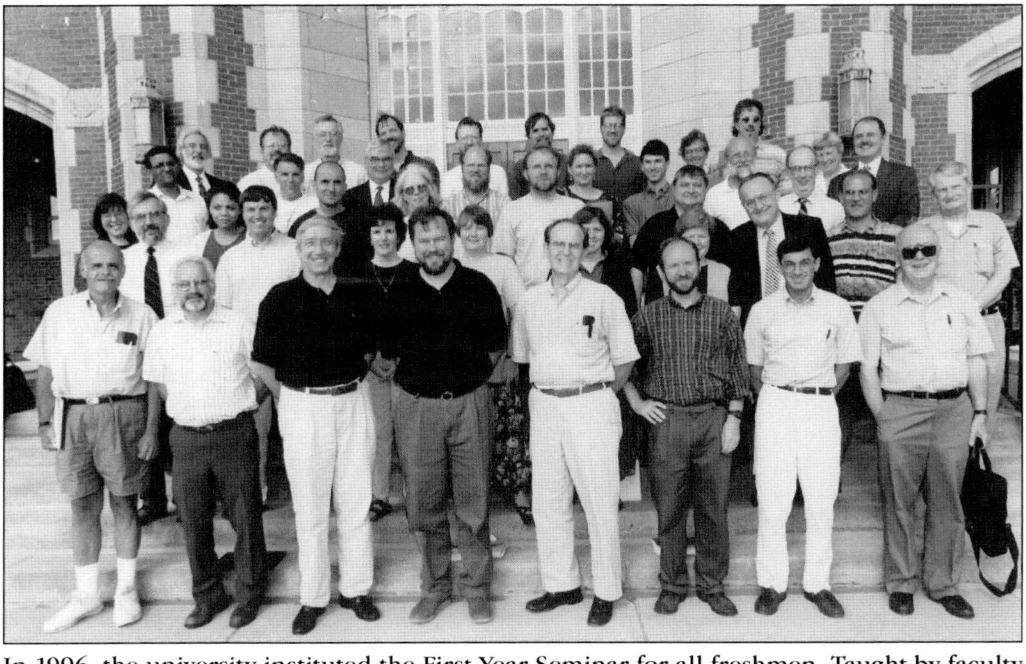

In 1996, the university instituted the First Year Seminar for all freshmen. Taught by faculty from across the disciplines, the course had a single theme; in the course's inaugural year, it was "The City: Past, Present, and Future." The course also included common readings and distinguished outside speakers. This photograph of the 1996 First Year Seminar faculty illustrates the growing predominance of lay faculty.

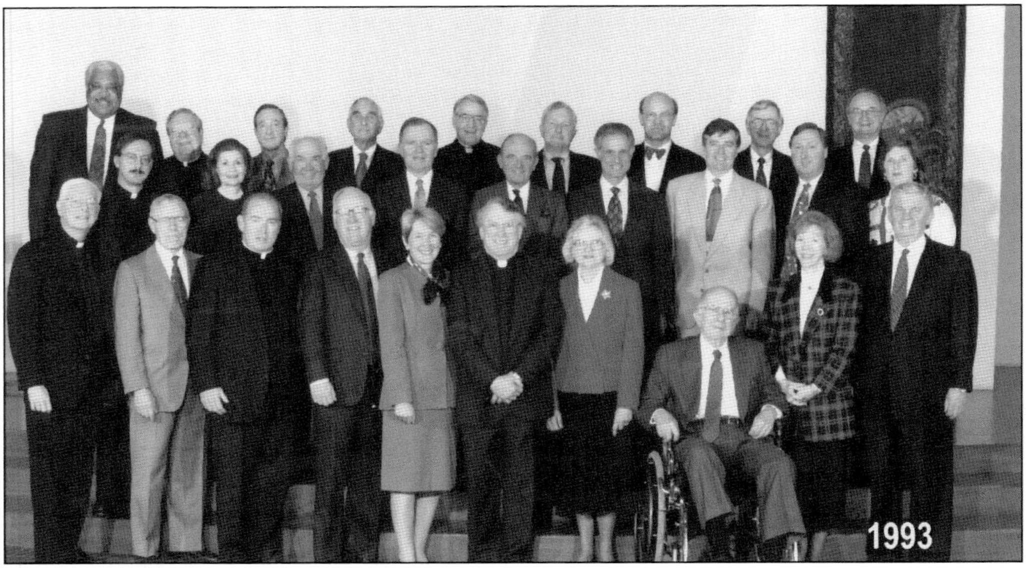

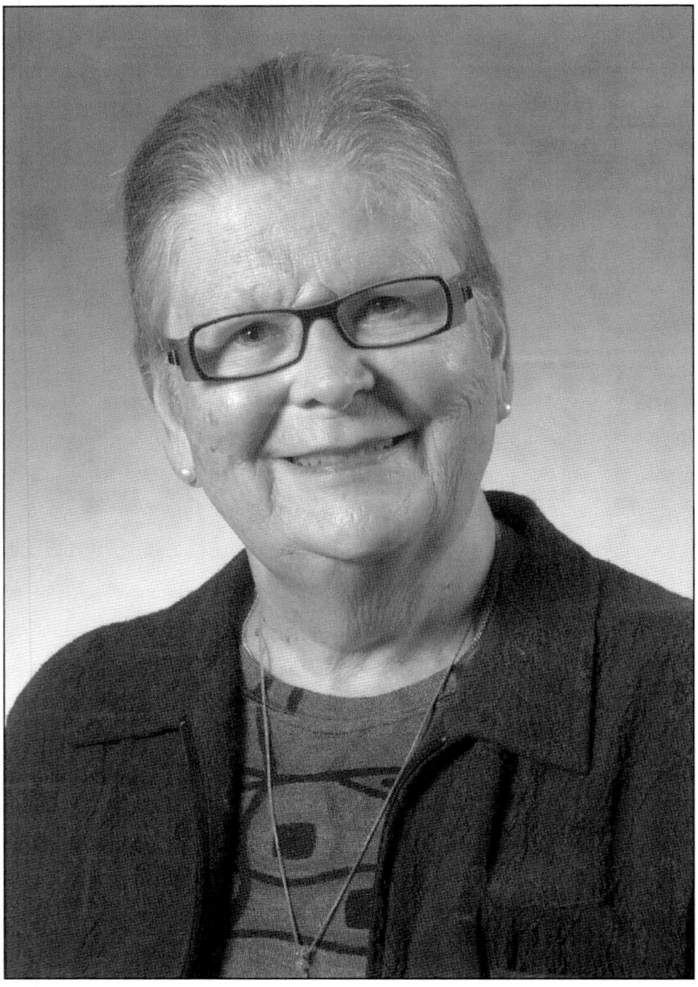

In 1969, the Board of Trustees had been reorganized to include three-fourths laypersons and one-fourth Jesuits. By 1993, the board also included several women. University president Rev. Michael J. Lavelle, SJ, is third from the left in the first row.

Dr. Sally Wertheim was a pioneer on campus as one of the university's first female deans. She served in many positions, including as dean of the Graduate School from 1986 to 1998, and again as interim dean in 2007. By 2011, three women were serving as deans: Dr. Jeanne Colleran, College of Arts and Sciences; Dr. Karen Schuele, Boler School of Business; and Dr. Sherri Crahen, Dean of Students.

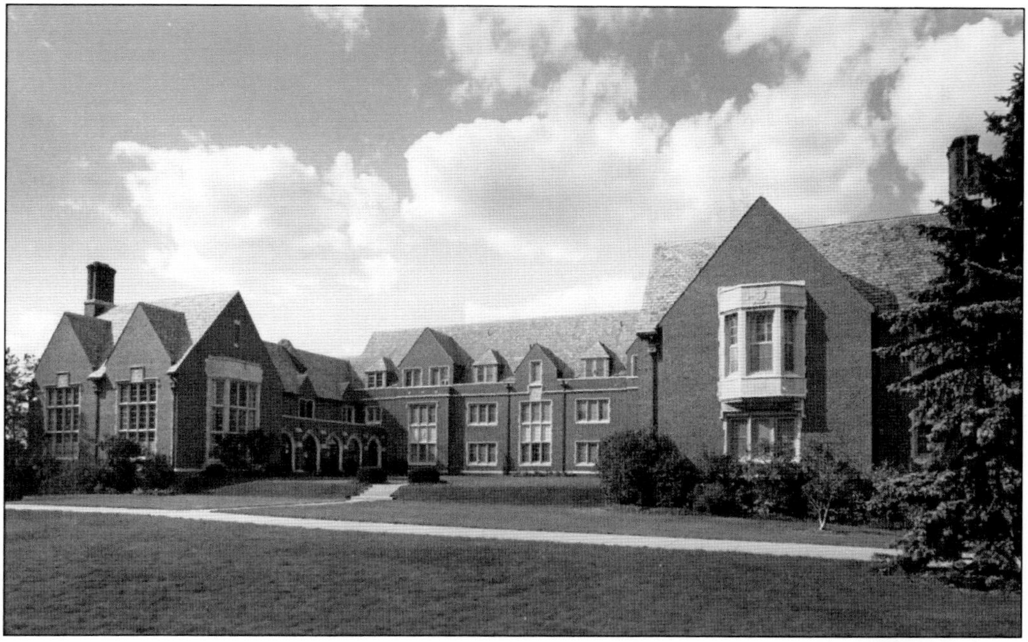

Rodman Hall, which was started in 1931 but not completely finished until it housed V-12 seamen during World War II, was intended to be a Jesuit residence. The imposing brick building now houses administrative and technical staff, not Jesuits. Graduation ceremonies are still held on its terrace.

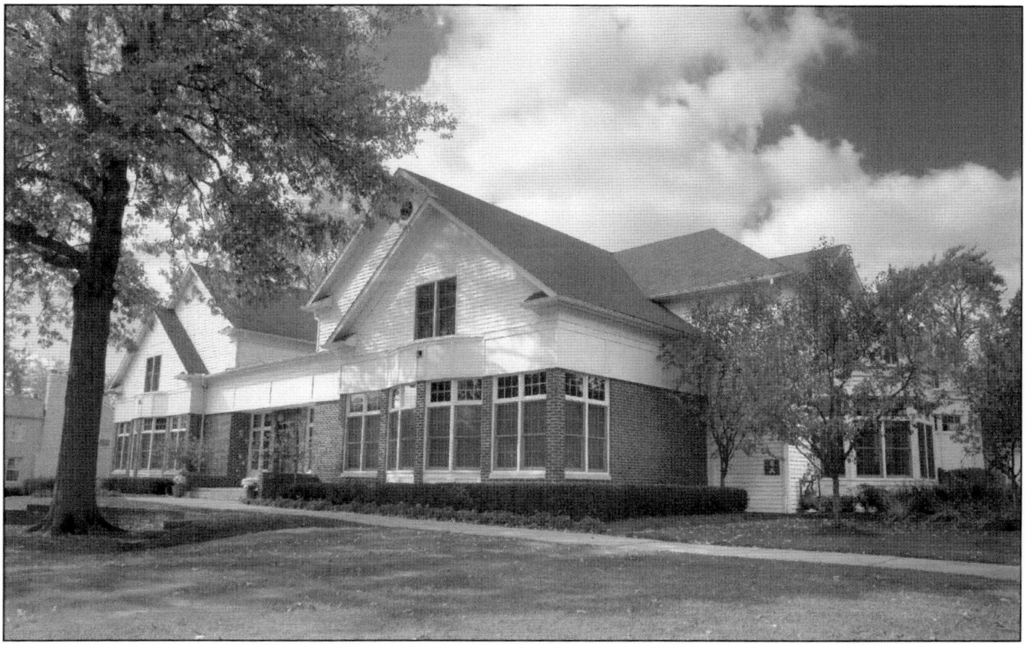

Schell House was completed in 1997 on Miramar Boulevard and named for Rev. Joseph O. Schell, SJ, former president and legendary Jesuit at John Carroll, who founded the university's Campus Ministry in 1971. Schell House now serves as the home of Jesuit faculty and administrators. The building is compatible with the single-family homes in the neighborhood.

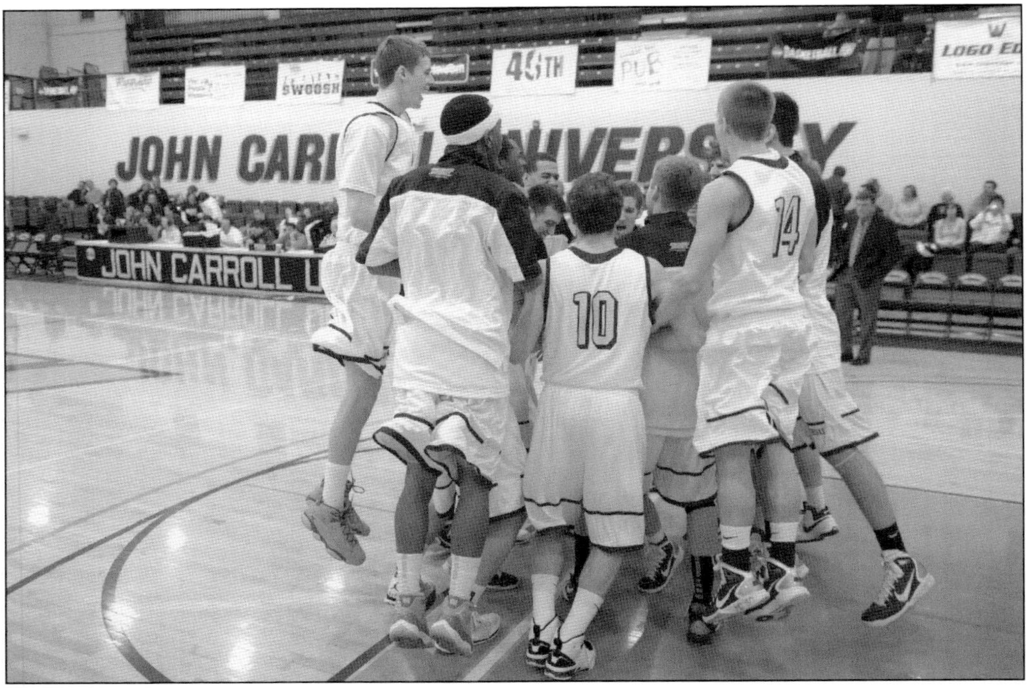

John Carroll fields men's varsity teams in baseball, basketball, cross-country, football, golf, swimming and diving, track and field, tennis, and wrestling. This is the 2007 varsity basketball team.

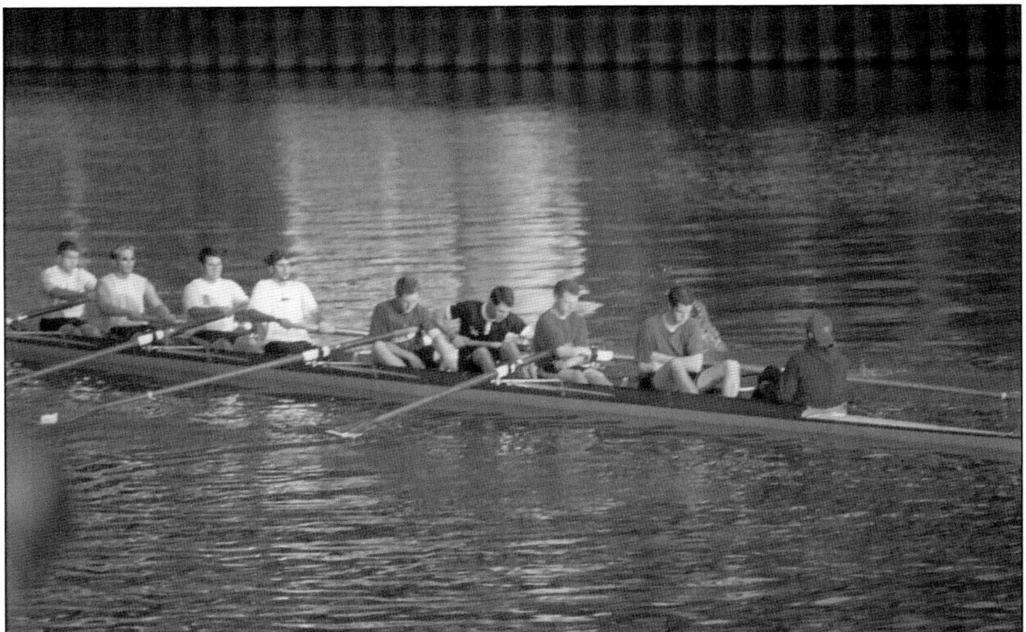

Crew is a club sport for both men and women. Practicing and competing on the Cuyahoga River as it winds through the Flats offers crew team members an opportunity to discover Cleveland's past and present.

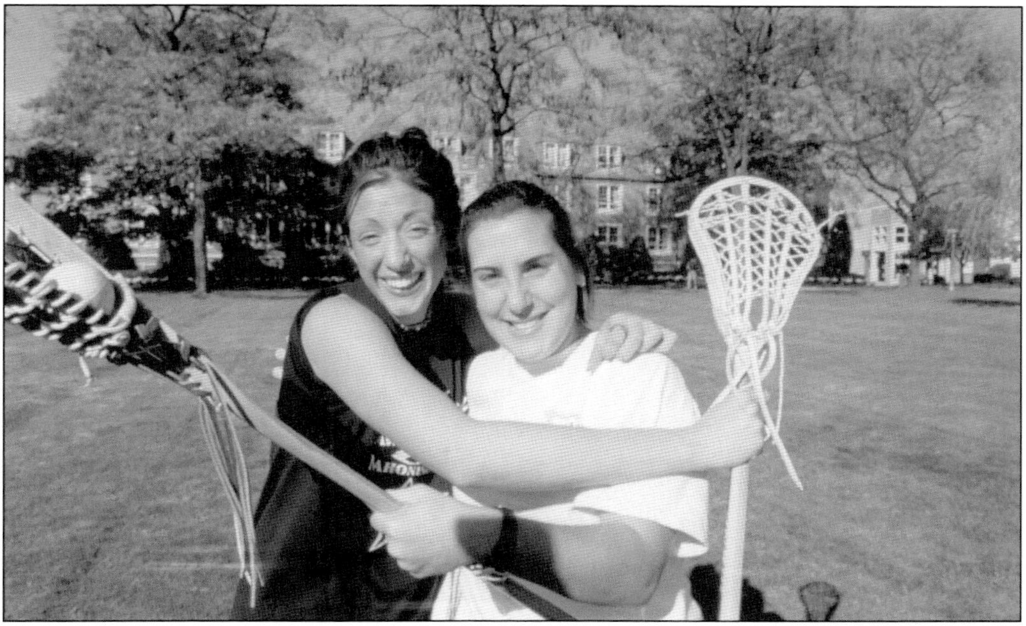

Like crew, lacrosse is a club sport for men and women; in 2014, it will become a varsity sport. The school also has women's varsity teams in basketball, cross-country, golf, soccer, softball, swimming and diving, tennis, track and field, and volleyball.

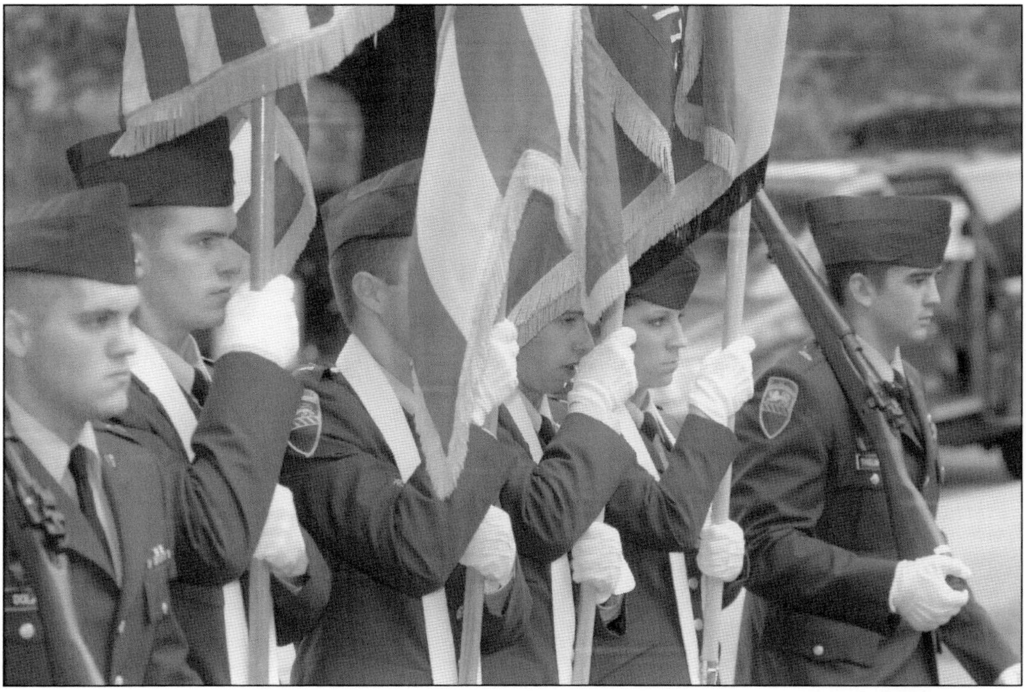

John Carroll has a long-standing history of hosting military programs. That history began with its World War I drill team and continued with the US Navy V-12 program during World War II and the establishment of an Army ROTC program in 1950. Today, both men and women participate in ROTC at John Carroll, and the university's WolfPack Battalion is the No. 1 ranked Army ROTC unit in Ohio.

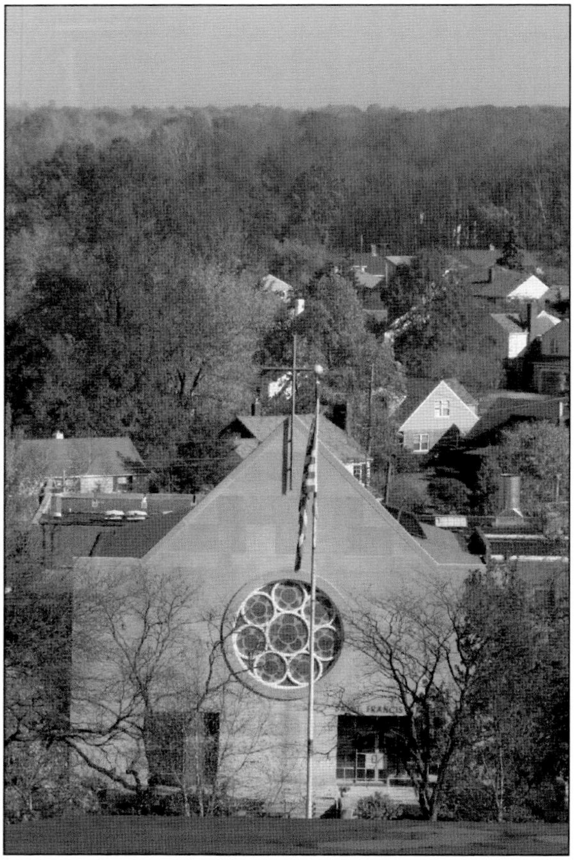

Saint Francis Chapel, which was completed in 1987, was made possible by gifts from Mrs. F.J. O'Neill and the F.J. O'Neill Charitable Corporation. It is the site of weekday Masses, a weekly and popular Sunday night Mass during the academic year, confessions, prayer services, weddings, and memorials. Its prominent location on campus, once intended for the Bishop's Chapel, is a reminder of the continued importance of religious faith on campus.

The "Christmas Carroll Eve" service (pictured below) is one of many opportunities students have to express their faith through music. Students also sing at Sunday Masses. The Chapel Ensemble, a vocal and musical group, performs at special liturgies.

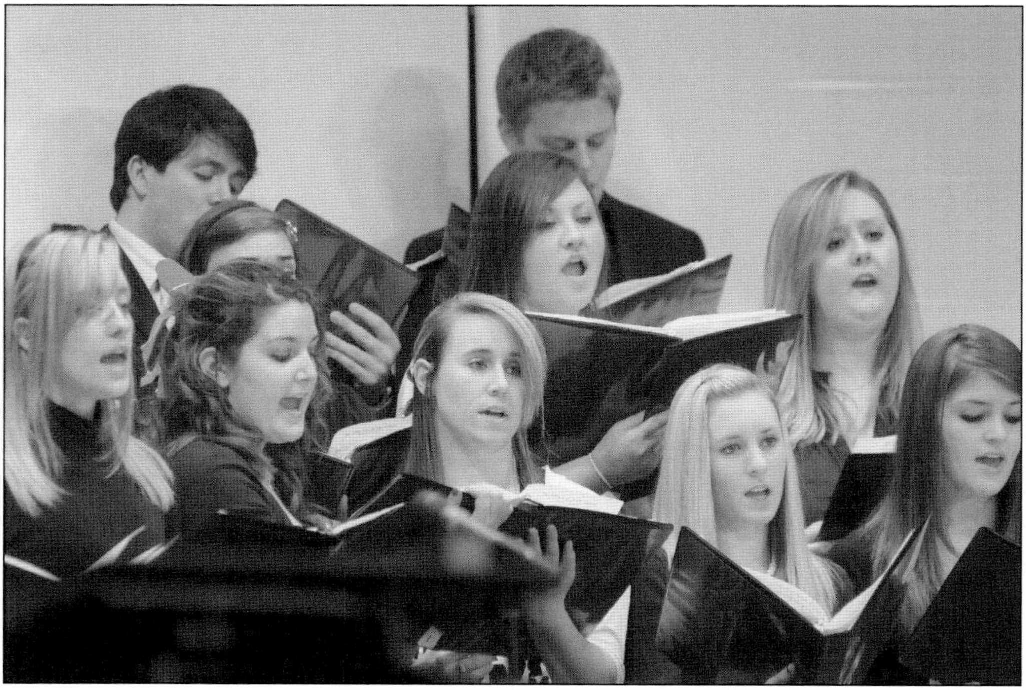

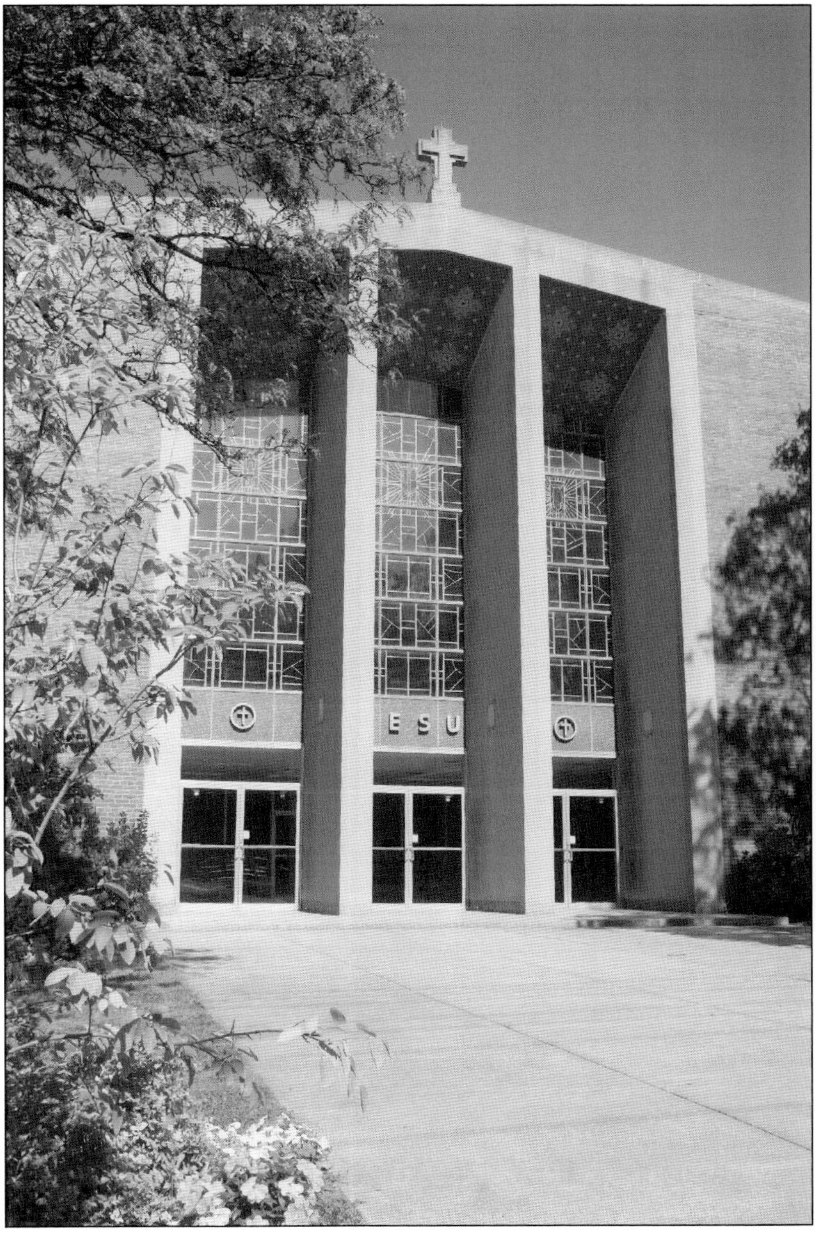

John Carroll and the Church of the Gesu, located adjacent to the campus, collaborate in many ways—including the annual Mass of the Holy Spirit, Reunion Mass, and Baccalaureate Mass—and Gesu serves as John Carroll's Parish of Record within the Diocese of Cleveland. The university and the church share a long history. The Jesuits got permission to establish the parish in 1925, although its boundaries were not yet firmly established. Masses were said in the University Heights City Hall until 1927, when the Cleveland Heights–University Heights Board of Education donated three portable buildings for the church and its school; the buildings were on the John Carroll campus. In 1937, the church purchased the current site on Miramar Boulevard, and during the 1940s, the congregation built its church-school building and a convent for the Sisters of Notre Dame, who staffed the school. The current church building was completed in 1958.

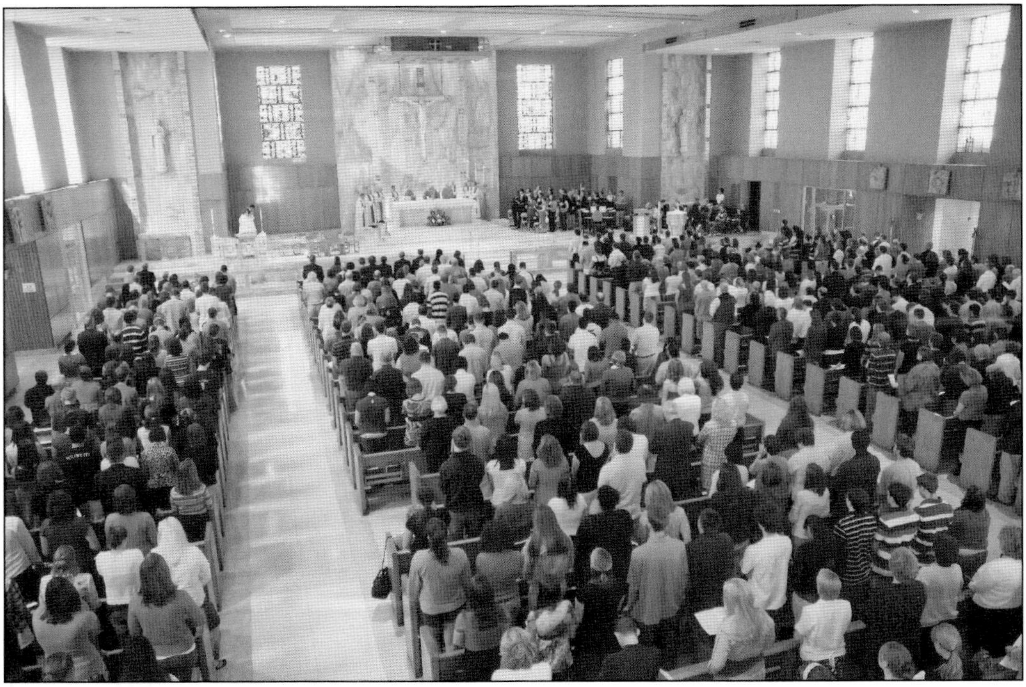

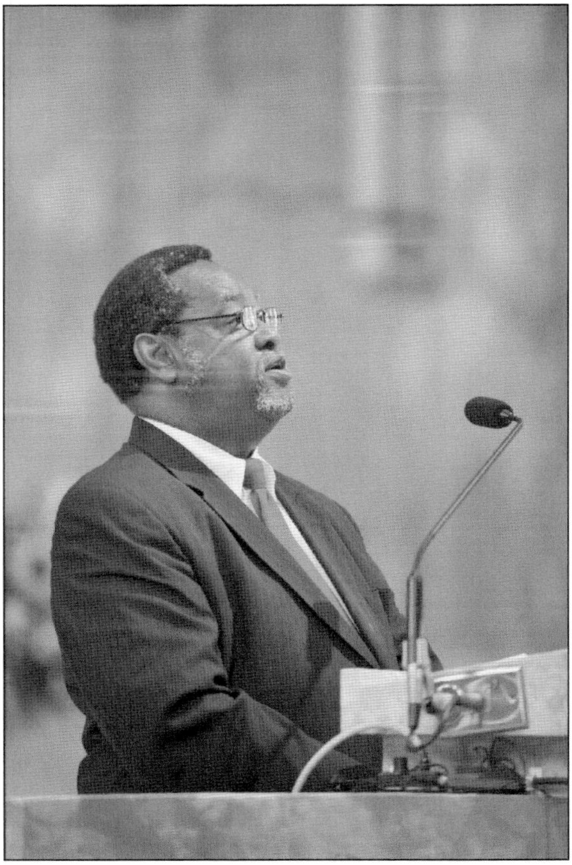

The Mass of the Holy Spirit is celebrated every fall to mark the beginning of another school year. The Mass is celebrated at the Church of the Gesu and welcomes John Carroll students, faculty, staff, and administrators of all faiths.

Rev. Dr. Valentino Lassiter, one of the participants in the Mass of the Holy Spirit, is John Carroll's current pastor in residence and a faculty member of the Department of Theology and Religious Studies. He is also the minister of the Eastview United Church of Christ in Shaker Heights.

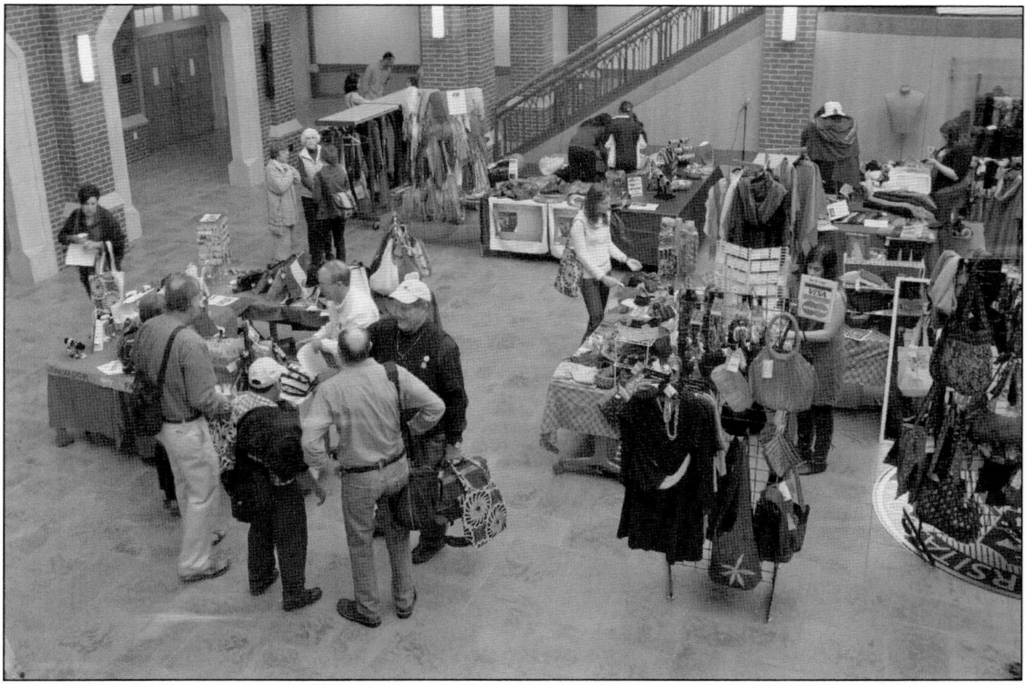

Campus Ministry sponsors many of John Carroll's social justice programs both on and off of the campus. These include this Fair Trade event, held in the Muldoon Atrium of the Dolan Center for Science and Technology, which features goods made in third world countries under fair trade conditions.

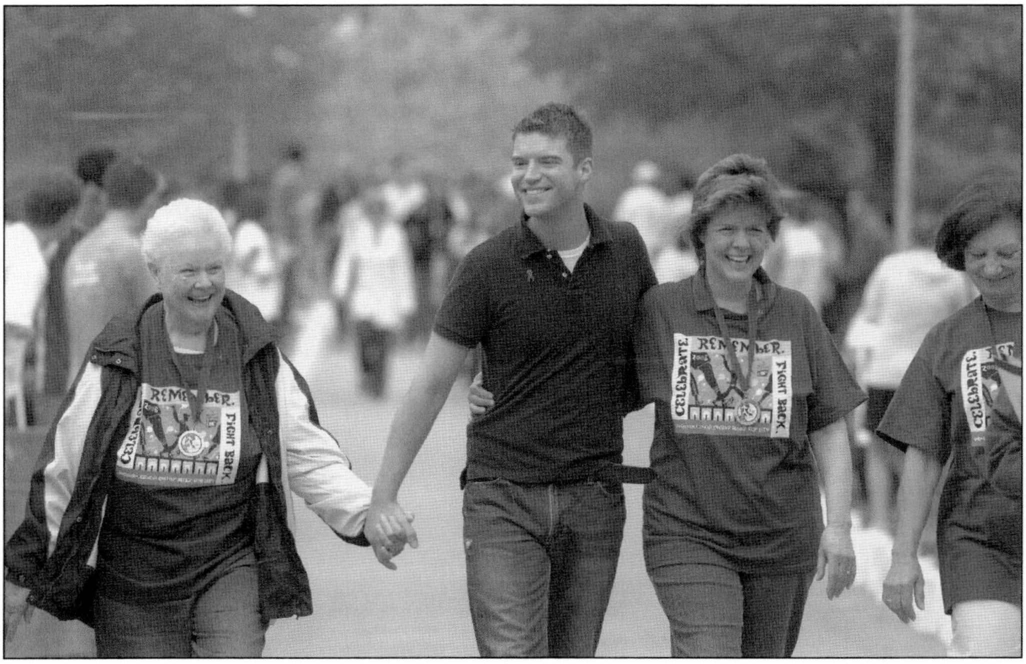

The Relay for Life is held on campus in the spring. The event raises funds for the American Cancer Society and engages people from the community as well as the university. Since 2007, John Carroll has raised a total of $300,000 for this cause.

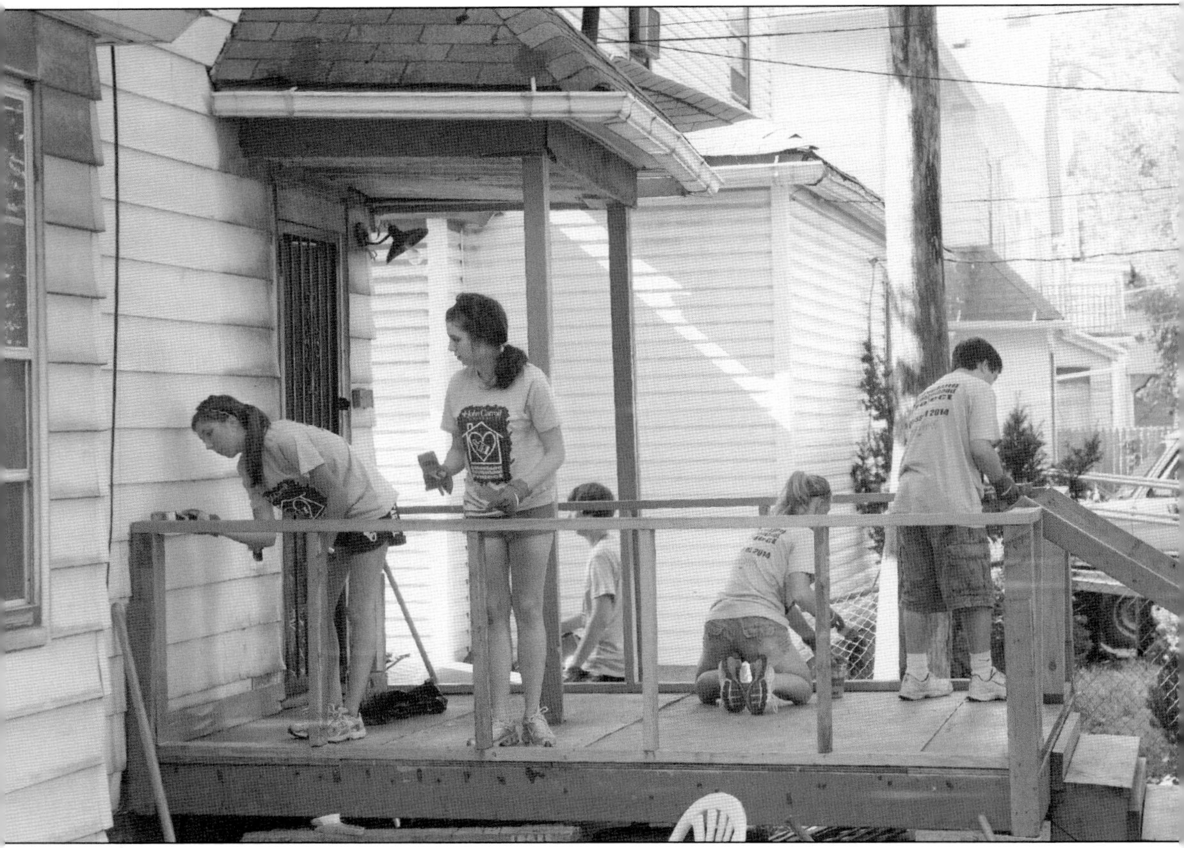

The Cleveland Neighborhood Project takes place in August on "Living the Mission Day." It introduces freshmen to some of the service possibilities that the university offers. Students, faculty, staff, and administration help to rehabilitate the Hough neighborhood's housing stock, most of which was built before the 1920s, when Hough was a middle-class neighborhood with a significant Catholic population. Hough is still the site of several Catholic institutions, including the Fatima Family Center; the Famicos Foundation, established by Sister Henrietta Gorris, CSA, and housed in the former Ursuline Academy on Ansel Road; Saint Thomas Aquinas School; and Saint Agnes–Our Lady of Fatima Church.

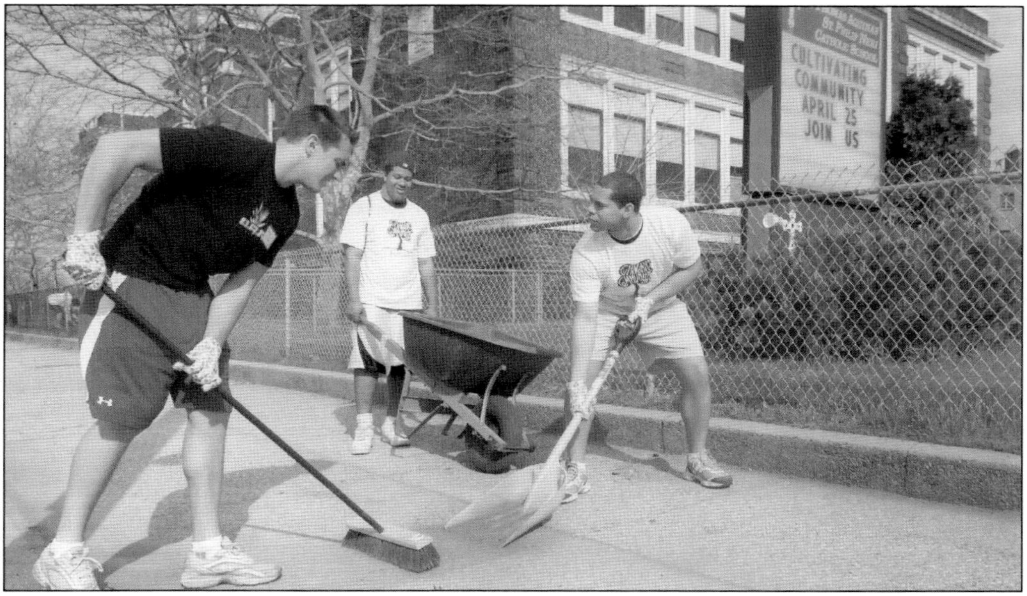

Cultivating Community is a service event sponsored by the Center for Service and Social Action that sends hundreds of students, faculty, and graduates into Cleveland neighborhoods each spring. Participants and residents rake leaves, mow grass, trim hedges, and plant gardens; the men pictured above are cleaning up the Saint Thomas Aquinas School playground.

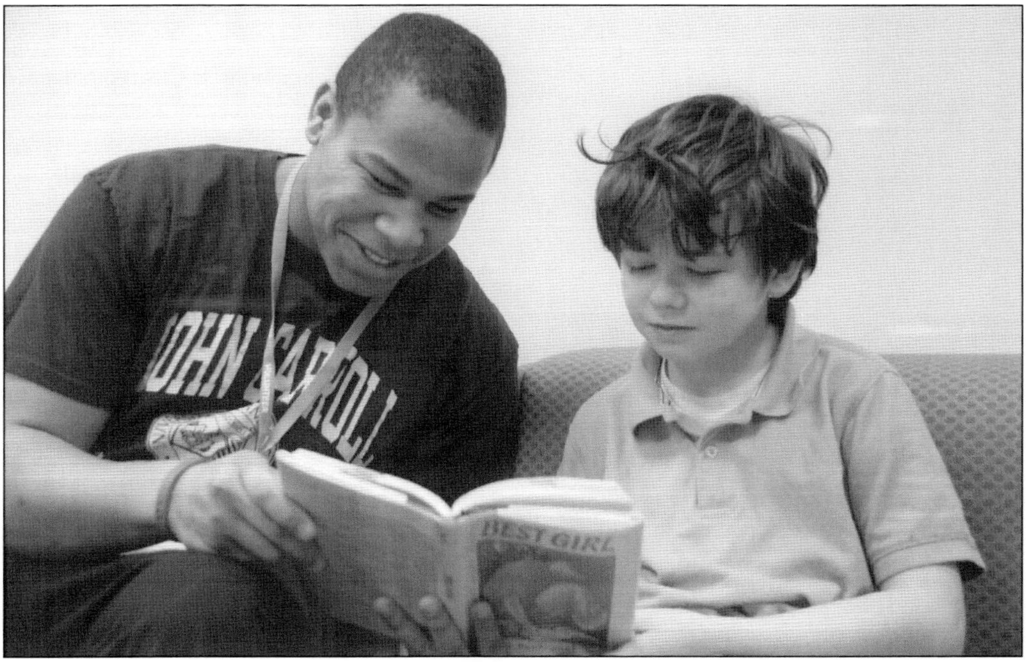

Carroll Reads is a federally funded program that provides children in parochial and charter schools with tutoring in math and reading. This picture was taken at the Intergenerational School. John Carroll has several programs that focus on K-12 education, including the Center for Mathematics and Science Education, the Cleveland Heights–University Heights School District Partnership, and the Institute for Educational Renewal.

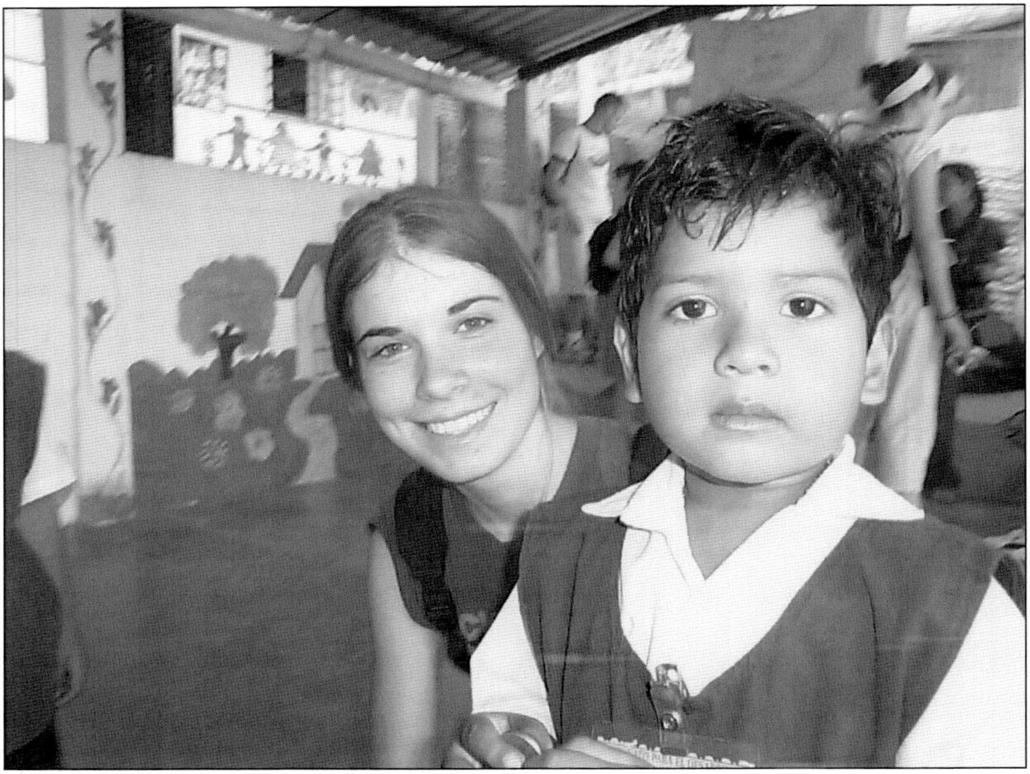

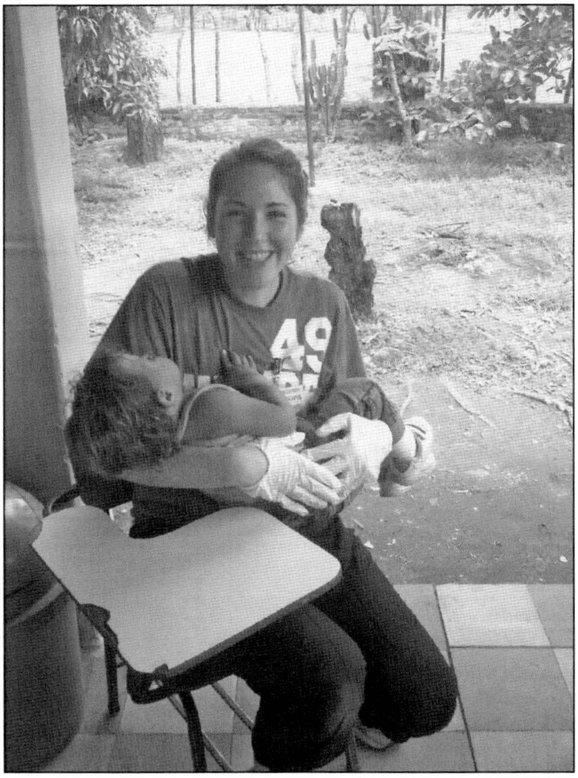

Under the auspices of the Center for Service and Social Action, students participate in immersion experiences, living with and learning from the people they are serving. This photograph was taken in El Salvador in 2004.

A medical immersion trip took this unidentified student to Honduras. In 2011, students also traveled to Ecuador, Jamaica, El Salvador, the Dominican Republic, and Nicaragua, as well as to New Orleans, Louisiana; Louisville, Kentucky; and Camden, New Jersey.

In spring 2008, these students took a class called "Islam and the EU" and visited the Grand Mosque in Paris. In an effort to globalize its curriculum, the university's study-abroad programs sent students to Central and South America, Africa, Australia, China, Japan, and all of the European countries and added majors in International Business with Language and Culture; Peace, Justice, Human Rights, and East Asian studies.

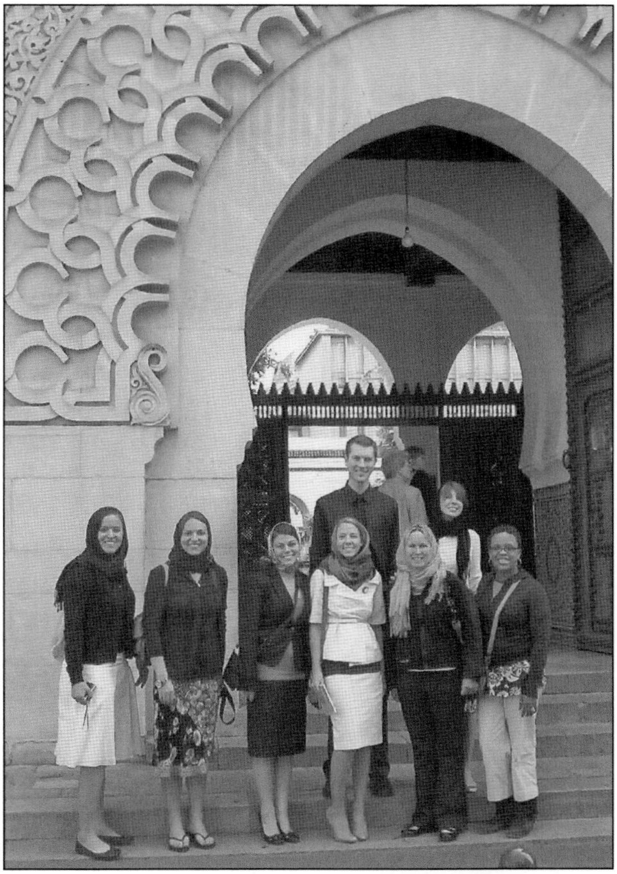

In March 2010, students and faculty traveled to Rome for a class called "Rome: City of Emperors, Saints, and Popes." The trip was partially funded by the Catholic Studies program.

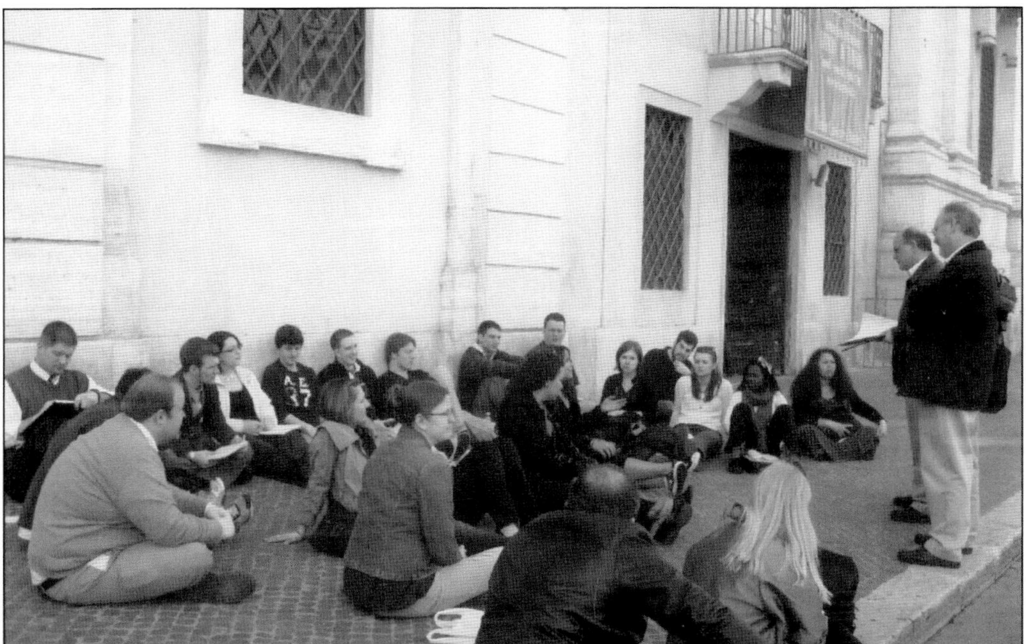

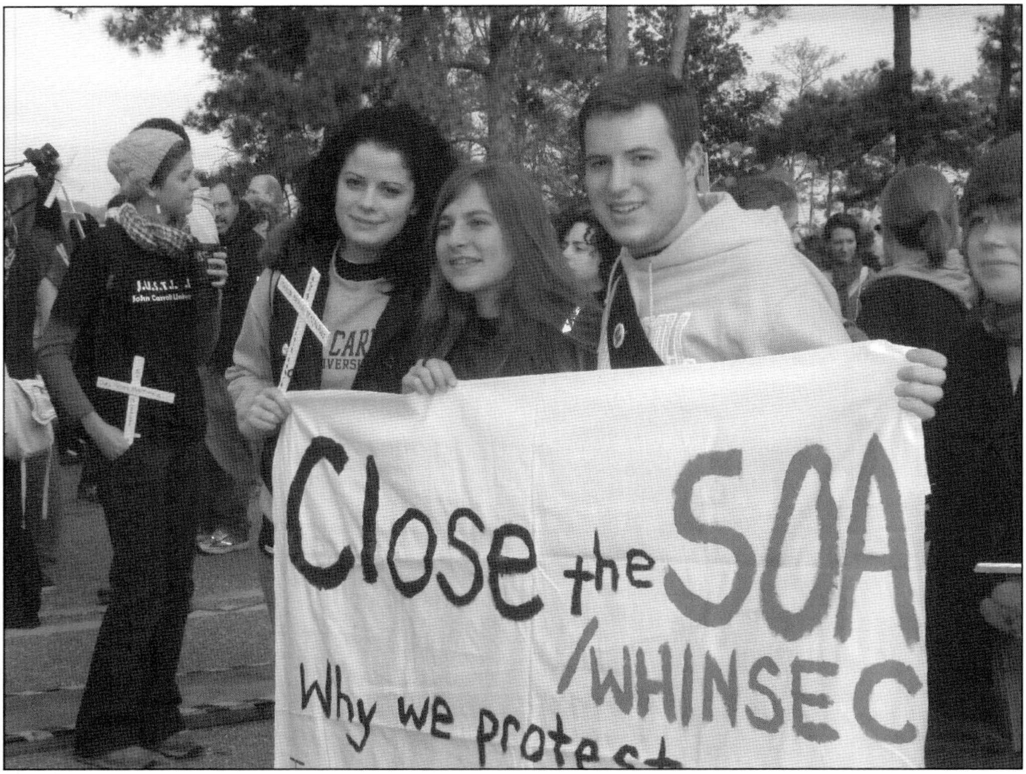

For several years, Campus Ministry sponsored trips to Fort Benning, Georgia, to protest the School of the Americas (now called the Western Hemisphere Institute for Security Cooperation), which was run by the US Army (WHINSEC is now under the administration of the US Department of Defense). Graduates of the SOA assassinated six Jesuit priests in 1989, as well as hundreds of other people. In partnership with the Ignatian Solidarity Network, John Carroll students now travel to Washington, DC, to continue education and advocacy with members of Congress about this and other issues.

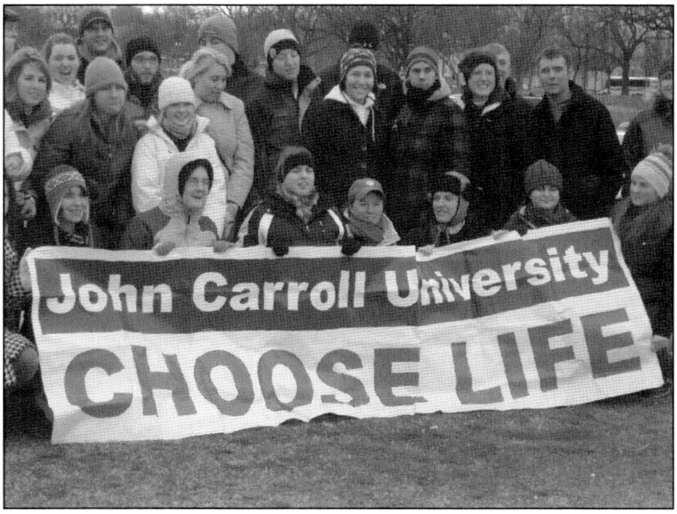

Campus Ministry also sponsored this January 2010 trip to Washington, DC, to protest the Supreme Court's 1970 *Roe v. Wade* decision, which legalizes abortions under certain conditions, counter to the teachings of the Catholic Church. Campus Ministry considers both of these trips integral to understanding what it means to be a Jesuit Catholic university and to the university's commitment to a faith that does justice.

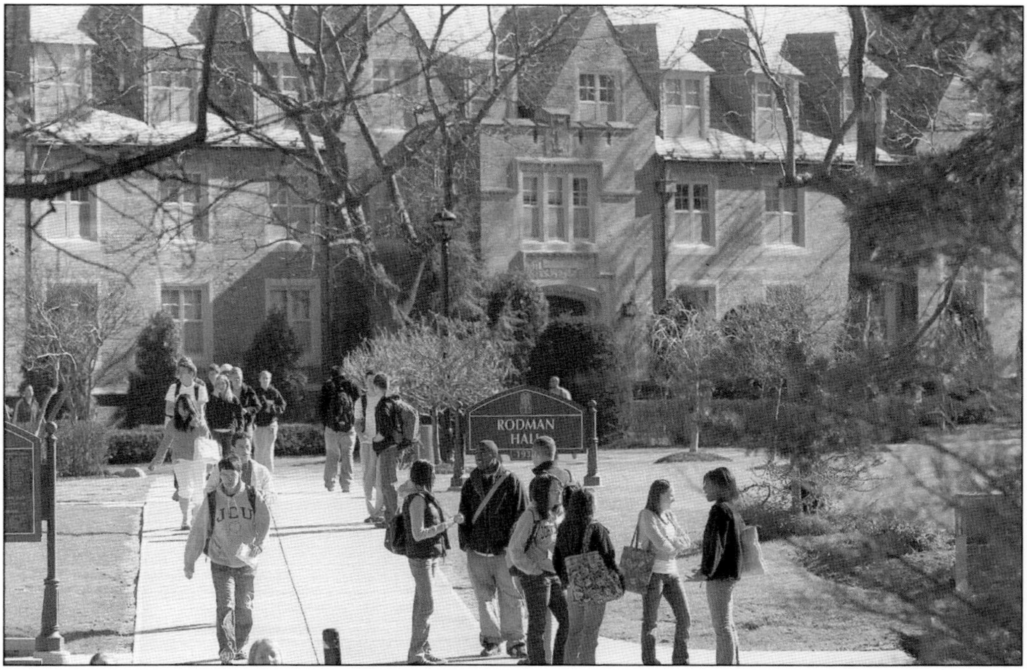

Enhancing the diversity of the campus culture was a priority for Pres. Rev. Robert L. Niehoff, SJ. To accomplish this, faculty, students, and administration held campus-wide town hall meetings and established an Office of Multicultural Affairs (later renamed The Center for Student Diversity and Inclusion) and several affinity groups.

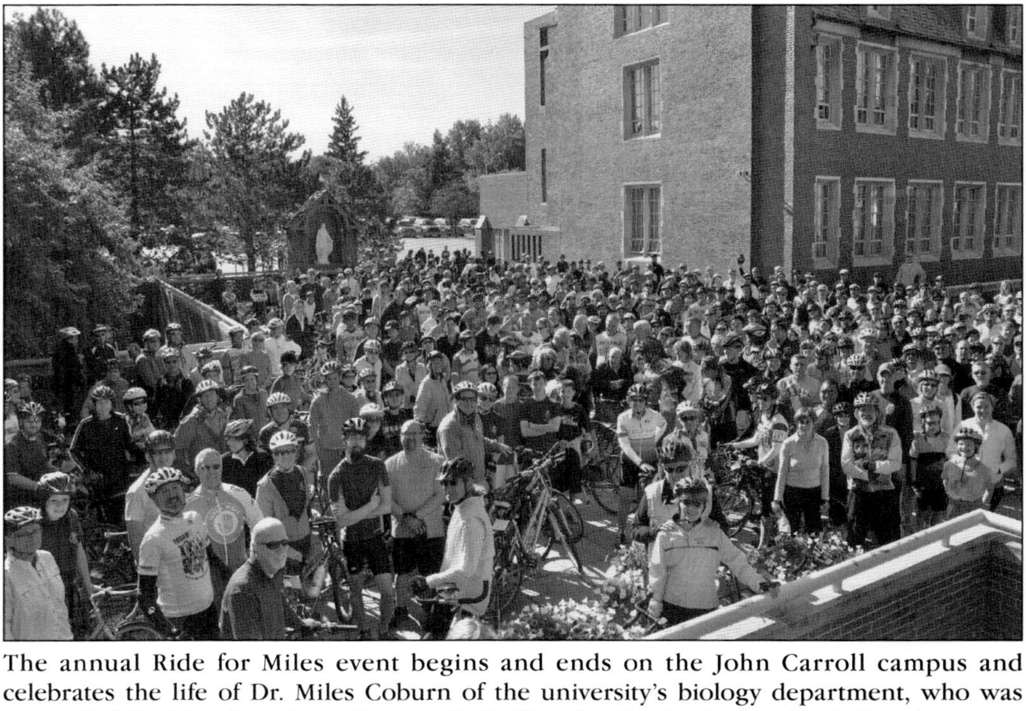

The annual Ride for Miles event begins and ends on the John Carroll campus and celebrates the life of Dr. Miles Coburn of the university's biology department, who was tragically killed in a bicycle accident in 2008. The 15-mile ride honors Dr. Coburn's passion for the environment and raises funds for the Dr. Miles Coburn Environmental Symposium.

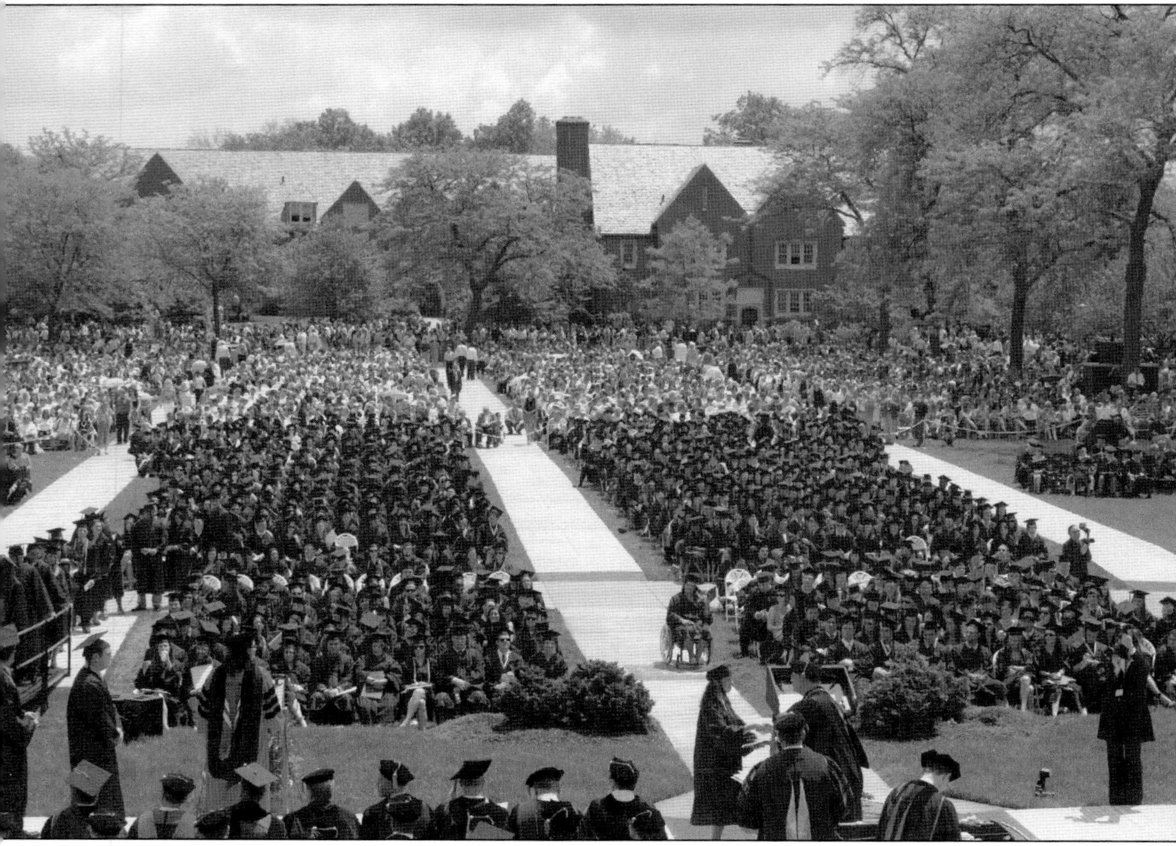

At the 2010 commencement, John Carroll granted 660 undergraduate degrees; 456 were bachelor's of arts, classics, or science degrees; 204 were bachelor's of science in business administration degrees. The university also awarded 239 master's degrees, including master's of arts, business administration, science, and education. This photograph offers an interesting contrast with the 1940 commencement photograph on page 58. In 2010, the lawn in front of Rodman Hall was full of proud families and friends, and the campus has been built out and shaded by tall trees. In 1940, on the brink of World War II, families and friends, equally proud, watched as 92 men, then the biggest graduating class in the university's history, picked up their diplomas.

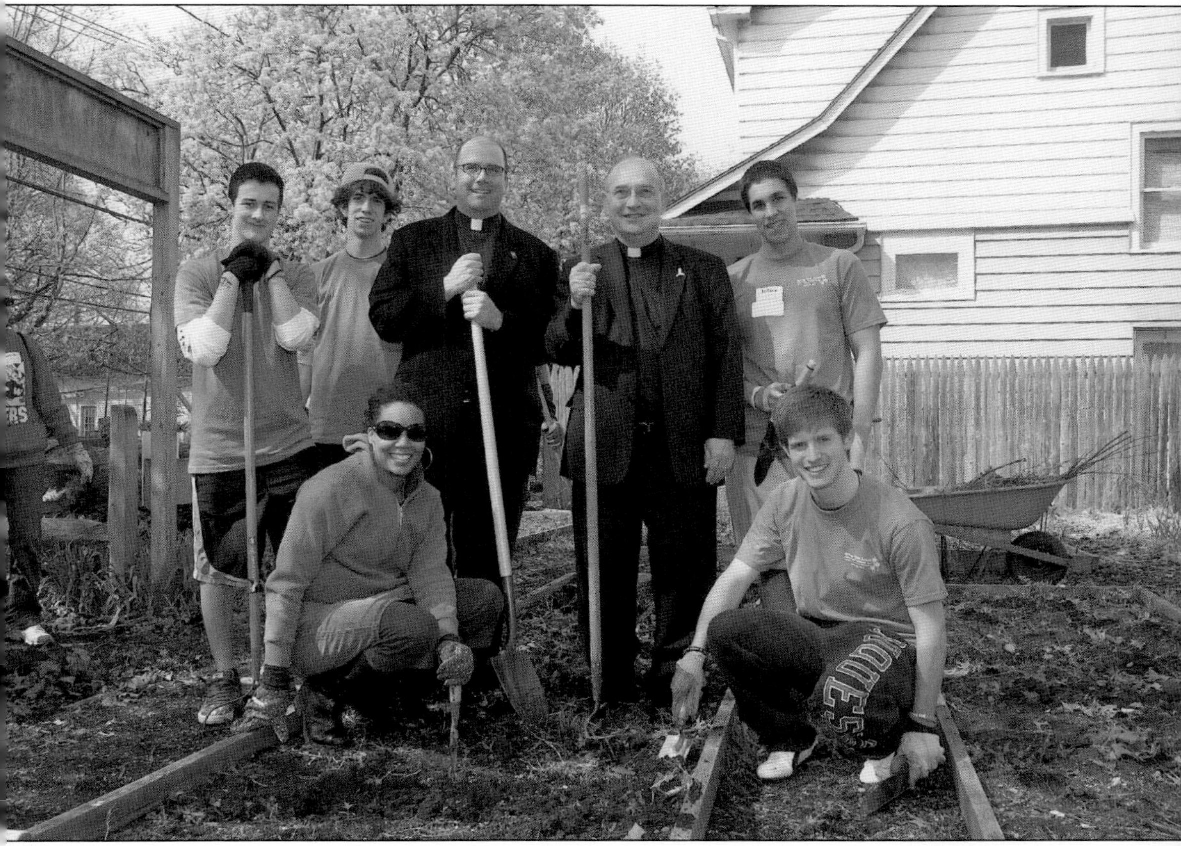

John Carroll returned to its Saint Ignatius roots when it celebrated its 125th anniversary in 2011. One of the events was a Cultivating Community Day that began at the high school where the university itself began. Rev. William J. Murphy, SJ, president of the high school (fourth from left) and Fr. Robert Niehoff, SJ, university president (fifth from left), participated in the event. Saint Ignatius High School has remained a stabilizing, energizing force in its Ohio City neighborhood. The 1891 building remains the heart of the campus. Saint Ignatius is still an all-boys school that finds its Jesuit identity in its rigorous academic program, in service to the community "For the Greater Glory of God," and through its Campus Ministry and spirituality programs for adults.

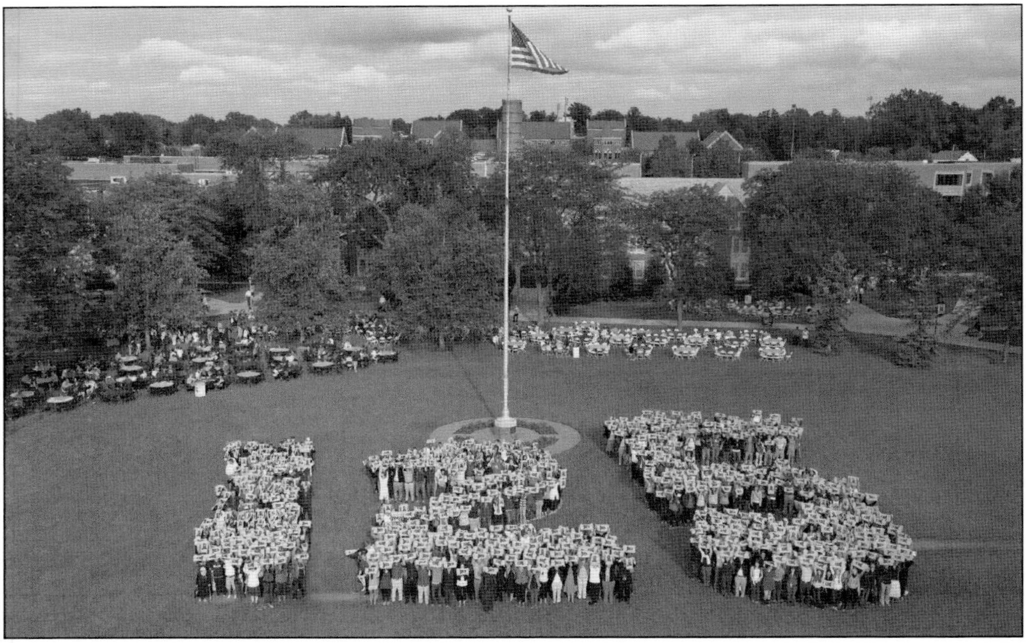

The 125th birthday celebration also involved the creation of this "125" sign by 700 alumni, students, faculty, staff, and administrators on the quadrangle behind the Administration Building.

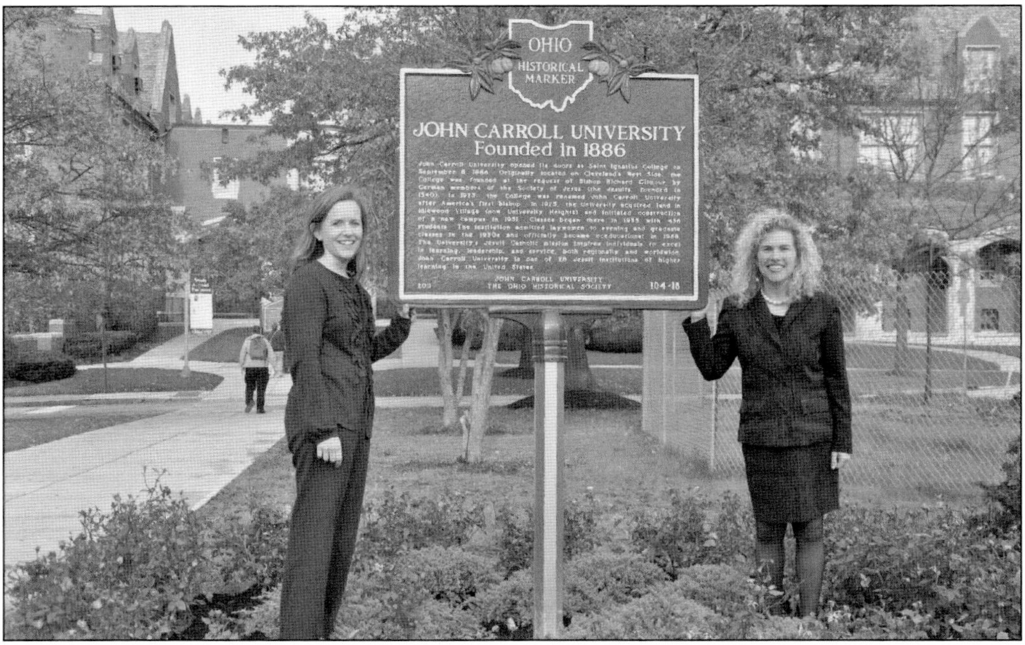

On the occasion of its 125th birthday, the university received this Ohio Historical Marker from the Ohio Historical Society. At left is Dora Pruce, John Carroll's director of government and community relations, and at right is University Heights councilwoman Frankie B. Goldberg. The marker, which was placed just outside of Grasselli Library, provides a brief history of John Carroll University and acknowledges the university's historic significance to its community and the state.

Six

John Carroll Graduates
Men and Women for Others

In October 1956, the *John Carroll Alumni News* listed 19 men who graduated from Saint Ignatius College or John Carroll University from 1914 to 1951 and were now priests in the Cleveland Diocese and 20 graduates from the classes of 1909 to 1949 who were running for public offices in the US House of Representatives, Cuyahoga County Commissioner, the Ohio Senate, the Ohio House of Representatives, and the Cleveland Municipal Court.

Over its 125 years in existence, Saint Ignatius College became John Carroll University; moved to the suburbs; hired more faculty; attracted a larger, more inclusive student body of men and women; and won national recognition. Throughout all this, its mission, restated in 2007, remained unchanged: "As a Jesuit Catholic university, John Carroll inspires individuals to excel in learning, leadership, and service in the region and in the world." Thousands of graduates have served their families, their professions, their university, their communities, and the world. The graduates recognized in this chapter are just a few of those who have chosen to become men and women for others.

Bishop Richard Gilmour and Rev. John B. Neustich, SJ, would have been proud. This was what the college was intended to do—educate and prepare people for a life of public service.

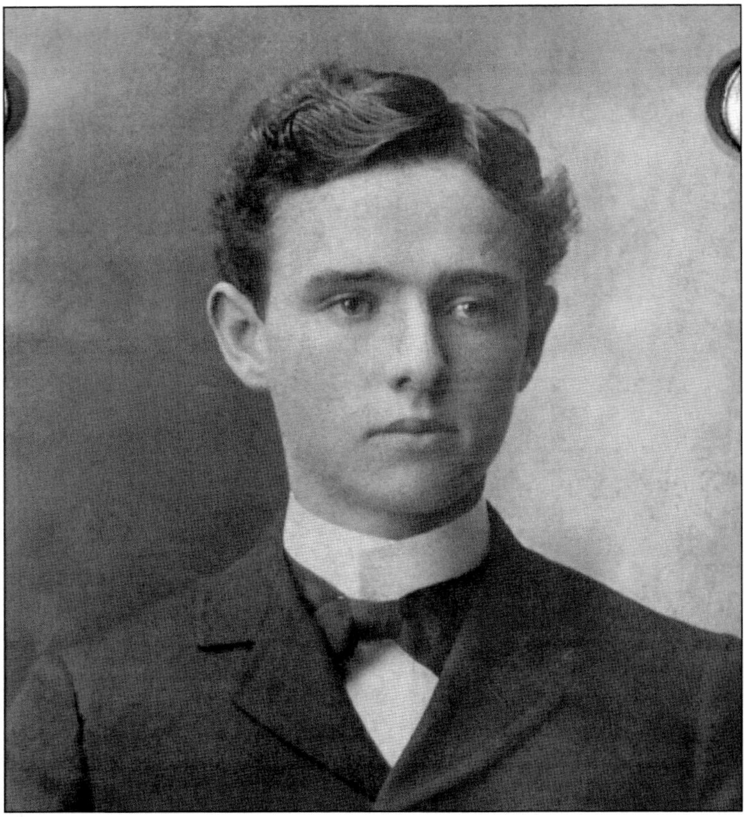

Ordained in 1905, Bishop James A. McFadden (class of 1899) became the first Clevelander to serve as auxiliary bishop in his home diocese in 1932. In 1943, he became bishop of the Diocese of Youngstown. McFadden was known for his acts of charity. His death on November 16, 1952, made front-page headlines in the *Cleveland Plain Dealer*: "Death yesterday stilled the kindly heart of James Augustine McFadden." (Courtesy of Cleveland State University Special Collections.)

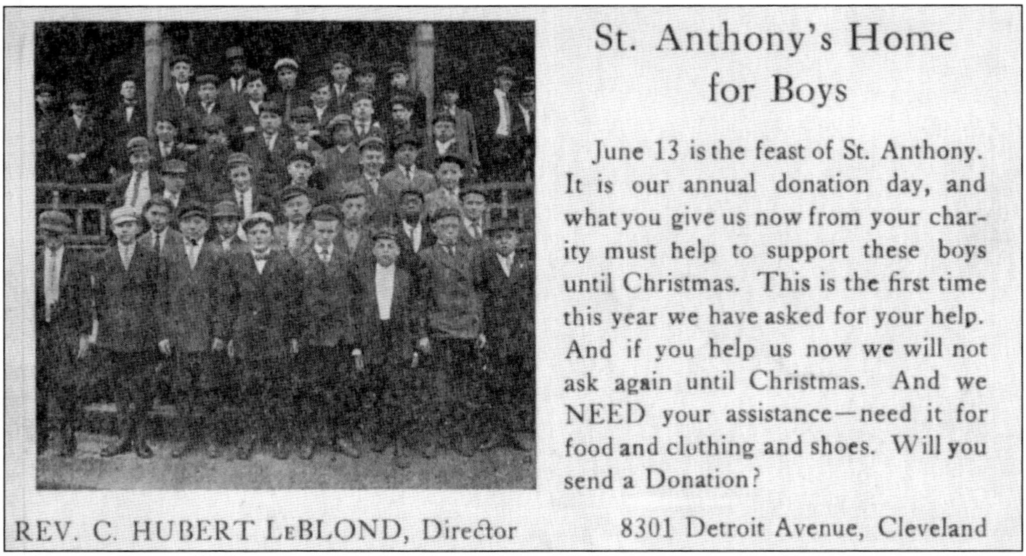

Bishop Charles Hubert LeBlond (class of 1903) became director of Saint Anthony's Home for Boys after his ordination in 1909. He was appointed the first director of Cleveland's Catholic Charities after its founding in 1910 and oversaw the funding of dozens of Catholic social welfare agencies. He was instrumental in the creation of Parmadale Children's Village (now Parmadale Institute). He was consecrated bishop of St. Joseph, Missouri, in 1933. (Courtesy of Cleveland State University Special Collections.)

Judge Joy Seth Hurd (class of 1906) is pictured in his capacity as presiding judge of the Ohio Court of Appeals as he swears in Judge Charles W. White (left). Hurd began his judicial career in 1935 on the Cuyahoga County Common Pleas Court and served there until he was named to the Ohio Court of Appeals in 1942. In 1960, Hurd was named "Catholic Man of the Year" by the Knights of Columbus, and he won the John Carroll Alumni Medal in 1962. (Courtesy of Cleveland State University Special Collections.)

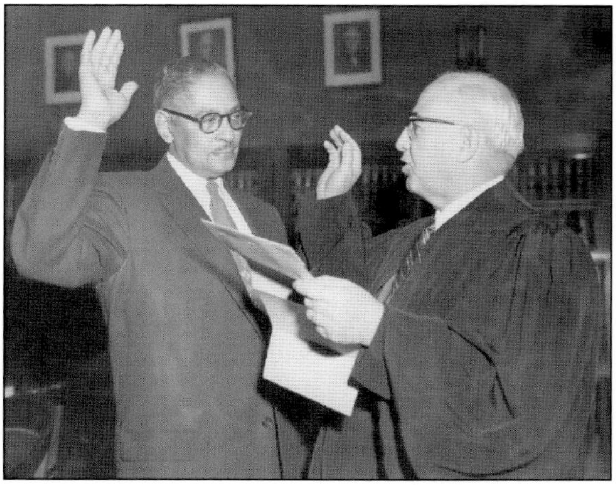

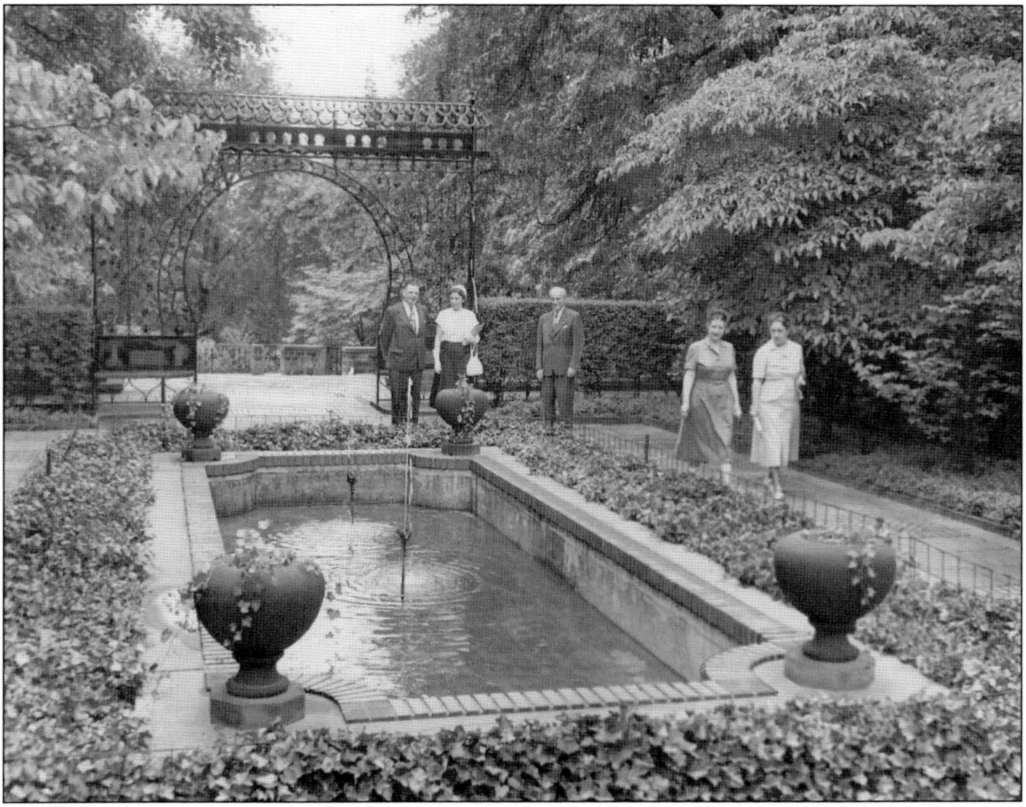

Louis Petrash (class of 1911) is the first person on the left in this photograph taken at the Hungarian Cultural Garden of Cleveland. Petrash was proud to be the first native-born Clevelander of Hungarian descent elected to Cleveland City Council, where he served from 1921 to 1931. Petrash was a municipal court judge from 1934 until his death in 1967. In 1960, John Carroll honored Petrash and Hurd at a special reception. Guests included nine other Carroll alumni who were also local judges. (Courtesy of Cleveland State University Special Collections.)

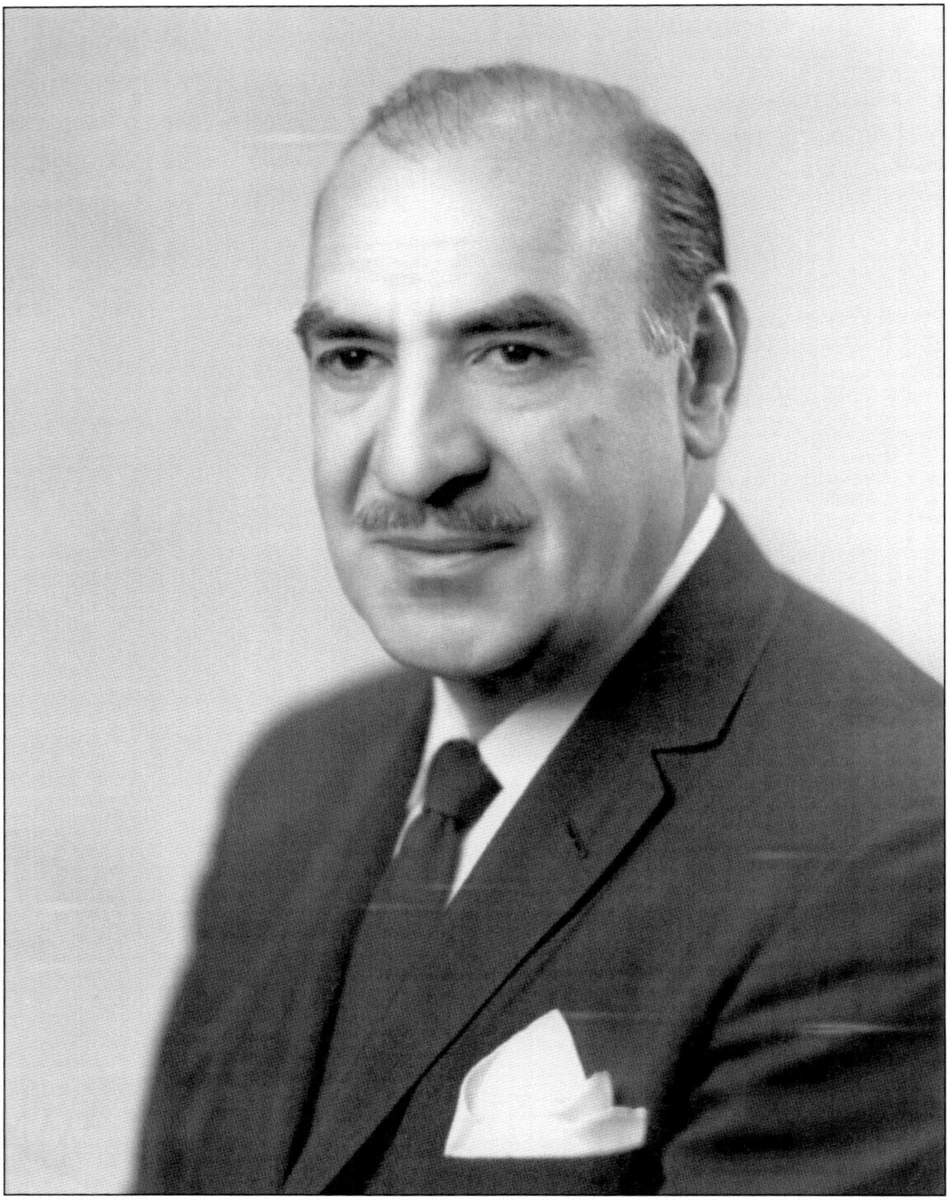

Anthony J. Celebrezze (class of 1934) was born in Anzi, Italy, in 1910 to Dorothy and Rocco Cilibrizzi. The name was Americanized when they immigrated to Cleveland in 1912. Anthony attended Fenn College for one year before transferring to John Carroll. After his graduation from Ohio Northern Law School in 1936, Celebrezze successfully ran for the Ohio State Senate in 1950 and 1952. In 1953, he was elected to his first of five terms as mayor of Cleveland. His achievements while in office included the promotion of the Saint Lawrence Seaway, the extension of the public transit system, and progress on the freeway system. In 1962, Pres. John F. Kennedy appointed him Secretary of the Department of Health, Education, and Welfare. In 1965, he was appointed a judge for the US Court of Appeals for the Sixth Circuit, where he served until his retirement in 1995. John Carroll awarded him the Alumni Medal in 1964 and made him an honorary doctor of laws in 1978. The federal building in downtown Cleveland is named for him.

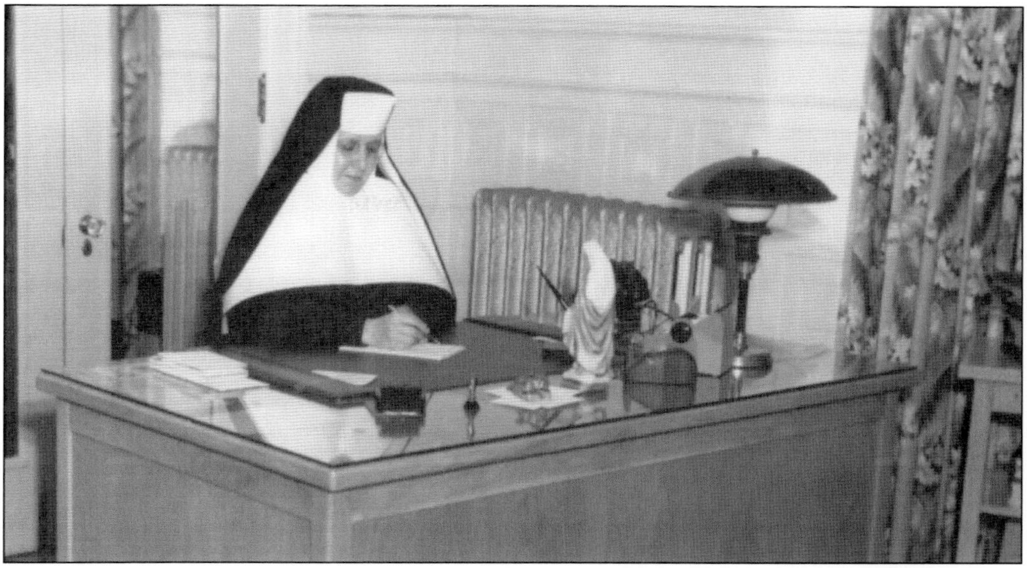

This is Sister Mary Fabian Catalano, OSU, who earned a bachelor's degree in 1933 and a graduate degree in 1939. She was possibly John Carroll's first female graduate and the first woman to earn two degrees from John Carroll. Sister Catalano taught at the now-defunct Sacred Heart Academy, Ursuline College, and Villa Angela and Beaumont High Schools. She was awarded the Alumni Medal in 1997 for "the positive influence she has had on generations of young women . . . and her dedication to Catholic education." (Courtesy of Cleveland Ursuline Sisters' Archives.)

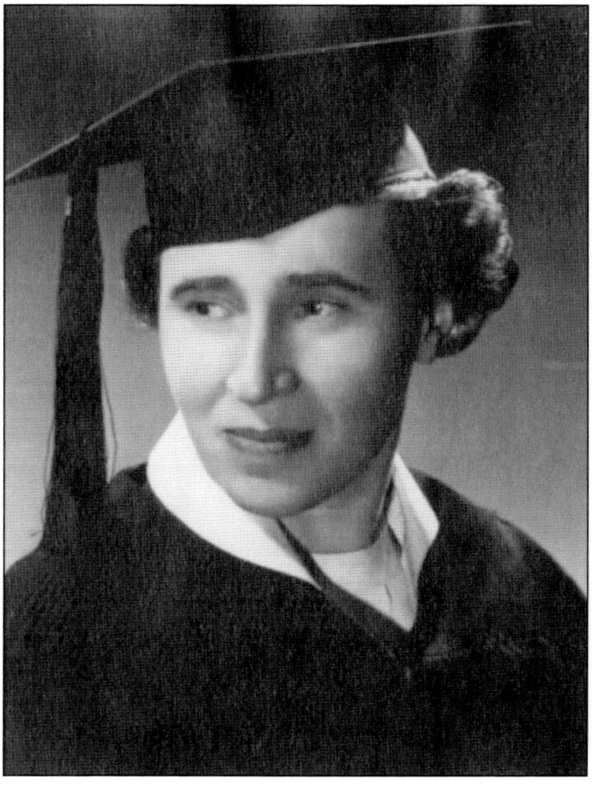

After fleeing Nazi Germany, Helen Kahn Weil (class of 1943) and her husband came to Cleveland in 1941, and she graduated from John Carroll two years later. This photograph was taken when she received her master's degree in social work from Western Reserve University. She specialized in social services for the elderly. She won the Alumni Medal in 1990 for her pioneering work in caring for the aging. (Courtesy of Western Reserve Historical Society.)

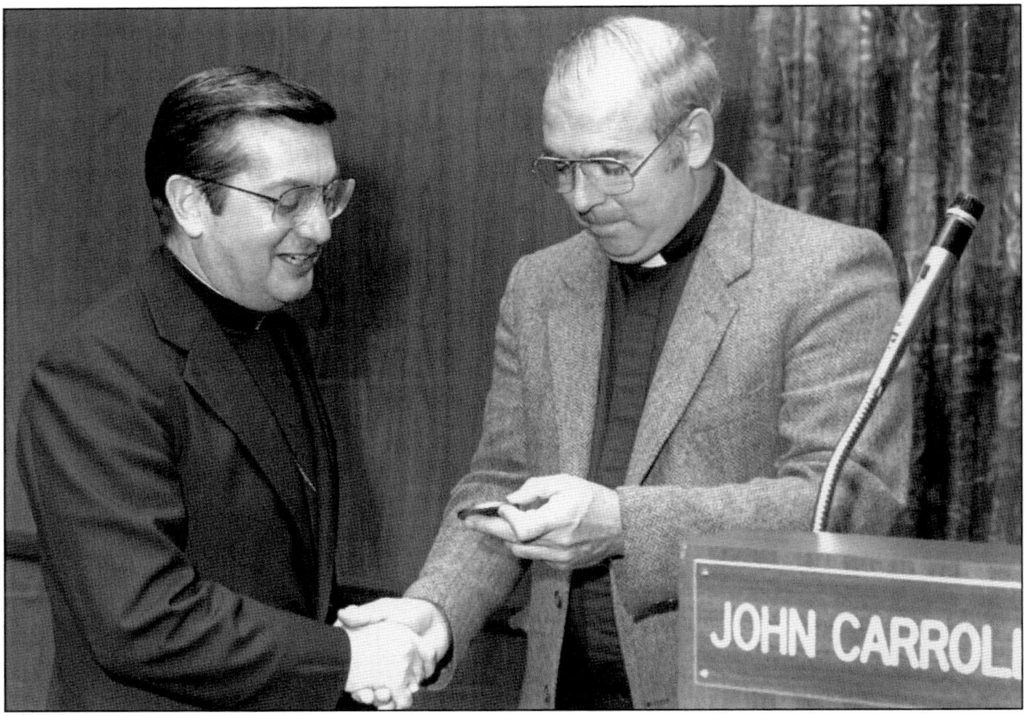

Native Clevelander Bishop Anthony M. Pilla (left), class of 1961 and Graduate School class of 1967, received his centennial medal from Rev. Michael J. Lavelle, SJ, another native Clevelander. Pilla served as Bishop of Cleveland from 1980 to 2006. In 1993, he published "The Church in the City," which urged his congregation to address the moral issues created by urban sprawl and the migration of Catholics from the city.

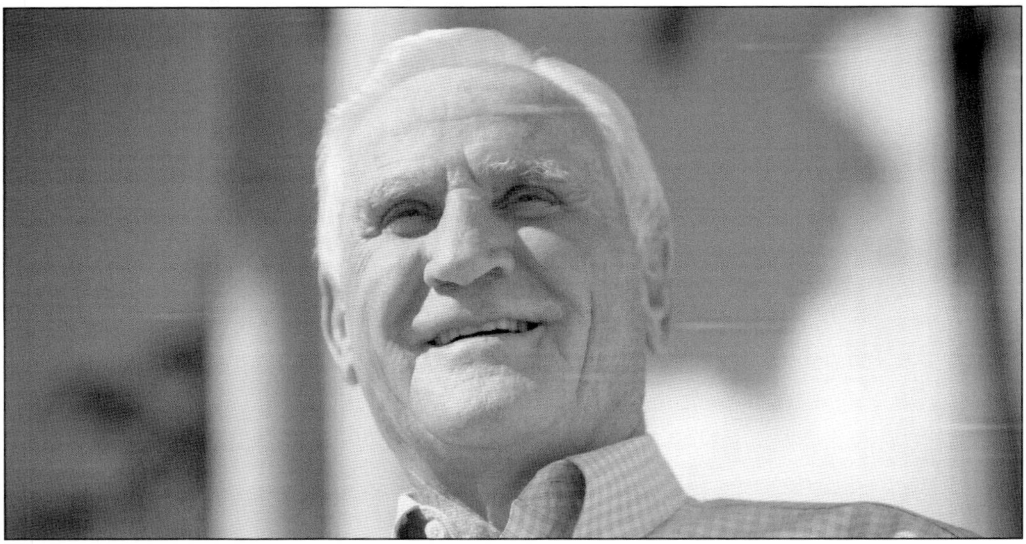

Don Shula (class of 1951) is best known as the coach of the Miami Dolphins. He coached in six Super Bowls (his team won two), and Don Shula Stadium at John Carroll's Wasmer Field is named after him. Shula's undergraduate philosophy classes at John Carroll inspired him to endow the Don Shula Chair in Philosophy, which presents programs of interest to philosophers and the general public.

Native Clevelander Rev. Casimir "Casey" Bukala, SJ (class of 1955), entered the Jesuit novitiate and was ordained in 1966. After doctoral studies at Boston College, Bukala joined the philosophy department at John Carroll. His many years of service and his devotion to the university and its students have won him the Distinguished Faculty Award, the Alumni Service Award, the Alumni Medal, and a centennial medal.

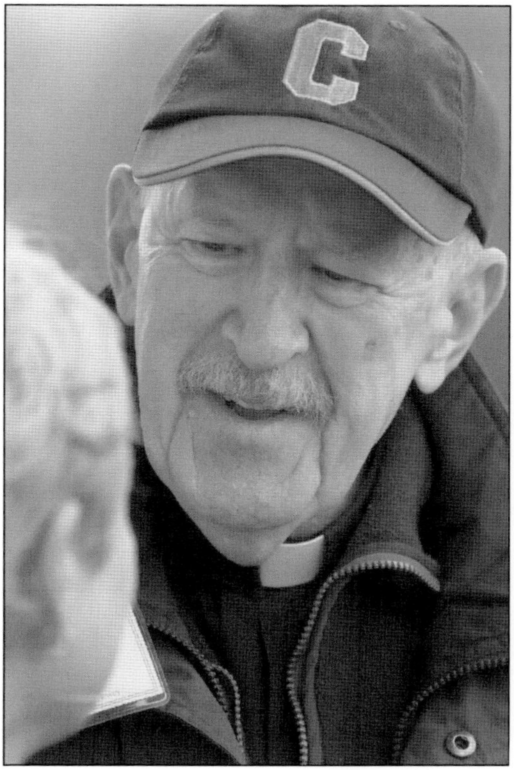

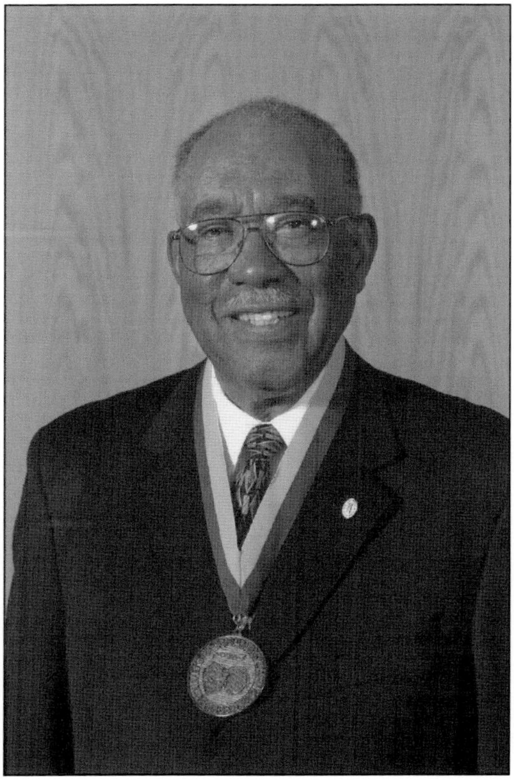

Rev. Wesley Toles (class of 1959) is an associate minister at Antioch Baptist Church who won the Alumni Medal in 2010. After his graduation from John Carroll, he served in the US Army's Medical Services Corps on active duty and active reserves for almost 40 years. He also serves Cleveland as a successful businessman.

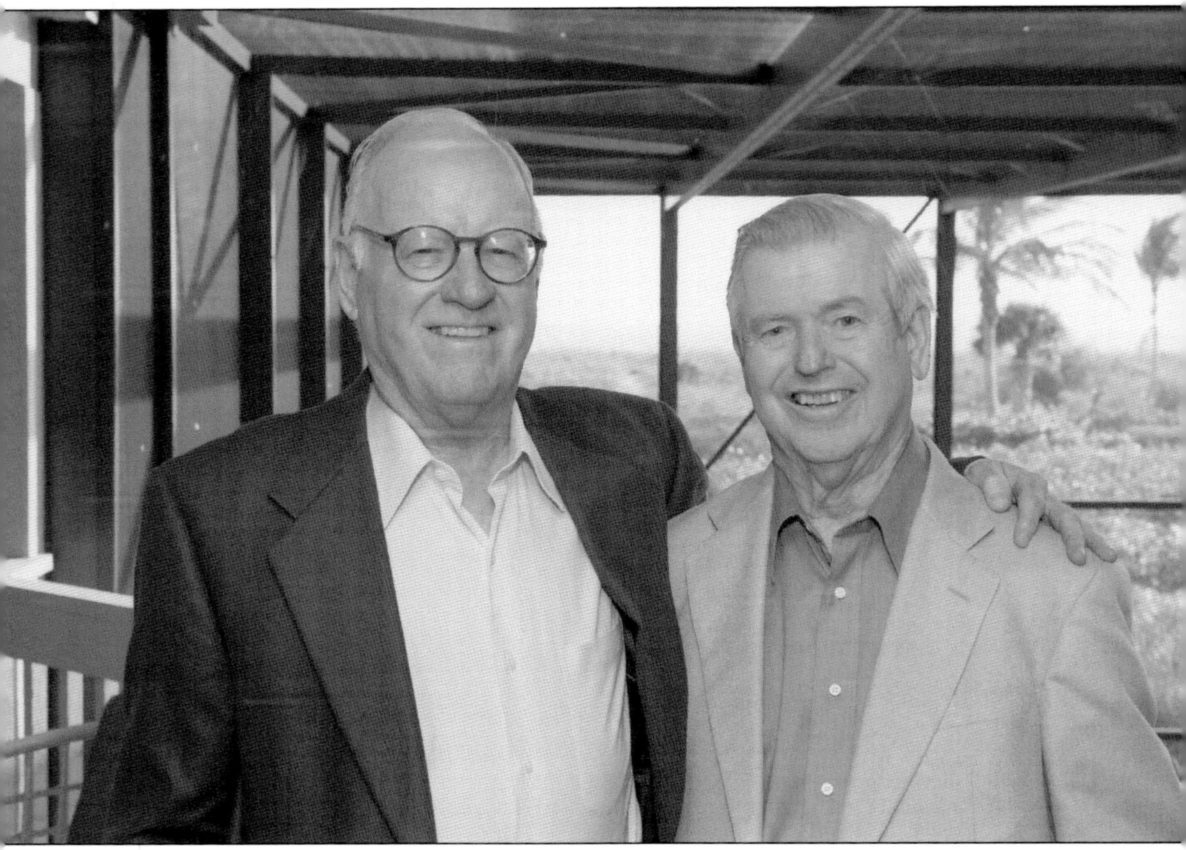

John G. "Jack" Breen (left) and John M. Boler both graduated from John Carroll in 1956. Breen served as president and CEO of Sherwin Williams from 1979 to 1999. He chaired the JCU Board of Trustees from 1991 to 1995 and the $50 million "Our Values, Our Responsibility" capital campaign. The Board of Trustees was renamed the Board of Directors in 2002. The generous gifts from Breen and his wife, Mary Jane (class of 1991 and Graduate School class of 1994), funded the John G. and Mary Jane Breen Learning Center and endowments that created the Institute of Catholic Studies and the Jack and Mary Jane Breen Chair in Catholic Systematic Theology at John Carroll. The generosity of John Boler, chairman of The Boler Company, and his wife, Mary Jo, includes a $10 million challenge grant that generated multiple gifts to the Boler School of Business—renamed in honor of the Bolers—and a gift for the D.J. Lombardo Student Center (named to honor Mary Jo's father), as well as other leadership gifts supporting the university over many decades. Breen and Boler, the John Carroll classmates and friends, won Alumni Medals in 2005, and both are director emeriti of the university.

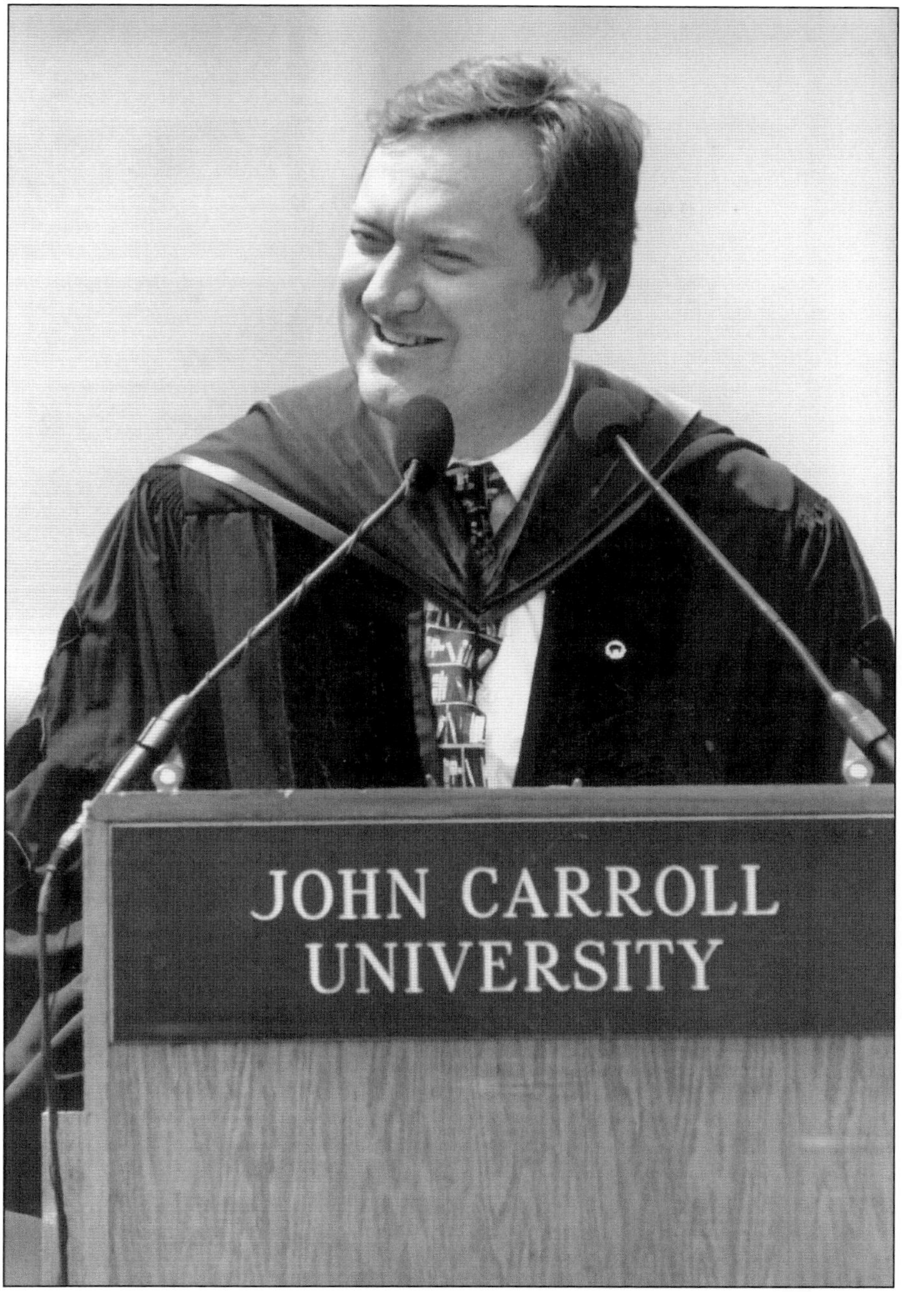

In this image, Timothy John "Tim" Russert (class of 1972) delivers the 1997 commencement address; at the time, he was a senior vice president and Washington bureau chief of NBC News. Russert was the president of the John Carroll Student Union from 1971 to 1972—tumultuous times at the university. He graduated from Cleveland-Marshall College of Law, with honors, in 1976. Russert became a best-selling author and the winner of many professional awards, but he was best known as the longtime moderator of NBC's *Meet the Press*. In 2009, John Carroll's Tim Russert Department of Communication and Theatre Arts was named in his memory, and NBC and the university created the *Meet the Press* fellowship, which is awarded annually to a John Carroll graduating senior.

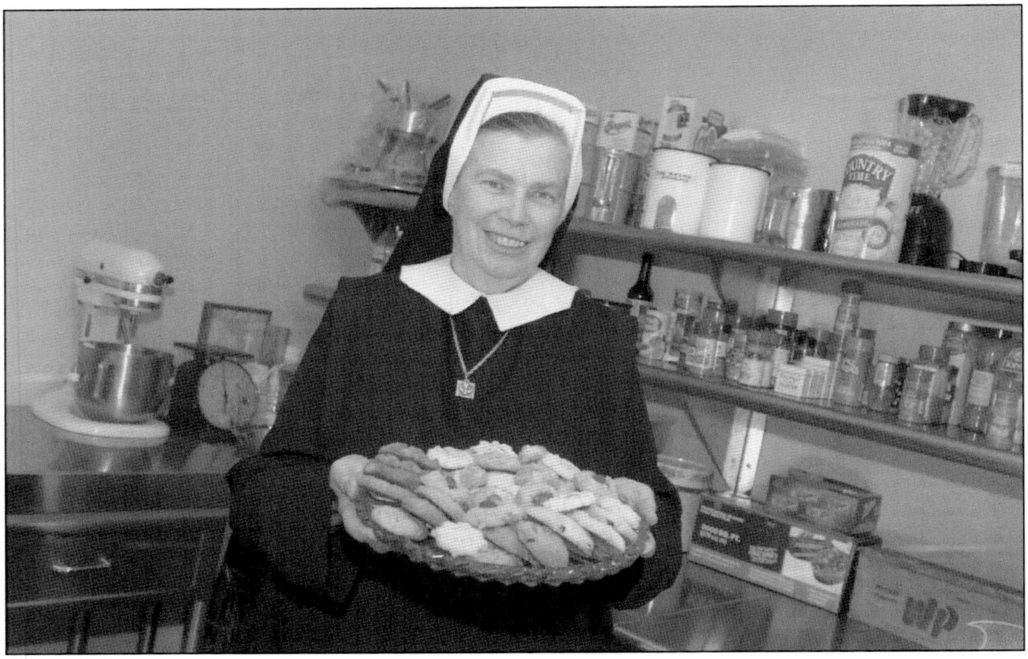

Sister Mary Assumpta (Graduate School class of 1973) and her small order, the Sisters of the Holy Spirit, administer at Jennings Hall, a nursing and assisted living facility in Garfield Heights. Her enthusiastic support of the Cleveland Indians and her chocolate chip cookies—known as "Nun Better"—that raised funds for Jennings Hall garnered local fame for Sister Assumpta. She won the Alumni Medal in 1998 in recognition of her generous support of the elderly.

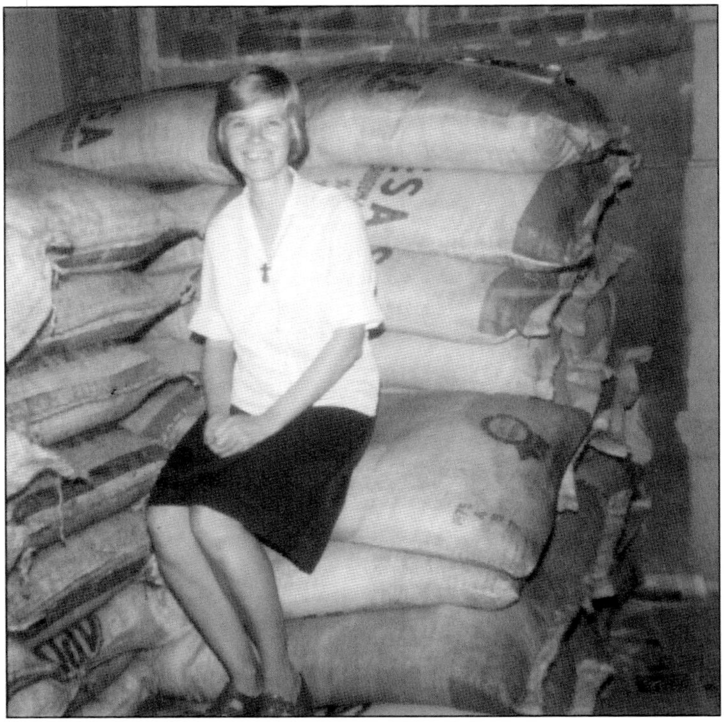

In 1974, Sister Dorothy Kazel, OSU (Graduate School class of 1974), joined the Cleveland Latin American Mission Team in El Salvador, where she worked with women and children. In 1980, Kazel, along with two other nuns and a lay missionary, was murdered by El Salvador National Guardsmen. The murders prompted a United Nations investigation and outrage against the US Army–run School of the Americas, where the guardsmen had trained. (Courtesy of Cleveland Ursuline Sisters' Archives.)

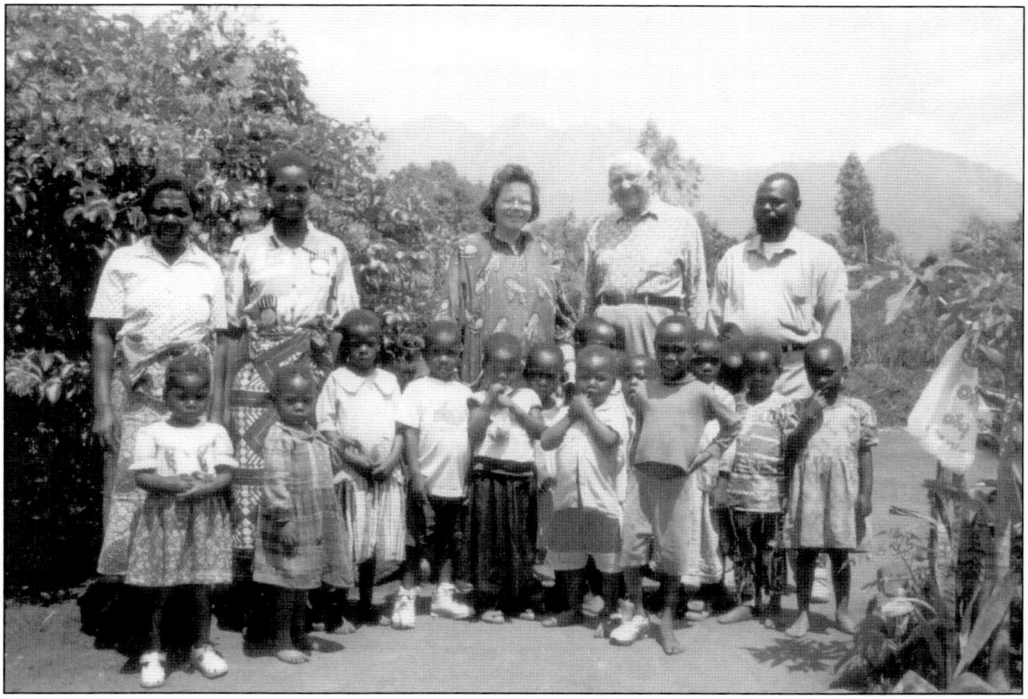

Dr. Beverly G. Hawk (class of 1975) majored in political science at John Carroll, received a master's degree in African studies from Howard University, and earned master's and doctoral degrees in political science from the University of Wisconsin-Madison. A specialist in African studies, Dr. Hawk received the Alumni Medal in 2004 for her work with AIDS orphans in Africa; she is pictured in the center of the back row among a group of orphans.

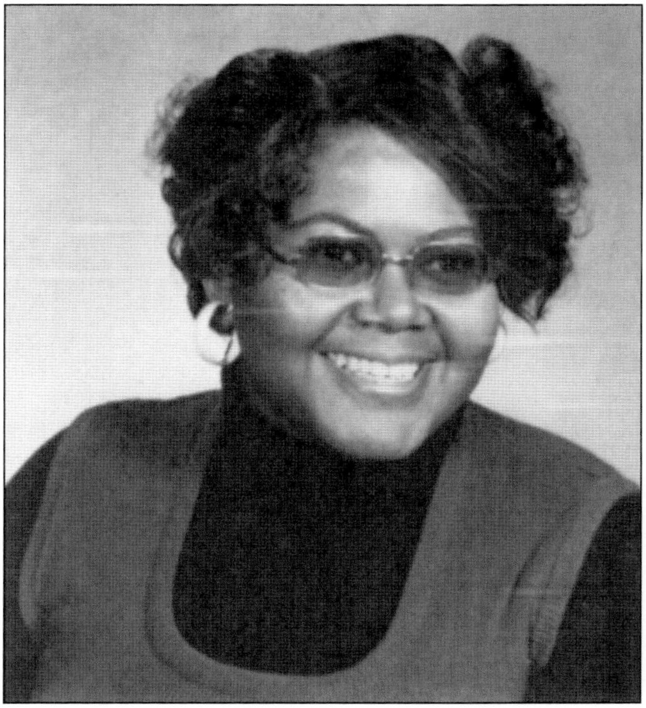

Pauline H. Tarver (class of 1975) received her law degree from Cleveland-Marshall College of Law, worked for the Cleveland Rape Crisis Center, and became executive director of the NAACP Cleveland Branch. She led a voter registration campaign in 2000 and designed an HIV/AIDS educational program. Tarver won the Alumni Medal in 2002 and was elected to Cleveland Municipal Court in November 2003.

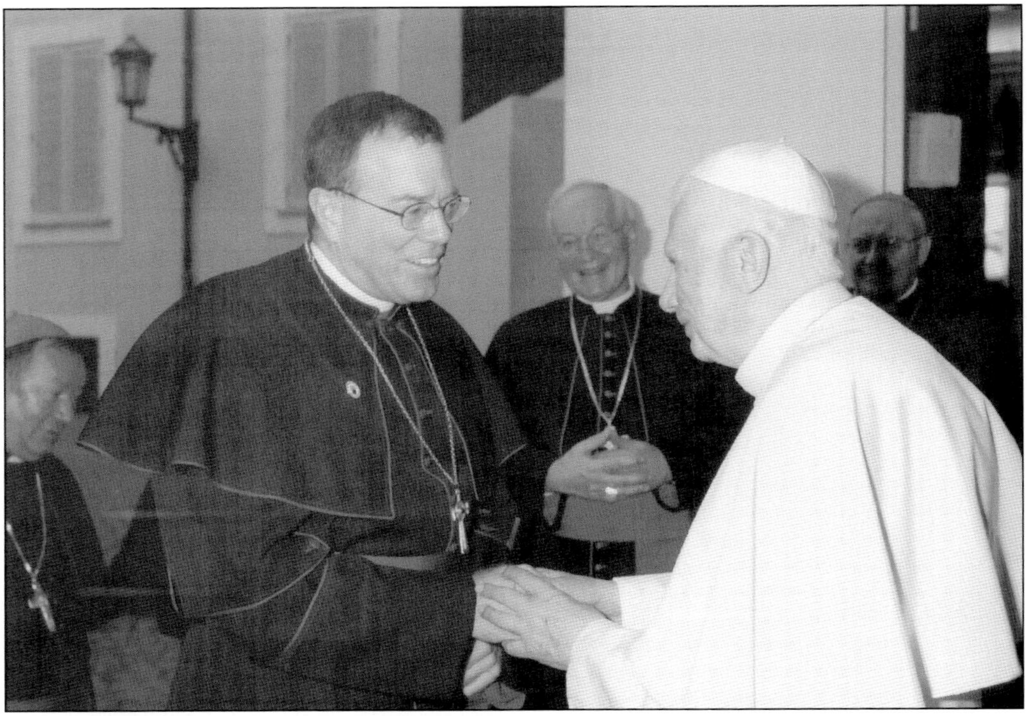

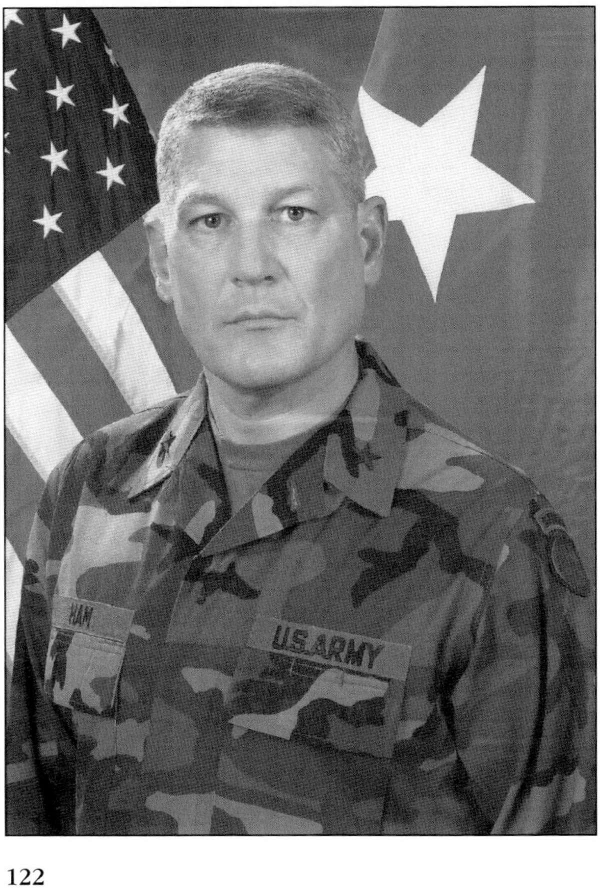

Bishop Neal Buckon (class of 1975) is pictured above with Pope Benedict XVI. In order to fulfill his ROTC commitment, Buckon went into the US Army after graduating from John Carroll. After active duty in Europe, Buckon resigned from the military and entered Saint Mary's Seminary. He was ordained a priest in 1995 and named an Army chaplain a year later. In 2011, he was appointed auxiliary bishop of the Archdiocese for the Military Services, USA.

Gen. Carter F. Ham (class of 1976) is so far the only graduate of John Carroll to hold the rank of four-star general. In 2009, he oversaw the investigation of the fatal shootings at the Fort Hood military base and was also appointed to the commission that investigated the military's "Don't Ask, Don't Tell" policy. In 2010, when Ham received the Alumni Medal, he was the commanding general of the US Army Europe and 7th Army.

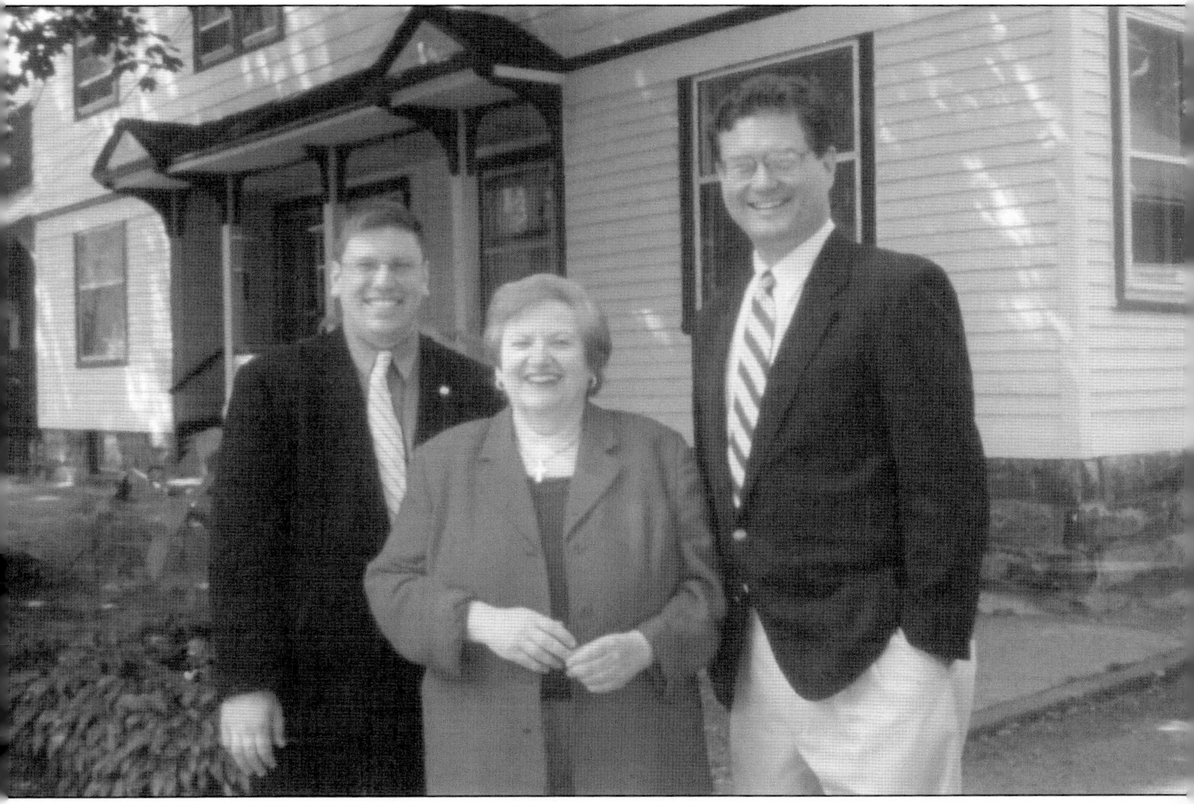

Pictured here are Joe Cimperman (left, class of 1992), Mary Rose Oakar (center, Graduate School class of 1966), and Ed Rybka (class of 1997). The careers of these three indicate that John Carroll graduates are still a force in Cleveland politics. After a stint in the Jesuit Volunteer Corps, Cimperman was elected to the Cleveland City Council in 1997. He is nationally recognized for his promotion of urban gardening. Oakar served on the Cleveland City Council from 1973 to 1976, in the US House of Representatives from 1977 to 1993, in the Ohio House of Representatives from 2000 to 2002, and on the Ohio State Board of Education. She became known as an advocate for women, health care, and the elderly. In 1985, Rybka was elected to Cleveland City Council, where he represented the Broadway-Slavic Village neighborhood. In 2005, he became the City of Cleveland's assistant director of city planning. In 2011, he was the city's director of the Department of Building and Housing.

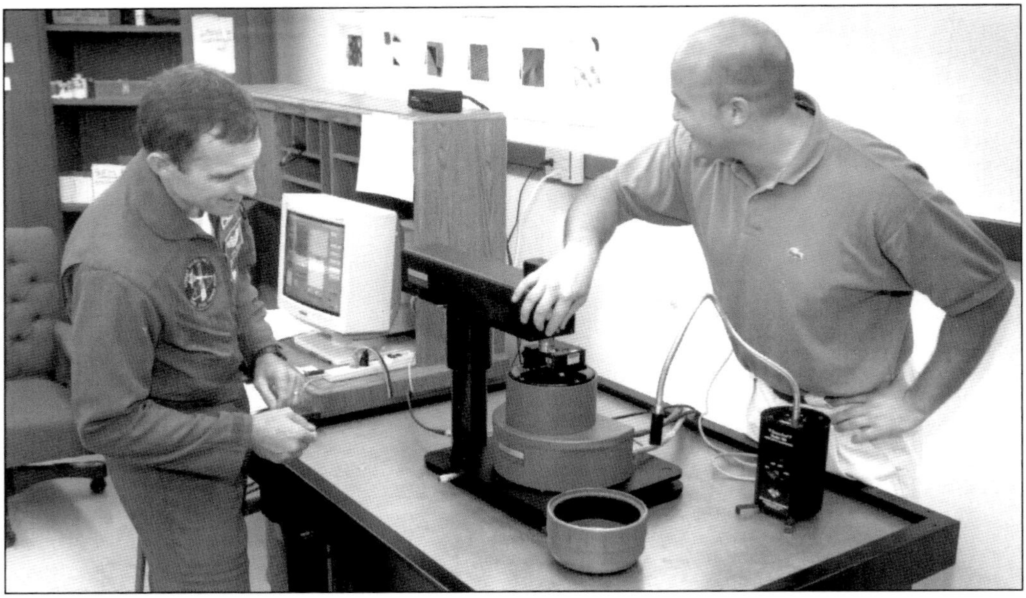

Retired US Air Force colonel Carl E. Walz (Graduate School class of 1979) is at left in this image. The former astronaut earned his master's of science in solid-state physics from John Carroll. In 1990, he was selected by NASA to make four trips into space. Walz was awarded four NASA Space Flight Medals, a NASA Distinguished Service Medal, and a NASA Exceptional Service Medal, as well as John Carroll's Alumni Medal (in 2002).

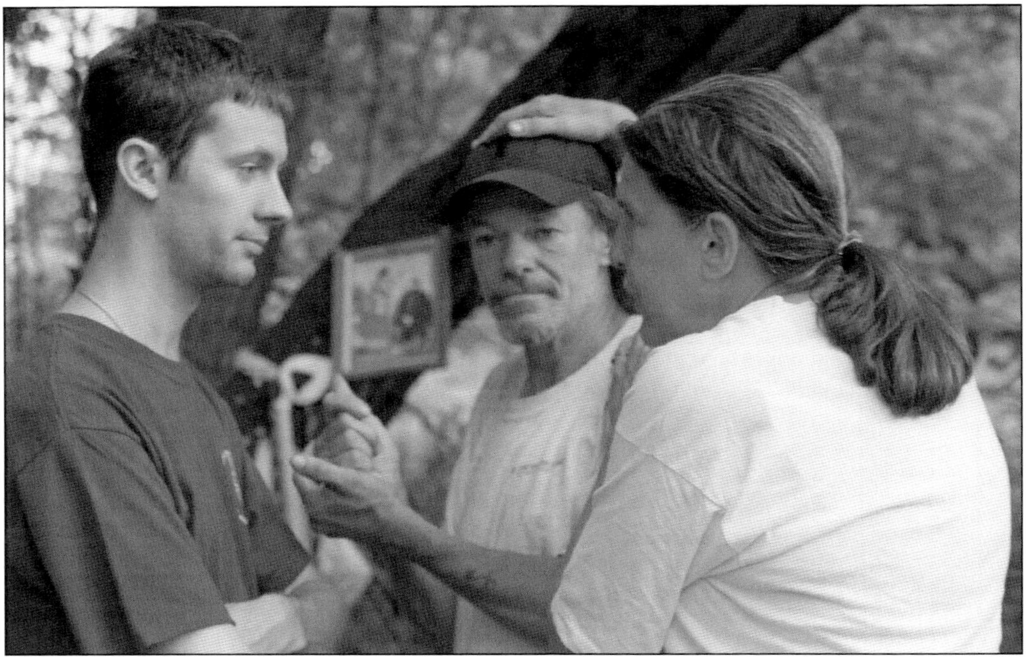

Bryan Mauk (left, class of 2008) was a founder of the Labre Project as an undergraduate and has won national awards, including the 2007 Howard R. Swearer Student Humanitarian Award and the 2007 Northeast Ohio Coalition for the Homeless Award. In 2008, he won the William E. Simon Fellowship for Noble Purpose, which came with a $40,000 cash grant that he applied toward his Metanoia Project for the homeless.

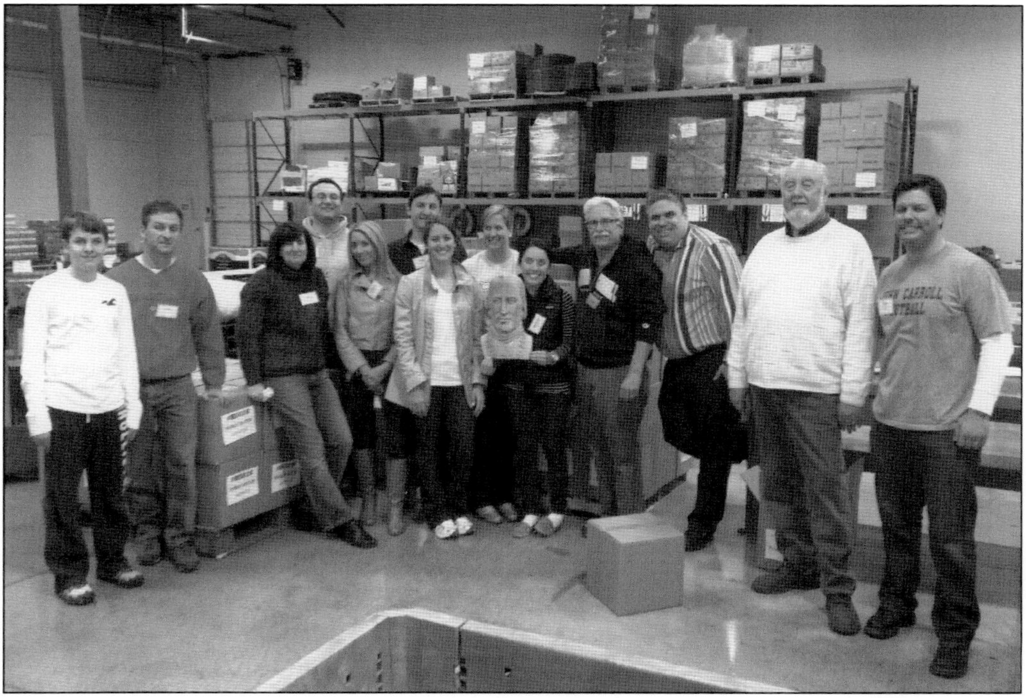

Many John Carroll graduates continue the tradition of community service that they engaged in at the university. Alumni events in 2011 included volunteering at the Cleveland and Pittsburgh Food Banks. In Cleveland (above), volunteers sorted and packed nonperishable food for distribution to local food pantries and shelters and assisted in preparing hot meals for local sites. In Pittsburgh (below), volunteers helped to pack and sort donated and purchased groceries. Without fanfare or public recognition, and like thousands of their fellow graduates, they remain men and women for others and representatives of the university's mission.

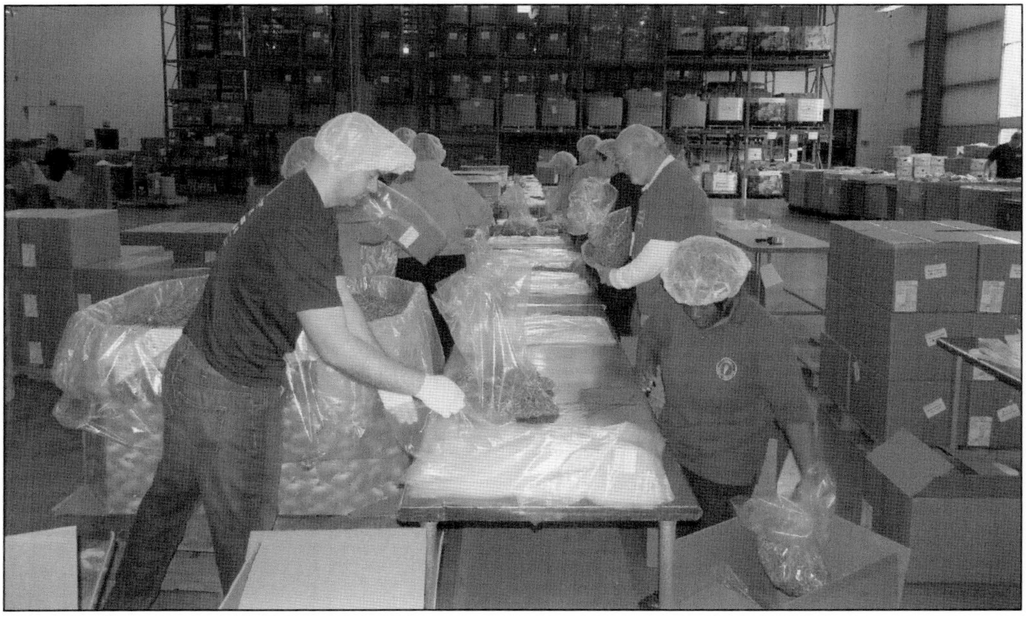

BIBLIOGRAPHY

Gallin, Alice, OSU. *Negotiating Identity: Catholic Higher Education Since 1960*. Notre Dame, Indiana: University of Notre Dame Press, 2000.

Gavin, Donald P. *John Carroll University: A Century of Service*. Kent, Ohio: Kent State University Press, 1986.

Gleason, Philip. "American Catholic Higher Education, 1940–1990: The Ideological Context," in George M. Marsden and Bradley J. Longfield, eds. *The Secularization of the Academy*. New York: Oxford University Press, 1992.

Grabowski, John J. *There Are No Strangers at the Feast: Catholicism and Community in Northeastern Ohio*. Cleveland: Western Reserve Historical Society, 2008.

Greeley, Andrew M. *From Backwater to Mainstream: A Profile of Catholic Education*. New York: McGraw-Hill Book Company. 1969

Hynd, Michael J. *History of the Diocese of Cleveland: Origin and Growth (1847–1952)*. Cleveland: World Publishing Co. 1953.

John Carroll Alumni News, 1944–2011.

Mahoney, Kathleen A. *Catholic Higher Education in Protestant America: The Jesuits and Harvard in the Age of the University*. Baltimore and London: The Johns Hopkins University Press, 2003.

Plain Dealer, 1886–2010.

Power, Edward J. *Catholic Higher Education in America: A History*. New York: Appleton-Century-Crofts, 1972.

Rudolph, Frederick. *The American College and University: A History*. Athens and London: University of Georgia Press, 1990.

Van Tassel, David D. and John J. Grabowski, eds. *Dictionary of Cleveland Biography*. Bloomington and Indianapolis, IN: Indiana University Press, 1996.

Van Tassel, David D. and John J. Grabowski, eds. *Encyclopedia of Cleveland History*. Bloomington and Indianapolis, IN: Indiana University Press, 1996.

Index

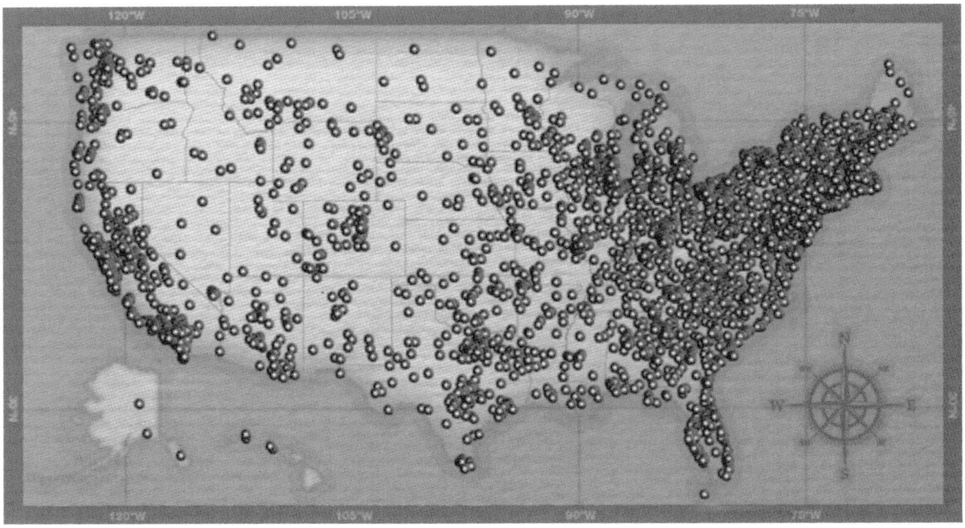